H. G. EARNSHAW

MODERN WRITERS

A Guide to
Twentieth-Century
Literature
in the
English Language

W. & R. CHAMBERS EDINBURGH & LONDON

The author and publishers are most grateful to all those who have kindly given permission for the reproduction of copyright material. A full list of acknowledgments appears on pages 265–6.

SBN: 550 71003 5

Printed in Great Britain by
Thomas Nelson (Printers) Ltd, London and Edinburgh

Preface

THIS book is intended for the general reader, not for the student specialising in Literature. A glance at the contents will show that I have chosen fifty or sixty writers of the twentieth century, English and American, because their work was important or interesting, or because their relationship to other writers of the period gave them some historical significance.

The process of selection was not easy. On the one hand, it is comparatively simple to pick six or eight or ten writers of outstanding importance and achievement, and concentrate on their work. Such a plan would, however, have been too restricted, and the treatment too detailed for the readers I had in mind. On the other hand, the number of books that might be thought worth a mention runs into hundreds; if they are each allotted a sentence or a paragraph, the result is little more than a catalogue.

My aim was to provide a guide and an introductory reading-list which would give the reader a general view of the century's writing in English. I have therefore compromised on a moderate number of writers, and for each of them I have usually selected one or two books, pointing out the qualities that might be looked for in them, rather than mentioning every book written. Once his interest is aroused, the reader will make further discoveries for himself. Believing that at this stage encouragement to read is the most useful service to offer, I have tried to stimulate pleasure and interest in preference to attempting a rigorous critical analysis.

As a schoolmaster, I hope that this book will be useful to senior pupils whose tastes and interests are beginning to develop. They may find the techniques of some of the writers difficult, and their subjects remote, but some knowledge of their work is essential to an understanding of the century's literature. A reading-list is given on pages 263–4.

I am grateful to my daughter Judith, who provided much of the material for the sections on Joyce, Yeats and Beckett, and whose comments were always stimulating.

H. G. E.

Contents

Introduction

IF you asked who were the most important writers of the nineteenth century, most readers would include in their lists the names of Wordsworth, Jane Austen, Dickens, Tennyson and Browning. Other writers—Sir Walter Scott, Coleridge, Shelley, Byron, Keats, Charles Lamb, Hazlitt, Thackeray, George Eliot, the Brontës and Matthew Arnold—would also be mentioned quite often. There would be occasional differences of opinion, but on the whole people would agree very closely. If, however, you asked the same question about writers of the twentieth century, you would find that far more names would be mentioned, and that the lists were often very different from each other. Why should it be so much harder to judge the writers of the age in which we live than those who lived a century ago?

In the first place, the man in the middle of events finds it hardest to see them clearly and in proportion. He is aware of movement rather than pattern. You will get a better view of a ballet from the circle than from the middle of the stage, and if you want to hear a piece of music as the composer intended it to be heard, you should not sit among the trombone-players. The outline of nineteenth-century literature seems quite clear now, but during their lives there was fierce argument about the work of Wordsworth, Keats and Browning. Some writers who were considered very important in their day, Carlyle for instance, have lost some of the reputation they then enjoyed, whilst Trollope's novels have risen in favour. A hundred years from now twentieth-century literature will present a much clearer picture than it does today. Some writers will be almost forgotten and others will stand out as greater figures than they now appear to be.

The number of books published, the number of authors and the number of readers have all greatly increased during the last hundred years. The world of books has become a more crowded one, because the world has become more crowded. The population of the English-speaking part of the world has expanded: through the spread of education a higher proportion of that increased population can read. English is now spoken, written and taught not only in the British Isles, in North America and in Australasia, but in many countries in Africa and Asia. Amongst all these millions of people who can read English, there are some who also have the urge to write books. Until the second half of the nineteenth century books in English were written almost exclusively by educated inhabitants of the British Isles, most of them males drawn from the upper and middle classes. This is no longer so.

In literature, as in other fields of human activity, the United States of America has advanced rapidly. Before this century a few American poets were known to the English reader—Longfellow, Edgar Allan Poe, Whittier, Whitman certainly—but both in number and in quality they were thought to compare badly with the native product. In prose there were Washington Irving, Poe, Nathaniel Hawthorne, Emerson, Herman Melville and Mark Twain to place beside the great English names. American writers sometimes settled in this country, as Henry James and T. S. Eliot did, because they thought their gifts would flourish more vigorously in a country with a literary tradition. More recently British writers, among them Aldous Huxley and W. H. Auden, have gone to live in the U.S.A., where they can enjoy more favourable living conditions, yet remain in touch with other writers and artists and scholars. Writers like William Faulkner, Eugene O'Neill and Robert Frost have been respected as among the most important writers of their day both in Britain and in America. The two countries are equal partners in the world of books, and the influence of an outstanding American writer in Britain is now as great as that of a British writer in the U.S.A.

These two countries are now the senior partners, but writers from Australia, India, the West Indies and South and West Africa have also been deservedly praised by critics. With the further passage of time some of these countries will also become forces in the development of English literature. As they do so, judgment will inevitably become more difficult, if only because there is more work to compare and judge.

Books are no longer the only, or even the principal, means of entertaining, informing, stimulating and delighting man. These functions are now shared by the cinema, radio and television. The newer media form part of the background of life for both readers and writers. Scott sometimes began his novels with long and leisurely descriptions of the scene and the characters. The modern reader goes to the cinema and watches television. There he is given the scene in one panoramic shot lasting perhaps a few seconds. He will not spend twenty minutes reading a description of the countryside. Nor does he need to: mention the scene—the Scottish Highlands or the Malayan jungle or the Sahara Desert—and he knows what it looks like from seeing such scenes in a film or a television programme. He knows also the manner of dress and speech of people from many parts of the world.

Film audiences adjust themselves rapidly to changes of scene. These changes are not usually sub-titled, but the experienced cinema-goer is quickly able to place the new scene. So, when he turns to a novel, he does not demand that the relation of each new incident to the last shall be spelled out for him. Successive chapters of Trollope's *The Last Chronicle of Barset* begin thus:

> At this time Grace Crawley was at Framley Parsonage.
>
> By some of those unseen telegraph wires which carry news about the country and make no charge for the conveyance, Archdeacon Grantly heard that his son the major was at Framley.
>
> The archdeacon, as he walked across from the Court to the parsonage, was very thoughtful and his steps were very slow.
>
> By the time that the archdeacon reached Plumstead his enthusiasm in favour of Grace Crawley had somewhat cooled itself.

Here each chapter is carefully linked to the last: the reader is told where the characters are, how they got there, and what purpose they had in going. Modern readers accept a more rapid, if less smooth, transition.

Films have also influenced the dialogue of both novels and plays. Film-producers usually take great pains to ensure that the settings are as detailed and accurate as possible. Against such realistic backgrounds characters must speak to each other in a way that convinces audiences that they too are real. Falseness is shown up without mercy. Consequently cinema technique avoids those perfectly rounded sentences which express the character's thoughts and feelings so much more precisely than is possible in real life, and novelists and playwrights have followed the example of the cinema in this respect. Parts of Nigel Balchin's novels, for instance, read like film-scripts.

On the face of it there is no reason why novels and plays should follow the example of cinema, radio and television, but in fact these new media have changed the public taste. Moreover, many writers have worked for films and radio. Christopher Fry, author of the verse-play *The Lady's not for Burning*, has written a number of film-scripts, and Louis MacNeice, best known perhaps as a poet, wrote several verse-plays for radio which are amongst the few classics of the air.

Radio, television and the cinema have introduced new means of expression for the writer. The area of human knowledge has also widened during the century. Psychology, for instance, is a twentieth-century study, taking for its subject the behaviour and the motives of human beings. One of the commonest themes in modern literature is the individual's need to assert his own personality, to defy the customs and the conventions of the society in which he lives. Other books trace the changes that take place in the relationships between members of a family, or the way in which men's behaviour and character are moulded by the pressures of industry, religion and politics. All these themes are taken from psychology. George Orwell's *1984* shows how the human personality can be crushed by political power. Scott Fitzgerald, Aldous Huxley and James Joyce were other writers whose work was influenced by their knowledge of psychology, whilst some of D. H. Lawrence's novels appear to be denials of the psychologists' teaching about human emotions.

Themes become exhausted with the passing of time. A masterpiece written on a certain theme may make later writers reluctant to challenge comparison of their own work with it. The example of *Hamlet* may have prevented other dramatists from attempting tragedies on the revenge theme. After Tennyson's *Idylls of the King* romantic treatment of the legend of King Arthur and the knights of the Round Table had had its day. Since then T. H. White has amused readers by re-telling part of the legend in a comic, fantastic, matter-of-fact way in *The Sword in the Stone*, and J. R. Tolkien has found a new approach to a legendary story in *The Lord of the Ring*. Trollope described the ambitions, intrigues, quarrels and family relations of the clergy in a cathedral city so effectively in his Barsetshire novels that he left little for his successors to work on. Time has flowed past the remote cathedral cities and the power of the clergy, and the struggles now take place within political parties, in factories and board-rooms, in centres of scientific research. C. P. Snow deals with intrigues not unlike those in Trollope's novels, but places them in different settings.

New themes crowd in to take the place of the old ones that have been exhausted. Science fiction has flourished in the twentieth century. The horrors of modern war have provided the material for many books and plays in the last fifty years. Many writers have warned man that the machines he has invented may threaten the things he values most in life. Then new developments such as television, advertising, public relations and big business have formed the backgrounds for many stories.

In addition to finding themes that belong to the twentieth century, writers have felt compelled to find distinctively modern ways of expressing their ideas. Writers like Dickens and Tennyson made this search inevitable. Tennyson's lyric, *The splendour falls on castle walls*, is as perfect in its own way as anything we can imagine. He has polished that particular jewel beyond the prospect of improvement, and later poets must seek another kind of perfection. What more can any writer do with the novel of plot and character than Dickens did in *Bleak House*? The scale is grand, the structure massive, the detail rich. Who else could add Chadband and Turveydrop as embellishments to the main design? The novelist who is ambitious to excel must move on and bring something new to the form of the novel. There are still good novels to be written in the manner of Dickens, but the times conspire against the writer who wants to equal him: modern life does not produce these contrasts, these eccentrics, as raw material for the story-teller.

It is the pace of change that makes the twentieth century so different from earlier ages. These changes have affected not only the conditions in which we live, but the ways in which we think. For this reason our own age has been a perplexing period to live in. We have seen great changes in industry, transport, entertainment and education; as soon as we have become used to a new invention or development, we are told that it is already out of date and warned to prepare ourselves for something even more modern. The artist lives in this world of change; it affects his work and is reflected in his work. If he is a musician, he may compose for films, radio or television as well as for the concert hall. The man who wishes to tell a story is no longer restricted to the novel and the ballad as his medium. Unless he deliberately chooses to cater for only a small section of the public, the artist now writes or paints or composes for a much wider public than did Jane Austen or Constable or Mozart.

Though it has been a century of ceaseless change in both literature and transport, the course of change in the two activities has been quite different. In transport there has been a consistent development, always towards greater range, higher speeds and more complicated machines. If you try to trace the changes that have taken place in English poetry, through John Masefield, Rupert Brooke, Wilfred Owen, T. S. Eliot, Robert Frost, W. H. Auden, Carlos Williams, Ted Hughes and the 'beat' poets, for instance, you will not find any trend that can be clearly stated. In 1922 two works distinctive of their period in mood and style were published: *The Waste Land* by T. S. Eliot and *Ulysses* by James Joyce. They were regarded as new points of departure in English literature. In his later poems and plays, however, Eliot wrote in a quieter, more sinewy style in which he seemed to draw back from some of the features most novel and most remarkable in *The Waste Land*. On the other hand, James Joyce's *Finnegan's Wake*, drafts of which began to appear in 1927 with the completed work published in 1939, went much further along the road of experiment than *Ulysses* had done. Since then few writers have tried to follow Joyce along this road, and little has come of his explorations so far. Perhaps the road will prove to have been a dead-end; perhaps his influence will be stronger in a later age. There are no revolutions in literature that make everything that has gone before look out of date, as Whittle's invention of the jet engine set the whole of the aircraft industry on a new line of development.

We look back on the nineteenth century as a time of settled beliefs, of fixed and seemingly permanent standards. Most English-speaking people were Christians; they believed that a man who did wrong was a sinner deserving punishment; the British Empire, protected by the Royal Navy, was a lasting power for good in the world; America was a land of expanding opportunity for the individual; democracy, based on the right of the citizen to use his vote freely, was the finest form of government and would spread over the whole earth as men and nations became capable of using their right to vote intelligently and responsibly; industry would grow more efficient in a world free from major wars, bringing prosperity to all nations, especially those enlightened enough to speak English. How many of these ideas survive? How many that survive are free from challenge? What beliefs have we put in place of those we have lost?

The old images have been broken in religion and politics. New images in plenty have been set up in their place, but these in their turn have been sharply rejected. Many people now cry, 'Down with images and public worship! Let every man fashion his own faith and live by that.' In art, too, the old standards have been assailed and shaken. New prophets have declared that a novel does not need a plot, that a good likeness is not the same as a good picture, that music can exist without a recognisable melody or theme, that poetic expression is thwarted by a regular form, and that plays of quite unactable length may nevertheless be masterpieces. The rebels have shown that there is some truth in their beliefs. Virginia Woolf wrote novels in which she revealed the minds of her characters in minute detail and in which the plot was of minor importance. D. H. Lawrence, like other poets before and after him, adopted a very free form in his poetry, without rhyme-schemes or fixed stanzas or lines of uniform length or a regular rhythm, but 'Snake' and 'Bavarian Gentians' are widely read and admired. Both Bernard Shaw and Eugene O'Neill have written plays of a length that cannot be fitted into the programme of any theatre, but whose force is undeniable.

During the same period poems that rhyme and scan, novels which entertain their readers through action and character, plays that stimulate and please audiences for two to three hours, have continued to be written. The surge of rebellion has perhaps slackened a little since the 1920s and 1930s. After restless movement there comes a time to take our bearings again. The twentieth century has firmly rejected many of the heirlooms of the nineteenth century. Now it has to decide what the new fashion is to be.

Of course our ideas about the nineteenth century would seem absurd to people who lived then. They did not think they were enjoying a period of security and placid belief. To them no doubt it was an age of bitter argument: they argued about the repeal of the law which forbade Catholics to hold official positions; about the admission of nonconformists to Oxford and Cambridge; about restrictions on the employment of boys and girls, and the provision of schools where instead they might enjoy the beginnings of an education; about the extension of the vote to men who were not the owners of property; about the right of workers to organise themselves into trade unions; about the Oxford movement as a threat to Protestantism and the theory of evolution as a threat to all religious belief. Though we think we live in an age that lacks a faith, we take many things for granted that would have been strange a hundred years ago: the right of boys and girls to the education that will benefit them most; the evil of hanging a man for stealing a sheep; the duty to provide medical attention for anyone who is sick.

Perhaps after all we delude ourselves in believing that the twentieth century is the most perplexing period in human history, different in almost every way from earlier times. It is true that the world described in the works of poets, novelists and dramatists is full of new inventions, that the problems they discuss have new settings. Yet books are still written about the joys and sorrows, the ambitions and the disappointments of men. Whilst we should certainly take notice of what is original in the technique of *The Waste Land* we should also reflect on what is similar in the theme of Eliot's poem to *Piers Plowman* written more than five hundred years earlier.

'Twentieth-century literature'—there are two points to bear in mind about this phrase, one about each part. First, that the twentieth century was not cut off from the nineteenth, and that in time it will overlap with the twenty-first. Many writers who were producing books in the years just before 1900 went on writing during 1901 and the years that followed. In fact, two poets whom we look upon as belonging to the twentieth century, Emily Dickinson and Gerard Manley Hopkins, died in 1886 and 1889 respectively, their works not being published until they had been dead for some years. Second, we should remember that 'literature' is an abstract word: books and their writers are real enough, but 'literature' is neither an object nor a person. It is merely a term which we find it convenient to use when we refer to all those different kinds of books written to please and delight their readers. Those who pride themselves on being students of literature should remind themselves that whilst novels, plays and poems exist, literature is an abstraction, and that any statement made about literature is almost certain to be partly false.

It is better to read books than to read books about books. There are two justifications for books about books: the first, that they introduce you to books you will enjoy reading; the second, that they help you to understand and appreciate books you have read. You, however, are the only person who can find out what a book means to you, and you should not accept anyone else's word for this.

PART ONE: 1901—1914

Rudyard Kipling

FROM now on the discussion will be about books published from 1901 onwards and about their authors. The first of these, *Kim* by RUDYARD KIPLING, appeared in that year. Its writer had been born in 1865 in Bombay, India, the son of an artist, John Lockwood Kipling, who became curator of Lahore Museum from 1875 to 1893. All these facts are important in the development of Kipling's work. He spent much of his childhood and youth in India; its scenes and people provide the material and the background for some of his best stories and poems. From his father he inherited the artist's eye for a striking or picturesque scene. In the very first sentence of *Kim* we meet the boy who is the hero of the book sitting on the great gun outside the Lahore Museum, and it is there that he meets the Tibetan holy man whom he accompanies from then onwards.

Kipling was sent to England to be educated, and he attended the United Services College at Westward Ho! in Devon. Here he made friends with two other boys, their adventures forming the basis of one of the best school stories in English, *Stalky and Co.*, published in 1899. Kipling also edited and contributed to a magazine at school. This experience filled him with the ambition to become a writer, a resolution from which he never turned back. When he went back to India, he became half the staff of the Lahore *Civil and Military Gazette*. In the course of his duties on this paper he met all kinds of people and saw many sides of life in India, an admirable training for a writer.

Kipling's first book was a collection of satirical poems, *Departmental Ditties* (1886), in which he poked fun at the way in which Indian civil servants schemed for promotion and exchanged gossip. Even in this early work Kipling shows that he can express an idea in a sentence that readers will remember. 'The Betrothed' tells of a man whose fiancée insists that he should give up cigars before she will marry him. The man decides that Maggie's attractions will wear off in time, but that cigars will always be the same:

And a woman is only a woman, but a good cigar is a smoke.

Between 1887 and 1889 seven of his stories, most of them about Englishmen who worked or served in India, were published, the best of these being *Soldiers Three*. The three were Mulvaney, an Irishman with an unquenchable thirst and a tireless tongue, Learoyd, a massive Yorkshireman and a great fighter, and Ortheris, a little Cockney who is the master-mind. Later Kipling wrote other stories about this trio.

These books won for Kipling recognition as a born story-teller, with a fertile imagination, a quick eye for character, and a vigorous style. He made a leisurely return to England to pursue his career as a writer. *Barrack Room Ballads* (1892) widened his reputation, this time as a writer of narrative verse. This collection includes perhaps more lines that have become known to most readers than any other work of its length, except *Hamlet*. Many people know these lines without realising where they come from:

For it's Tommy this, an' Tommy that, an' 'Chuck him out, the brute!'
But it's 'Saviour of 'is country' when the guns begin to shoot. . . .
('Tommy')

So 'ere's *to* you, Fuzzy-Wuzzy, at your 'ome in the Soudan;
You're a pore benighted 'eathen, but a first-class fightin' man. . . .
('Fuzzy-Wuzzy')

Though I've belted you and flayed you
By the livin' Gawd that made you,
You're a better man than I am, Gunga Din!
('Gunga Din')

On the road to Mandalay,
Where the flyin'-fishes play,
An' the dawn comes up like thunder outer China 'crost the Bay!
('Mandalay')

We're poor little lambs who've lost our way,
Baa! Baa! Baa!
We're little black sheep who've gone astray,
Baa-aa-aa!
Gentlemen-rankers out on the spree,
Damned from here to Eternity,
God ha' mercy on such as we,
Baa! Yah! Bah!
('Gentlemen-Rankers')

They are hangin' Danny Deever, they are marchin' of 'im round,
They 'ave 'alted Danny Deever by 'is coffin on the ground;
An' 'e'll swing in 'arf a minute for a sneakin' shootin' hound—
O they're hangin' Danny Deever in the mornin'!
('Danny Deever')

Oh, East is East, and West is West, and never the twain shall meet,
Till Earth and Sky stand presently at God's great Judgment Seat;
But there is neither East nor West, Border, nor Breed, nor Birth,
When two strong men stand face to face, tho' they come from the ends of the earth!

('The Ballad of East and West')

For the female of the species is more deadly than the male.

('The Female of the Species')

Many of the ballads are written in the language of the ordinary soldier, slangy, strongly rhythmical, humorous, earthy, shrewd, sympathetic, but always memorable. Many of the lines jump up from the page and hit you; it is verse that is meant to be spoken and that refuses to be forgotten. In these ballads Kipling expresses his intense patriotism, made all the keener for the years he has spent in a distant land. 'What should they know of England who only England know?' he asked in *The English Flag.* Kipling recognises the courage and cleverness of foreigners, but for all their good points, and for all the weaknesses of the English, they *are* foreigners and we *are* English. That made all the difference in the world to Kipling.

One of the most astonishing things about Kipling at that time was his ability to follow up one success with another of a completely different kind. In 1894 *The Jungle Book* appeared, to be followed by *The Second Jungle Book* in 1895. These books tell how the human child, Mowgli, was brought up in the jungle by wolves, learning from them the law of the jungle. These stories have delighted children of every generation since they were written. Animals which live in a different world from men, but which in many ways behave like human beings, have fascinated children from the sixth century B.C. when Aesop composed his fables. Children also like a story to have a moral: in *The Jungle Books* Mowgli learns that 'The Law of the Jungle—which is by far the oldest law in the world—has arranged for almost every kind of accident that may befall the Jungle People, till now its code is as perfect as time and custom can make it.' The animals themselves—Akela, Baloo the bear, Toomai, Rikki-tikki-tavi and others—are creatures that children have grown up with in imagination, and who have helped children to grow up by extending the range of their imagination.

But in the end children and grown-ups read *The Jungle Books* with a warm feeling of pleasure because every word is right. Here is part of 'Red Dog' from *The Second Jungle Book* describing how the dholes chased Mowgli:

They gave one deep howl, and settled down to the long, lobbing canter that can at the last run down anything that runs. Mowgli knew their pack-pace to be much slower than that of the wolves, or he would never have risked a two-mile run in full sight. They were sure that the boy was theirs at last, and he was sure that he held them to play with as he pleased. All his trouble was to keep them sufficiently hot behind him to prevent their turning off too soon. He ran cleanly, evenly, and springily; the tailless leader not five yards behind him; and the pack tailing out over perhaps a quarter of a mile of ground, crazy and blind with the rage of slaughter. So he kept his distance by ear, reserving his last effort for the rush across the Bee Rocks.

No one needs to read this passage twice to understand it. Kipling chooses simple words, places the pauses skilfully, the sentences do not tail away. The paragraph moves on.

Kipling married an American, Miss Caroline Balestier, in 1892 and lived for a few years in Vermont, a state in the north-east of the United States on the border with Canada. By American standards Vermont is no great distance from the scene of Kipling's next novel, *Captains Courageous*, a story of the Grand Banks. The story tells how Harvey Cheyne, the spoilt son of an American multi-millionaire, makes himself sick by smoking a cigar whilst crossing the Atlantic. He falls overboard and is picked up in the nets of a Newfoundland fishing-schooner, the *We're Here*. There was no ship's wireless in those days, so Harvey had to remain on board until the schooner returned to port. The simple life, hard work, sea air and discipline make a man of Harvey before he is restored to his parents. The story records a way of life and a kind of character in a remote part of North America that was fading away even in Kipling's day.

The ways of Vermont did not suit Kipling, and his own ways did not please his wife's family, so he left the U.S.A. to return to England, paying a visit to South Africa en route. *Stalky and Co.* was published in 1899 and *Kim*, of which more is to be said later, in 1901. The *Just So Stories* (1902) were written for rather younger children than *The Jungle Books*; they give unlikely explanations of such mysteries as 'How the leopard got his spots', 'How the camel got his hump' and 'How the whale got his throat'. Kipling tells his fantastic stories with their absurd details in a mock-serious manner. The style is grand and dignified, but even the young reader sees that Kipling does not mean the stories and the language to be taken seriously. The stories are full of fine phrases and sentences that remain with the reader: the mariner who was 'a man of infinite-resource-and-sagacity', and 'The great grey-green, greasy Limpopo river, all set about with fever-trees'.

Kipling eventually settled in a house called 'Bateman's' at Burwash in

Sussex. Visitors to this delightful village are allowed to see the house and grounds on payment of an entry-fee. The many historical associations of Sussex set Kipling's imagination working to produce *Puck of Pook's Hill* (1906). In this book Puck, whom we always think of as a particularly English fairy, appears to two children, Dan and Una, and reveals to them scenes and events in England's history. The first story is set at Pevensey Bay, not far from Burwash. Through all the stories runs a pride in England's history and a sense of its continuity. In many ways the situation of the Romans in England is like that of English soldiers in India, the Roman Wall like the North-West Frontier. In this book and its successor, *Rewards and Fairies* (1910), Dan and Una see people from history and learn to appreciate how they make decisions when much depends on the course they choose. At the end they have learned what kind of people the English are, what kind of a land they live in, and how the country came to produce the people.

After 1910 Kipling's period of achievement appears to have been exhausted, except for a few short stories such as *The Bull that Thought*. The world changed and Kipling did not like the changes. The British Empire was no longer impregnable after the Boer War; its air of permanence had gone. Kipling cut himself off from India from where his inspiration had flowed so freely. He went on writing, but his touch was not so sure, the boyish enjoyment of life had evaporated, the humour was often rather sour. The style was still vigorous, but his sentiments now made many of his countrymen rather uncomfortable. Perhaps Kipling no longer felt sure enough of himself to write another 'Ballad of East and West' or *Kim*.

Mowgli and Kim were both boys brought up in different worlds from those natural to their birth and ancestry. Kimball O'Hara was the son of an Irish soldier who had stayed on and died in India after his discharge. Kim had been left with a half-caste woman and was brought up as an Indian boy until he was caught hanging about the camp by the padre of his father's old regiment. The regiment then sent him to Saint Xavier's to receive the education that befitted a young sahib. Kim's schooling was, however, only a small part of his education. On the day when the story opened Kim had met two very different men: the Teshoo Lama, a Tibetan holy man, from whom Kim received his moral education whilst they wandered together through India. The lama dedicated his life to the search for the River of the Arrow, for 'whoso bathes in it washes away all taint and speckle of sin'. On the same day as Kim became the lama's *chela*, or disciple, he saw an old friend, Mahbub Ali, a Pathan horse-dealer and member of the Indian secret service, who gave Kim 'the pedigree of the white stallion' to take to Colonel Creighton, head of the service. Kim quickly realises that the 'pedigree' is a paper for which Mahbub's enemies would kill him. This is Kim's initiation into 'the Great Game' of counter-espionage, for which he also has to be educated. In the end the lama finds the River of the Arrow, and Kim accomplishes his first mission in 'the Great Game'. Kim learns from the lama the lessons of humility and self-control, but like Mowgli he responds to the call of his own ancestry when the time comes for choice.

Kim has some exciting adventures: he saves the life of his fellow-agent on the train by disguising him as a Saddhu; he steals the *kilta* containing all the Russian agent's secret papers: but *Kim* is more than an adventure story. It is a gallery of characters, all of them more than life-size and vividly impressive. There is Lurgan Sahib, the healer of sick pearls, who in a strange scene tests Kim's powers of resistance to hypnosis; Huneefa, the blind woman, who had the secret of a colour that catches: 'a huge and shapeless woman clad in greenish gauzes, and decked, brow, nose, ear, neck, wrist, arm, waist, and ankle with heavy native jewellery. When she turned it was like the clashing of copper pots.' Hurree Chunder Mookerjee, 'whose name on the books of one section of the Ethnological Survey was R 17', a fat man who was by nature fearful, but who faced hardship and danger whilst inwardly quaking. Hurree Babu (a Babu is a Bengali with an English education) speaks an English of his own:

This is fine! This is finest! Mister O'Hara! You have—ha! ha!—swiped the whole bag of tricks—locks, stocks, and barrels. They told me it was eight months' work gone up the spouts! By Jove, how they beat me! . . . Look, here is the letter from Hilâs! Mister Rajah Sahib has just about put his foot in the holes. He will have to explain offeecially how the deuce-an'-all he is writing love-letters to the Czar. And they are very clever maps . . . and there is three or four Prime Ministers of these parts implicated by the correspondence. By Gad, sar! The British Government will change the succession in Hilâs and Bunâr, and nominate new heirs to the throne. 'Trea-son most base' . . . but you do not understand? Eh?

The gallery contains more than portraits: there are also landscapes and interiors—the Kashmir Serai, the bazaar, the 'te-rain', and the Grand Trunk Road, which presents India in miniature:

This broad, smiling river of life was a vast improvement on the cramped and crowded Lahore streets. There were new people and new sights at every stride—castes he knew and castes that were altogether out of his experience.

They met a troop of long-haired, strong-scented Sansis with baskets of lizards and other unclean food on their backs, their lean dogs sniffing at their heels. These people kept their own side of the road, moving at a quick, furtive jog-trot, and all other castes gave them ample room; for the Sansi is deep pollution. Behind them, walking wide and stiffly across the strong shadows, the memory of his leg-irons still on him, strode one newly released from the jail; his full stomach and shiny skin to prove that the Government fed its prisoners better than most honest men could feed themselves. Kim knew that walk well, and made broad jest of it as they passed. Then an Akali, a wild-eyed, wild-haired Sikh devotee in the blue-checked clothes of his faith, with polished-steel quoits glistening on the cone of his tall blue turban, stalked past, returning from a visit to one of the independent Sikh States, where he had been singing the ancient glories of the Khalsa to College-trained princelings in top-boots and white-cord breeches. Kim was careful not to irritate that man ; for the Akali's temper is short and his arm quick. Here and there they met or were overtaken by the gaily dressed crowds of whole villages turning out to some local fair; the women with their babes on their hips, walking behind the men, the older boys prancing on sticks of sugar-cane, dragging rude brass models of locomotives such as they sell for a halfpenny, or flashing the sun into the eyes of their betters from cheap toy mirrors. . . . A solid line of blue, rising and falling like the back of a caterpillar in haste, would swing up through the quivering dust and trot past to a chorus of quick cackling. That was a gang of *changars*—the women who have taken all the embankments of all the Northern railways under their charge—a flat-footed, big-bosomed, strong-limbed, blue-petticoated clan of earth-carriers, hurrying north on news of a job, and wasting no time by the road. They belong to the caste whose men do not count, and they walked with squared elbows, swinging hips, and heads on high, as suits women who carry heavy weights. A little later a marriage procession would strike into the Grand Trunk with music and shoutings, and a smell of marigold and jasmine stronger even than the reek of the dust. One could see the bride's litter, a blur of red and tinsel, staggering through the haze, while the bridegroom's bewreathed pony turned aside to snatch a mouthful from a passing fodder-cart. Then Kim would join the Kentish-fire of good wishes and bad jokes, wishing the couple a hundred sons and no daughters, as the saying is. Still more interesting and more to be shouted over it was when a strolling juggler with some half-trained monkeys, or a panting, feeble bear, or a woman who tied goats' horns to her feet, and with these danced on a slack-rope, set the horses to shying and the women to shrill, long-drawn quavers of amazement.

The reader can see, hear and smell the Grand Trunk Road; he can even understand some of its life and movement.

This passage illustrates, as almost every page that Kipling wrote does, his craftsmanship with words; his skill in choosing the right words and building them into sentences and paragraphs that are both firm and shapely. Both the beginning and the end of his sentences are admirable; there is no fumbling for words here.

Kipling is a boy's writer, clear, lively, exciting. His mind was neither flexible nor subtle; although the times changed, his ideas persisted. His career traces almost a perfect curve, reaching its peak in the middle years of his life. After that his beliefs and attitudes became unfashionable, and his popularity declined. But no writer who can handle words and tell a story as Kipling could deserves to be neglected, and the literary snob who despises him cuts himself off from a great deal of pleasure.

Henry James

HENRY JAMES (1843–1916) is a link between the nineteenth and the twentieth centuries, between America and Europe. His career as a writer extended from the time of the American Civil War to the First World War; he was born in the state of New York, but lived for most of his life in England. Shortly before his death he became a British citizen and was admitted to the Order of Merit. He was never a popular author during his lifetime, but his reputation has steadily risen during the fifty years that have followed his death.

His early life resembled in several respects that of Virginia Woolf, a later writer whose work James influenced. His father, a writer and lecturer on theology, was comfortably off, and his ability was inherited by his sons, William, a year older than Henry, who became famous as a psychologist and a philosopher, and Henry. William seems to have been the more robust in outlook and once told Henry, 'I play with boys who curse and swear'. The younger brother had a sheltered upbringing, being educated by private governesses and tutors, mainly in Europe, where the family travelled. His principal recreation was reading. His interest in literature was made keener by his frequent meetings with well-known writers who visited his father. In his adult life in Europe Henry James cultivated the acquaintance of literary figures, meeting amongst others Turgenev, Flaubert, Browning, Robert Louis Stevenson, Conrad, Kipling and H. G. Wells. Although he remained a bachelor, he led a busy social life as an assiduous diner-out and conversationalist.

The most important decision he took in his life was to settle in Europe; from 1869 onwards he lived mainly in England, first in London, later at Rye in Sussex. He appears to have found the American preoccupation with material progress and expansion at that time unsympathetic to the artist, whilst in Europe it was easier to find a circle of people with intellectual and literary interests, and a cultural tradition which could absorb him. Although he was not dependent on his royalties for his livelihood, he became in outlook the most professional of writers. He used his own background and experience as material for a number of his novels dealing with the impact of Europe on American citizens, and with the impact of Americans on Europeans. These include some of his best work in *The Portrait of a Lady* (1881), *The Wings of a Dove* (1902) and *The Ambassadors* (1903). Other well-known works included *Washington*

Square (1880), *The Bostonians* (1886) and the macabre ghost-story *The Turn of the Screw* (1898).

James regarded the novel, not primarily as a story, but as a means of depicting in detail the interaction of characters. Their range was restricted mostly to middle-class Americans and more sophisticated Europeans; the Americans often rather naive, the Europeans touched with corruption. The problems of American heiresses who are courted for their fortunes particularly concerned him. *The Portrait of a Lady* treats this subject with great delicacy, playing subtle variations on the theme. In his later work James required a central character and a situation—a populated situation—rather than a plot to work out. The examination of human behaviour becomes almost microscopic in its attention to detail. Some readers think that James became tedious and verbose as he grew older, but those who admire him most think that his qualities are shown fully developed in *The Ambassadors.* Lambert Strether, editor of an American review, is sent over to Paris by his patron, a wealthy widow called Mrs Newsome who expects to marry Strether. His task is to persuade Mrs Newsome's son, Chad, to return to take his part in the running of the prosperous family business in Woollett, Massachusetts; in the course of this he is expected to disentangle Chad from a supposed infatuation with a Frenchwoman. When he meets Chad, however, Strether finds him greatly improved by his sojourn in Paris, and he gives a good deal of credit for the improvement to the Comtesse de Vionnet. Mrs Newsome grows impatient with her ambassador's failure to complete his mission and sends over her daughter, Sarah, to deliver an ultimatum to Strether. In the end Chad remains in Paris, but Strether returns without enthusiasm to Woollett. Life in Paris has made him realise how dull was his life in Massachusetts, and how much he has missed. He tells a young American artist living in Paris, Little Bilham, not to repeat his mistakes: 'Live all you can; it's a mistake not to. It doesn't so much matter what you do in particular, so long as you have your life. If you haven't had that what *have* you had?' This is the message of the book.

It will be seen that, though this is a fairly long novel, not a great deal happens. Each chapter is a scene in which there is a meeting or a discussion or an incident; the thoughts, the feelings, the motives, the doubts, the suspicions of the characters concerned are minutely examined with reference to their past actions and histories, and with speculation about the possible consequences for their future of the incident or encounter. From all this comes a well-rounded picture of characters firmly set against a detailed and convincing background. Here is an account of a meeting between Strether and his friend Waymarsh, whose sympathies are now entirely with Mrs Newsome and her daughter, when Waymarsh comes to tell him that Sarah would like to see him:

He was never in the morning very late, but Waymarsh had already been out, and after a peep into the dim refectory, he presented himself there with much less than usual of his large looseness. He had made sure, through the expanse of glass exposed to the court, that they would be alone; and there was now in fact that about him that pretty well took up the room. He was dressed in the garments of summer; and save that his white waistcoat was redundant and bulging these things favoured, they determined, his expression. He wore a straw hat such as his friend hadn't yet seen in Paris, and he showed a buttonhole freshly adorned with a magnificent rose. Strether read on the instant his story—how, astir for the previous hour, the sprinkled newness of the day, so pleasant at that season in Paris, he was fairly panting with the pulse of adventure and had been with Mrs Pocock, unmistakably, to the Marché aux Fleurs. Strether really knew in this vision of him a joy that was akin to envy; so reversed as he stood there did their old positions seem; so comparatively doleful now showed, by the sharp turn of the wheel, the posture of the pilgrim from Woollett. He wondered, this pilgrim, if he had originally looked to Waymarsh so brave and well, so remarkably launched, as it was at present the latter's privilege to appear. He recalled that his friend had remarked to him even at Chester that his aspect belied his plea of prostration; but there certainly couldn't have been, for an issue, an aspect less concerned than Waymarsh's with the menace of decay. Strether had at any rate never resembled a Southern planter of the great days—which was the image picturesquely suggested by the happy relation between the fuliginous face and the wide panama of his visitor.

Strether then goes on to speculate on the part that Sarah (Mrs Pocock) had played in the blossoming of Waymarsh, and to reflect on the reversal of his and Waymarsh's roles, for Strether was being blamed for self-indulgence whilst in fact the formerly sedate Waymarsh was the one who was enjoying life without either a care or a word of criticism. The whole scene is described from Strether's point of observation—James thought that a definite viewpoint was of the utmost importance in describing a scene—and his thoughts and feelings traced in every step. This technique was later developed further by Virginia Woolf in the 'interior monologues' of her characters. Certainly James's later work has greatly interested many twentieth-century novelists, and he has rightly been called 'a novelist's novelist'.

His skill in the portrayal of character is shown here in the variety he brings to the numerous Americans in Paris whom he describes—Strether, Waymarsh, Chad, Sarah, her husband, Jim Pocock, Mamie, sister of Chad and Sarah, Maria Gostrey, Little Bilham. They are all distinctively American; on most of them Paris has an effect; but they are kept wonderfully clear and separate. The reader who does not demand that novels shall be broad in their conception, sweeping in their effects, and written with unflagging vigour, will find a great deal to enjoy at his leisure in the novels of Henry James.

Thomas Hardy

THE last years of the nineteenth century marked a turning-point in the career of THOMAS HARDY (1840–1928), just as they did in James Barrie's. Until 1897 Hardy was known as a novelist; afterwards he devoted his talent to poetry. In other ways the two writers could hardly have contrasted more strongly: Barrie was the most sentimental, Hardy the least sentimental of writers.

Hardy was born at Higher Bockhampton, a village near Dorchester, in 1840, and remained a Dorset man by birth, upbringing and feeling throughout his life. His father's craft as a stonemason and his hobby as leader of the local church choir both influenced Hardy. The craft gave him an interest in buildings which led Hardy to become an architect, and he inherited his father's liking for music. Stinsford Church, where his father led the choir, was the model for Mellstock, the village whose choir is so amusingly and lovingly described in *Under the Greenwood Tree.* Hardy's heart is buried in Stinsford churchyard.

He was articled to an architect in Dorchester, a neighbour of William Barnes, the Dorset poet. Although Hardy himself began to write poetry at the age of about seventeen, he took the advice of his friends to continue his training as an architect as a surer way of earning a living. At the age of twenty-two he sought to widen his professional experience by working in London as assistant to Arthur Blomfield, a famous architect. Hardy won a prize and a medal for his work, but fell ill and returned to work in Dorset. In the next few years he wrote several stories, achieving his first success with *Under the Greenwood Tree* in 1872. During the next twenty-five years he established himself as one of the leading novelists of the age with *Far from the Madding Crowd* (1874), *The Return of the Native* (1878), *The Trumpet-Major* (1880), *The Mayor of Casterbridge* (1886), *Tess of the D'Urbervilles* (1891) and *Jude the Obscure* (1896). The last two are harsh tragedies in which the principal characters bring about their own downfall by flouting the moral code of the society in which they live. Hardy showed plainly the part that sexual instinct played in the destruction of Tess Durbeyfield and Jude Fawley without condemning them outright. As a result the novels were widely denounced as immoral. The last sentence of *Tess* after she has been hanged, 'The President of the Immortals had finished His sport with Tess,' was regarded as blasphemous and earned Hardy the reputation of being an atheist. He now abandoned the writing of novels to return to poetry. Six volumes of verse were published between 1898 and 1928 as well as the epic poetic drama, *The Dynasts* (1903–8).

Many of the poems published during this period had been written many years before, but Hardy continued to write almost until his death. The following poem, subtitled 'A Reflection on my Eighty-sixth Birthday', expresses his view on life clearly:

He Never Expected Much

Well, World, you have kept faith with me,
                    Kept faith with me;
Upon the whole you have proved to be
                    Much as you said you were.
Since as a child I used to lie
Upon the leaze and watch the sky,
Never, I own, expected I
                    That life would all be fair.

'Twas then you said, and since have said,
                    Times since have said,
In that mysterious voice you shed
                    From clouds and hills around:
'Many have loved me desperately,
Many with smooth serenity,
While some have shown contempt of me
                    Till they dropped underground.

'I do not promise overmuch,
                    Child; overmuch;
Just neutral-tinted haps and such,'
                    You said to minds like mine.
Wise warning for your credit's sake!
Which I for one failed not to take,
And hence could stem such strain and ache
                    As each year might assign.

This is the distillation of a lifetime's experience: Hardy accepted the world, not demanding too much from it. By not expecting more from life than it was likely to give him, Hardy avoided extremes of disappointment and joy. His freedom from illusion braced him to withstand the minor crises of life. He does not pass judgment on the way life has treated him; he is neither indignant nor servile. His attitude is that of a man whose mild curiosity about the scheme of things has been satisfied.

The language is for the most part simple, the words and the sentence rhythms those of everyday speech. The rather awkward phrase, 'just neutral-tinted haps and such', stands out from the rest of the poem in a manner typical of Hardy. The effect is not musical, and the rhymes are a little forced. This is a poem, not because it sounds pretty, but because Hardy says something important about life with conviction. Like many of Hardy's poems it gives the impression of being compressed.

Most readers think that Hardy is a pessimist. In his poems he sees both aspects of life, its pangs and its pleasures:

Any Little Old Song

Any little old song
    Will do for me,
Tell it of joys gone long,
    Or joys to be,
Or friendly faces best
    Loved to see.

Newest themes I want not
    On subtle strings,
And for thrillings pant not
    That new song brings:
I only need the homeliest
    Of heart-stirrings.

In fact, many of Hardy's most familiar poems tell of his delight in simple things: 'The Darkling Thrush', 'Weathers', 'Snow in the Suburbs', for instance. These can be found in many anthologies.

On the other hand, he notes the apparently senseless destruction of beauty by the passage of time. In a sonnet called 'Hap' he says that the destruction of joy and hope would be easier to bear if there seemed to be any design in it, even a malevolent design, but he concludes:

These purblind Doomsters had as readily strown
Blisses about my pilgrimage as pain.

Man's fate appeared to be determined by sheer chance. A similar idea is worked out in the following poem:

God's Education

I saw him steal the light away
    That haunted in her eye:
It went so gently none could say
More than that it was there one day
    And missing by-and-by.

I watched her longer, and he stole
    Her lily tincts and rose:
All her young sprightliness of soul
Next fell beneath his cold control
    And disappeared like those.

I asked: 'Why do you serve her so?
    Do you, for some glad day,
Hoard these her sweets—' He said, 'O no,
They charm not me; I bid Time throw
    Them carelessly away.'

Said I: 'We call that cruelty—
    We, your poor mortal kind.'
He mused. 'The thought is new to me.
Forsooth, though I men's master be
    Theirs is the teaching mind!'

Hardy doubted whether life had any lessons to teach; life could only be accepted for what it was. The teaching mind was man's, not God's.

The next little poem has a charming, almost a romantic, idea as its theme: a boy's belief that there was only the one same cuckoo that returned year after year. One boy embraced the idea, the other scorns it; Hardy himself expresses no opinion:

Boys Then and Now

'More than one cuckoo?'
And the little boy
Seemed to lose something
Of his spring joy.

When he'd grown up
He told his son
He'd used to think
There was only one,

Who came each year
With the trees' new trim
On purpose to please
England and him:

And his son—old already
In life and its ways—
Said yawning: 'How foolish
Boys were in those days!'

Hardy's reputation for pessimism arises partly from his awareness of death in the midst of life, as revealed in this poem:

A Thought In Two Moods

I saw it—pink and white—revealed
Upon the white and green;
The white and green was a daisied field,
The pink and white Ethleen.

And as I looked it seemed in kind
That difference they had none;
The two fair bodiments combined
As varied miens of one.

A sense that, in some mouldering year,
As one they both would lie,
Made me move quickly on to her
To pass the pale thought by.

She laughed and said: 'Out there, to me,
You looked so weather-browned,
And brown in clothes, you seemed to be
Made of the dusty ground!'

Only the third verse here is gloomy; for the rest, Hardy is struck by the oddity of the resemblance between the two young people and the earth beneath their feet. In his novels the idea of death is not usually terrifying; often it seems the destination of life. 'A Thought In Two Moods' also expresses the kinship that Hardy believed to exist between man and the land where he lived.

This interest in death appears also in the last of Hardy's poems to be quoted here. It is typical also in its use of the device of question and answer, the most familiar example of which is 'Men who march away'.

'Who's in the next room?—who?'

'Who's in the next room?—who?
I seemed to see
Somebody in the dawning passing through,
Unknown to me.'
'Nay: you saw nought. He passed invisibly.'

'Who's in the next room?—who?
I seem to hear
Somebody muttering firm in a language new
That chills the ear.'
'No: you catch not his tongue who has entered there.'

'Who's in the next room?—who?
I seem to feel
His breath like a clammy draught, as if it drew
From the Polar Wheel.'
'No: none who breathes at all does the door conceal.'

'Who's in the next room?—who?
A figure wan
With a message to one in there of something due?
Shall I know him anon?'
'Yea he; and he brought such; and you'll know him anon.'

The matter-of-fact tone of the replies makes them seem the more certainly final.

Hardy's most ambitious work is *The Dynasts, An Epic-Drama of the War with Napoleon, in Three Parts, Nineteen Acts, & One Hundred & Thirty Scenes.* His interest in Napoleon had earlier been shown in his novel, *The Trumpet-Major*. Dorset, as a probable scene of invasion, was particularly stirred by the Napoleonic Wars, and, of course, Nelson's flag-captain at Trafalgar was also a Dorset man called Thomas Hardy. The drama unfolds the career of Napoleon from Trafalgar to Waterloo, showing also the reactions of the English rank and file to their experiences as soldiers and deserters, and the comments of their relatives in Wessex. Hardy also 'thought proper to introduce, as supernatural spectators of the terrestrial action, certain impersonated abstractions, or Intelligences, called Spirits', whose function was to explain the significance of the events of the drama.

Hardy rightly said that *The Dynasts* is intended for mental performance, and not for the stage. No one can doubt the grandeur of the conception, but the characterisation is monotonous and Hardy's resources of language unequal to the great task he set himself. There is clarity and eloquence in some of the scenes where characters confer, and there is humour in the rustic scenes, but these are not enough to carry through a work of this size. It is easier to admire the conception than to read the work itself. As a poet, Hardy's skill seemed to lie in condensing his ideas rather than in expanding them.

J. M. Barrie

KIPLING wrote both verse and fiction successfully. Many other writers have also applied their talents to two branches of literature, and a few, amongst them Dryden, Goldsmith and T. S. Eliot, have gained distinction in prose, poetry and drama. JAMES MATTHEW BARRIE (1860–1937) had two literary careers, the first as a novelist, the second as a playwright. His novels belong to the nineteenth century, but the plays he wrote after the turn of the century have lasted better. His birthplace was Kirriemuir, a small town in Angus, Scotland, which figured in several of his stories as Thrums. The death of his brother, when Barrie was only six years old, appears to have been a shock both to Barrie and to his mother whom the author idolised. After attending school in Kirriemuir and at Dumfries Academy, Barrie studied at Edinburgh University where he graduated at the age of twenty-two. He worked as a journalist in Nottingham for eighteen months before he settled in London in 1885 to work as a free-lance journalist, that is, a writer who offers his stories and articles to any periodical likely to be interested, but who is not regularly employed by any paper. Barrie was able to sell what he wrote and had none of the struggles that many authors have undergone. He soon turned to the writing of novels based on his early life in Kirriemuir, the best-known of these being *A Window in Thrums* and *The Little Minister* (1891). These homely stories of life in an obscure Scottish town, described with sentiment and humour, were said by critics to belong to the 'Kailyard School' of literature, a kailyard being a patch of land on which cottagers grew cabbages.

The Little Minister was so popular as a novel that Barrie adapted it as a play in 1897, so setting out on the road to a career as a popular dramatist. His best-known play is undoubtedly *Peter Pan* (1904), but among his other plays *The Admirable Crichton* and *Quality Street* (both 1902), *What Every Woman Knows* (1908), *Dear Brutus* (1917), *Mary Rose* (1920) and several of his one-act plays are still remembered and sometimes acted. Each of these plays has its admirers, but none of them has been generally accepted as Barrie's masterpiece.

Peter Pan, who said, 'I want always to be a little boy and to have fun', is one of those characters in English literature, like Falstaff and Mr Pickwick, who are known to all readers. This yearning for youth appears in several other characters in Barrie's plays. *Mary Rose* is about a young wife who disappears on an island in the Hebrides for twenty-five years, then reappears not a day older, though her infant son is now a man. Miss Phoebe Throssel, the heroine of *Quality Street*, masquerades as her own niece, Livvy, to win the love of Captain Valentine Brown after he has commented on the way in which she has aged during his absence fighting in the Napoleonic Wars. In *Dear Brutus* several people who have made a mess of their lives are given a second chance to avoid their past errors, only for most of them to repeat their mistakes, so proving that

> The fault, dear Brutus, is not in our stars,
> But in ourselves. . . .

Maggie, the heroine of *What Every Woman Knows*, is haunted by the knowledge that she is older than her husband and devoid of charm, so that she has to use all her wits to protect and keep him. Barrie in these plays struggled against the idea of advancing age and the changes that it brings. Perhaps *Peter Pan*, in which the ever-youthful Peter routed the seedy, middle-aged pirate, Captain Hook, symbolises this struggle.

Peter Pan took Wendy and her brothers to the Never-Never Land, where they met pirates, redskins, a mermaid and a fairy. The play has been regularly produced each Christmas, appropriately because it contains many of the ingredients of pantomime, including Nana, the Newfoundland dog who acts as nursemaid to the children. Several of Barrie's other plays are set in never-never lands of his own imagination. Acts II and III of *The Admirable Crichton* take place on a desert island in the Pacific where the Earl of Loam with his family, friends and servants is shipwrecked. On this island Crichton, the butler, shows he is master, and in a topsy-turvy world his former employers are humbly grateful for the chance of serving him. The characters in *Dear Brutus* are offered their second chance in an enchanted wood where the manservant becomes a financier and the deceived wife is now the deceiver. Mary Rose falls under a fairy spell on an island in the Hebrides. Barrie's romantic nature disliked the world as it really was, and he recreated it to his own satisfaction.

Because he was a romantic, Barrie spread the sentiment so thickly in his plays that in anyone else the effect would be embarrassing for the audience. He himself so obviously believes in, and beams at, this lavish sentiment that he often carries the audience along with him. Even so, it is a little difficult to listen without wriggling to lines like these of Peter Pan: 'When the first baby laughed for the first time, the laugh broke into a thousand pieces and they all went skipping about, and that was the beginning of fairies.'

In Barrie's world evil does not exist as a force; there are no convincing villains. Captain Hook is a comic character who crumples at the sight of danger, whilst Smee, his henchman, proves to be a sound nonconformist fond of needlework. *Peter Pan* is a pantomime without a demon king. Old Lob, who schemes all the trouble in *Dear Brutus*, is a mischievous spirit, quite content to nod in his chair whilst his guests torment each other. Nor indeed are the men in these plays, even those sympathetically portrayed, particularly forceful or heroic. As soon as the rescue boat calls in at the desert island, Crichton's little empire collapses, and he becomes a servant once more. Simon, Mary Rose's husband, for all his reputed gallantry as a naval officer, does nothing to save her from the spell of the island. Some of Barrie's best-drawn characters are fussy, elderly people, mildly spiteful towards their friends—Mr Morland and Mr Amy in *Mary Rose*, the gossips in *Quality Street*, Coady in *Dear Brutus.*

It is an interesting question whether Barrie's was a woman's world, or a sexless world in which male and female qualities were not made distinct from each other. Peter Pan is a boy, but his part is written for, and played by a girl. The most forceful and the most attractive of his characters is Maggie in *What Every Woman Knows.* The story and background of this play lay within Barrie's experience: a poor, but talented, young Scotsman follows a path from an insignificant Scottish town to a position of comfort and influence in London. Here Barrie is writing about the kind of people he knows, and the background is much more convincing than that of the country house in *Dear Brutus.* John Shand, a brilliant scholar by his own admission, but too poor to continue his education at the university, is offered £300 by the Wylie family to finance his education and first steps in the world, on condition that Maggie Wylie is given an option to marry him in five years' time. Shand fulfils David Wylie's expectations: 'A young Scotsman of your ability let loose upon the world with £300, what could he not do? It's almost appalling to think of; especially if he went among the English.'

The rest of the play is an illustration of David's other comment: 'There are few more impressive sights in the world than a Scotsman on the make.'

In his progress Shand is unobtrusively helped at every stage by Maggie, who is too wise to let her husband realise what she is doing for him. It is only when Shand tries to strike out without Maggie that he begins to suspect how important her help is to him. He then learns 'what every woman knows': 'Every man who is high up loves to think that he has done it all himself; and the wife smiles, and lets it go at that. It's our only joke. Every woman knows that.'

This is the play of Barrie's liked best by some; it is about a world that really existed, peopled by characters whose ambitions, humour and feelings the author understood.

Barrie was much more skilful at imagining situations than at working out plots; even *What Every Woman Knows* consists of two situations—the initial offer to Shand, and the crisis in which he sees Maggie's true worth—rather than a connected story. For that reason, he was a master of the one-act play. Two of these are well worth reading—*The Twelve-Pound Look* and *The Old Lady Shows her Medals*, the first for its amusing deflation of a successful man by his former wife, and the other for its mixture of pathos and humour in the picture of an old lady who has in her imagination claimed a young soldier as her son.

Barrie's 'whimsy', a mixture of strange imagination and sentiment, is unlikely to return to fashion, but his plays act better than they read, and one or two of them are likely to remain as minor curiosities in our literature. He was an odd man, as can be seen from reading an amusing account of a week-end with him described by Neville Cardus in his *Autobiography*.

George Bernard Shaw

THERE was a gap of over 100 years between the careers of GEORGE BERNARD SHAW (1856–1950) and the last great dramatist in English before him, Sheridan. There was also a link between them, for both were born in Dublin and achieved their fame in London. Shaw served a long apprenticeship to greatness and at the age of thirty not only had he accomplished very little, but he seemed likely to spend the rest of his life wasting his talents.

After losing a comfortable post in the Dublin Law Courts, Shaw's father became a wholesale corn-merchant, a business of which he knew nothing and which he was too indolent to learn. What little money he had went mostly on drink, so Shaw's mother had to fend for herself and her three children. A strong-minded woman with musical talent, she was able to make a living as a singer and a teacher of singing. This work left her with little time to look after her son, who to a great extent brought himself up. He attended several schools where, except in composition, he did badly. 'I cannot learn anything that does not interest me,' he said later, and he educated himself from an early age by wide reading, especially of Shakespeare and Dickens, by listening to the music which flooded his home, and by visiting the theatre to see operas and plays. Any weakness in mathematics at school proved no handicap later in life, for Shaw became a very shrewd business-man in the handling of his own plays. The contempt he often expressed for scientists was based on his youthful ignorance.

After leaving school Shaw became junior clerk to a land agent, one of his duties being the collecting of rent from poor tenants. The sudden departure of the cashier, a key man, caused a crisis in the office, and Shaw, though still only sixteen, was given the job on trial; he held the position successfully for four years. By the time he was twenty he was earning a salary of £84 a year, then a comfortable income, in a profession which offered glowing prospects in Ireland for a young and able man. In 1876, however, Shaw suddenly resigned his position to follow his mother and sisters to London where they had gone four years earlier. Mrs Shaw had become a successful music-teacher there, and Shaw's sister was a promising singer who later appeared in musical comedy.

During his first nine years in London Shaw earned almost nothing and in fact lived on his mother. He wrote five novels in which none of the many publishers to whom he sent them showed the slightest interest. Shaw put the novels away in a cupboard, but even the mice which nibbled at them were unable to finish them. Jack Tanner, the hero of Shaw's play, *Man and Superman*, was expressing the views the author had himself put into practice when he said, 'The true artist will let his wife starve, his children go barefoot, his mother drudge for his living at seventy, sooner than work at anything but his art.'

Shaw was now a non-smoker, a teetotaller, a vegetarian, a socialist and a religious sceptic, all his beliefs outraging the standards of the society on whose outskirts he existed. He spent a good deal of his time speaking in public to any audience he could find, at street-corners or in halls, in support of his views. Even his friends regarded him at this time as a crank.

In 1884 he joined the Fabian Society, a group of socialist intellectuals formed a few months earlier. Its members included a future Prime Minister, Ramsay MacDonald, a poet, William Morris, a subsequent Cabinet Minister, Sydney Webb, and other men and women distinguished in journalism, the Civil Service and politics. Shaw's transformation from a talented ne'er-do-well to a successful reviewer and playwright began when he joined the Fabians. The pamphlets and reports he wrote for the Society clearly showed his ability as a writer, and from 1885 onwards work as a journalist began to come to him. Once the door opened to him, his talent with words, his capacity for hard work and his efficiency led straight to success. Editors soon learned that Shaw would produce well-written work at the time he had promised it. As a socialist Shaw showed the qualities of a successful capitalist.

In 1888 Shaw became music critic on *The Star*, writing under the name of Corno di Bassetto, an obsolete wind instrument. His criticism was always lively and amusing, often shocking to the musical opinion of the day. Of an oratorio by Gounod he wrote, 'If you will only take the precaution to go in long after it commences and to come out long before it is over you will not find it wearisome.' Shaw often took the unpopular and unconventional view, notably in championing the operas of Wagner who was regarded as a lunatic by some critics and scholars.

As dramatic critic of *The Saturday Review* from 1895 onwards, Shaw lampooned some of the popular idols of the London stage, especially Henry Irving who, he said, had 'simply no brains, all character and temperament'. He also recognised and proclaimed the genius of the Norwegian playwright, Henrik Ibsen, who had been branded as an incompetent dramatist with shockingly immoral ideas.

It was his support for Ibsen that led Shaw to write his first play. J. T. Grein had produced Ibsen's *Ghosts* for the Independent Theatre, but could not find an English play to follow it. Shaw, having praised Ibsen's work, thought it his duty to provide a successor, so he completed a half-written play for Grein. This was *Widowers' Houses* which attracted a great deal of attention, most of it hostile.

Once he had begun writing plays, Shaw brought to the work his formidable energies, and with his fourth play, *Arms and the Man* (1894), he began to attract a wider public, although the play was not at its first production a financial success. On the first night the play was warmly applauded by the audience, except for one man who booed vigorously. In his curtain speech Shaw addressed this man: 'I quite agree with you, my friend, but what can we two do against a whole houseful of the opposite opinion?'

Arms and the Man was quickly followed by *Candida*, *You Never Can Tell* and *The Devil's Disciple*. The last play was produced in New York by Richard Mansfield with great success in 1897, giving Shaw for the first time popular success and financial security. Shaw had now written eight plays in five years with the result that overwork brought on a serious illness. An Irish heiress, Charlotte Payne-Townshend, insisted on rescuing him from the squalid conditions in which Shaw had continued to live and took him away to nurse him to recovery. In these circumstances Shaw found it simplest and very convenient to marry the lady, and from then onwards they lived very comfortably together.

When he had recovered from his illness the flow of plays resumed with little interruption for thirty years. They included *Caesar and Cleopatra*, in which Shaw made historical characters human beings who shared the feelings and language of the rest of mankind; *Man and Superman*, which illustrated the working of the Life Force, the nearest Shaw came to a religious belief; *Major Barbara*, about which more will be said later on; *Androcles and the Lion*, a comedy about the persecution of the early Christians which includes some delightful scenes; *Pygmalion*, which showed that the key to English society is not birth or breeding or ability, but the right accent; *Heartbreak House*, a parable about the Europe that was destroyed in the First World War; *Back to Methuselah*, a working out of Shaw's belief in Creative Evolution as the key to man's development through the ages—a very long play, but not tedious to read; and *Saint Joan*, the greatest of his plays in popular opinion. Shaw was still writing plays after he had passed his eightieth birthday.

In a long and productive life Shaw changed people's ideas of what a play is. Instead of plots in which the action built up to a climax, after which the author tidily rounded off the play and paired off the characters, Shaw gave his audiences ideas, discussion and debate of themes, comment on religion, politics and society, and lively and intelligent conversation. It was not that Shaw could not work out a plot: *The Devil's Disciple* strings together many of the stock situations of melodrama in a most effective theatrical manner. Nor was Shaw unable to create interesting characters; Doolittle, Lady Cicely Waynflete, Captain Shotover, Joan of Arc, Andrew Undershaft, all prove this. But they are characters who interest us more in what they think and the way in which they express and apply their ideas than by their physical appearance or odd habits. In some of his plays Shaw does delight in standing ideas on their heads and turning them round through all angles rather more than his audience does; sometimes that flow of words goes on and on without saying much that is either important or convincing. Some of the characters appear to exist solely in order to express Shaw's own ideas and have no life of their own. But in his better plays Shaw persuades the audience to accept his view that a play is anything which will keep them in the theatre, and that nothing is more entertaining than good talk.

Many of the themes of his own life are reflected in the plays. He enjoyed shocking people by his beliefs and appearance. Lanky, pale-faced with a red beard, he exaggerated his own oddity by wearing Jaegers, strange, knitted, one-piece, woollen garments combining trousers, jacket and waistcoat. Similarly, his plays were full of ideas that then seemed outrageous expressed in pungent style—women in pursuit of men, doctors guided by their own fads and superstitions, a king who threatens to get himself elected as Prime Minister.

His experience as a public speaker is exploited in every scene he wrote. The rhythms of speech came naturally to his mind and were readily translated to his pen. He was a gifted writer of prose who chose drama as his medium. Whether in dialogue or in the longer set speeches he so often introduces, what Shaw wrote was always very speakable. The lines speak for themselves if the actors do not try to force them, and the laughs come where Shaw planned them. The emphasis, the repetition, the balance, the pauses, the variation, all work together to ensure that.

As a young man in the estate business, a socialist worker, a councillor in the Saint Pancras area of London, Shaw knew what poverty and bad housing meant, and he uses his knowledge in plays like *Widowers' Houses* and *Major Barbara*. His own parents may be involuntarily recalled in the gallery of formidable women in his plays—Lady Cicely, Lady Britomart, Ann Whitefield, Saint Joan—and some of the ineffective men.

Major Barbara and *Saint Joan* are the plays now to be discussed in a little more detail. Both appear to be plays on religious themes, but the main theme of *Major Barbara* is the relation between money and power. Andrew Undershaft, the wealthy manufacturer of armaments, unashamed of the vast profits he makes from death and destruction, says:

Food, clothing, firing, rent, taxes, respectability and children. Nothing can lift those seven millstones from Man's neck but money; and the spirit cannot soar until the millstones are lifted. I lifted them from your spirit. I enabled Barbara to become Major Barbara; and I saved her from the crime of poverty.

CUSINS: Do you call poverty a crime?

UNDERSHAFT: The worst of crimes. All the other crimes are virtues beside it: all the other dishonours are chivalry itself by comparison. Poverty blights whole cities; spreads horrible pestilences; strikes dead the very souls of all who come within sight, sound, or smell of it. What you call crime is nothing; a murder here and a theft there, a blow now and a curse then: what do they matter? They are only the accidents and illnesses of life: there are not fifty genuine professional criminals in London. But there are millions of poor people, abject people, dirty people, ill fed, ill clothed people. They poison us morally and physically: they kill the happiness of society: they force us to do away with our own liberties and to organise unnatural cruelties for fear they should rise against us and drag us down into their abyss. Only fools fear crime: we all fear poverty. Pah! (*turning on* BARBARA) you talk of your half-saved ruffian in West Ham: you accuse me of dragging his soul back to perdition. Well, bring him to me here; and I will drag his soul back again to salvation for you. Not by words and dreams; but by thirty eight shillings a week, a sound house in a handsome street, and a permanent job.

Undershaft's daughter, Barbara, had become an enthusiastic member of the Salvation Army, but when the Army accepts money from a whisky distiller and an armaments manufacturer, she leaves. She realises that the work done by the Army depends on the money given by sinners. Undershaft tells her that to do good man needs power, and that power comes from money. After a struggle with herself Barbara decides that her father is right, and decides to apply the lesson he has taught her in her own fashion. Here is the conflict on which drama depends, a conflict of ideas not personalities, for Barbara is like her father in character. And how amusing the conflict is.

There is the dialogue; here is a passage between Undershaft and his son, Stephen, a rather stuffy young man who is appalled by his father's frank speaking:

UNDERSHAFT: It is settled that you do not ask for succession to the cannon business.

STEPHEN: I hope that it is settled that I repudiate the cannon business.

UNDERSHAFT: Come, come! don't be so devilishly sulky: it's boyish. Freedom should be generous. Besides, I owe you a fair start in life for disinheriting you. You cant become prime minister all at once. Havent you a turn for something? What about literature, art, and so forth?

STEPHEN: I have nothing of the artist about me, either in faculty or character, thank Heaven!

UNDERSHAFT: A philosopher, perhaps? Eh?

STEPHEN: I make no such ridiculous pretension.

UNDERSHAFT: Just so. Well, there is the army, the navy, the Church, the Bar. The Bar requires some ability. What about the Bar?

STEPHEN: I have not studied law. And I am afraid I have not the necessary push—I believe that is the name barristers give to their vulgarity—for success in pleading.

UNDERSHAFT: Rather a difficult case, Stephen. Hardly anything left but the stage, is there? (STEPHEN *makes an impatient movement.*) Well, come! is there anything you know or care for?

STEPHEN (*rising and looking at him steadily*): I know the difference between right and wrong.

UNDERSHAFT (*hugely tickled*): You dont say so! What! no capacity for business, no knowledge of law, no sympathy with art, no pretension to philosophy; only a simple knowledge of the secret that has puzzled all the philosophers, baffled all the lawyers, muddled all the men of business, and ruined most of the artists: the secret of right and wrong. Why, man, youre a genius, a master of masters, a god! At twentyfour, too.

LADY BRITOMART (*uneasily*): What do you think he had better do, Andrew?

UNDERSHAFT: Oh, just what he wants to do. He knows nothing; and he thinks he knows everything. That points clearly to a political career. Get him a private secretaryship to someone who can get him an Under Secretaryship; and then leave him alone. He will find his natural and proper place in the end on the Treasury bench.

The play is full of passages like these. There is, too, an array of characters to be enjoyed. Lady Britomart imposes her will on most people, but is outmatched by her cool and wily husband; Andrew and Barbara, his daughter, choose their own ways to follow; Stephen makes pompous speeches, but Cholly Lomax, for all his drivel, acts shrewdly when necessary; in the Salvation Army hostel we have the contrast between Snobby Price and Rummy Mitchens with their false and lurid confessions and Peter Shirley, the poor but honest workman, whom Undershaft saves, as he promised to do, by giving him a steady job; Bill Walker's physical strength is no match for Barbara's tongue; finally, we have a glorious character who never appears, perhaps because in the flesh he could not hope to equal the legend—Sergeant Todger Fairmile, who won £20 by standing up at the Music Hall against a Japanese wrestler, and who prayed for Bill Walker's soul whilst kneeling on his head.

In one sense *Major Barbara* is not a religious play, but a materialist's play. Shaw teaches that man can be saved by security and comfort, that the human soul is rotted by poverty and the diseases that poverty brings, not by unbelief.

Saint Joan is a play about a girl and a saint who achieves miracles by her faith. It is also, like many of Shaw's plays, about power. Joan's voices gave her the inspiration to seek glory and victory, for herself, for her country, and for God. As long as she was successful she had power. She clashed with the Church, whose power over its members was threatened by Joan's claim that her voices (i.e. her individual conscience) must be obeyed even when they conflicted with the teachings of the Church. If you wish to understand fully the themes of the play you should read Shaw's preface in which he explains these ideas and much else that is in the play. But you should see the play first if you can, then read it, then read the preface, with a final visit to a performance or a re-reading of the play. Even if you do not understand Shaw's views on authority and the human conscience, you will be moved by the tragedy of Joan.

It might seem that a play which takes a famous man or woman as its principal character starts with a great advantage—the audience is already interested in the character. In fact, this is not the case. The playgoer expects evidence of greatness from the very beginning and for this to be maintained throughout the play. The everyday affairs of a clerk may be made interesting, but we expect to be impressed by an emperor or a saint or a genius. Although we realise that if Julius Caesar in Shakespeare's play dominated the first three acts, his murder would leave the rest of the play empty, we are still disappointed that he does not appear a greater man.

Shaw solved this problem of portraying greatness as he tried to solve most problems—unexpectedly. We think of a saint as saintly, and when we use the word 'saintly' we think of someone not of this world, perhaps timid and hesitant in dealing with the affairs and people of this world. This view is, of course, nonsense; saints do more than think of God in a vague way: they are prepared to suffer anything for their belief in God. The real Joan was a country girl, a farmer's daughter, a young woman who gloried in the struggle and was able to lead and command tough soldiers. This comes out in her first scene in the play with Captain Robert de Baudricourt:

JOAN (*bobbing a curtsey*): Good morning, captain squire. Captain: you are to give me a horse and armour and some soldiers, and send me to the Dauphin. Those are your orders from my Lord.

ROBERT (*outraged*): Orders from your lord! And who the devil may your lord be? Go back to him, and tell him that I am neither duke nor peer at his orders: I am squire of Baudricourt; and I take no orders except from the king.

JOAN (*reassuringly*): Yes, squire: that is all right. My Lord is the King of Heaven.

ROBERT: Why, the girl's mad. (*To the* STEWARD) Why didn't you tell me so, you blockhead?

STEWARD: Sir, do not anger her: give her what she wants.

JOAN (*impatient but friendly*): They all say that I am mad until I talk to them, squire. But you see that it is the will of God that you are to do what He has put into my mind.

ROBERT: It is the will of God that I shall send you back to your father with orders to put you under lock and key and thrash the madness out of you. What have you to say to that?

JOAN: You think you will, squire; but you will find it all coming quite different. You said you would not see me; but here I am.

STEWARD (*appealing*): Yes, sir. You see, sir.

ROBERT: Hold your tongue, you.

STEWARD (*abjectly*): Yes, sir.

ROBERT (*to Joan, with a sour loss of confidence*): So you are presuming on my seeing you, are you?

JOAN (*sweetly*): Yes, squire.

ROBERT (*feeling that he has lost ground, brings down his two fists squarely on the table, and inflates his chest imposingly to cure the unwelcome and only too familiar sensation*): Now listen to me. I am going to assert myself.

JOAN (*busily*): Please do, squire. The horse will cost sixteen francs. It is a good deal of money; but I can save it on the armour. I can find a soldier's armour that will fit me well enough: I am very hardy; and I do not need beautiful armour made to my measure like you wear. I shall not want many soldiers: the Dauphin will give me all I need to raise the siege of Orleans.

ROBERT (*flabbergasted*): To raise the siege of Orleans!

JOAN (*simply*): Yes, squire: that is what God is sending me to do. Three men will be enough for you to send with me if they are good men and gentle to me. They have promised to come with me. Polly and Jack and—

ROBERT: Polly! You impudent baggage, do you dare call squire Bertrand de Poulengey Polly to my face?

JOAN: His friends call him so, squire: I did not know he had any other name. Jack—

ROBERT: That is Monsieur John of Metz, I suppose?

JOAN: Yes, squire. Jack will come willingly: he is a very kind gentleman, and gives me money to give to the poor. I think John Godsave will come, and Dick the Archer, and their servants, John of Honecourt and Julian. There will be no trouble for you, squire: I have arranged it all: you have only to give the order.

ROBERT (*contemplating her in a stupor of amazement*): Well, I am damned!

JOAN (*with unruffled sweetness*): No, squire: God is very merciful; and the blessed saints Catherine and Margaret, who speak to me every day (*he gapes*), will intercede for you. You will go to paradise; and your name will be remembered for ever as my first helper.

ROBERT (*to the steward, still much bothered, but changing his tone as he pursues a new clue*): Is this true about Monsieur de Poulengey?

STEWARD (*eagerly*): Yes, sir, and about Monsieur de Metz too. They both want to go with her.

ROBERT (*thoughtful*): Mf! (*He goes to the window, and shouts into courtyard*) Hallo! You there: Send Monsieur de Poulengey to me, will you? (*He turns to Joan*) Get out; and wait in the yard.

JOAN (*smiling brightly at him*): Right, squire. (*She goes out.*)

Here Shaw does two things: he writes a boisterous comic scene, and he introduces a saint. The saint is quite different from the one we had expected to see: she is in fact rather like the Principal Boy in a pantomime, but she impresses us by her faith. Joan performs a small miracle in the first scene in persuading Robert to help her. This small miracle prepares us for the bigger ones she performs later in lifting the siege of Orleans and breathing courage into the Dauphin. If Joan had come on to the stage and made a rousing speech about the glories of France and her mission in accomplishing the defeat of the English, we should not have been convinced of her greatness, for it is easier to make a speech than to perform miracles, even small ones. Henry V's speech before Harfleur is an exciting one, but the king's greatness is more truly seen in the scene with Bates, Court and Williams on the eve of Agincourt.

In the first scene Shaw makes us believe in Joan's faith, courage and determination, but the mood of the scene is a long way away from tragedy. The change comes gradually. In the court scene, though Joan triumphs, we see the opposition she is creating both in the court and in the Church. After the coronation of the Dauphin, in the discussion with the Archbishop, Dunois and the Dauphin, the possibilities of tragedy are made clear; the Archbishop says, 'The pit is open at her feet; and for good or evil we cannot turn her from it.' The trial follows.

Through these scenes Joan's character also deepens. At the beginning she is carried forward by excitement and success; later she comes to see that the first interruption in her run of success will lead to her death. Her faith and courage remain, but her faith is now in rights of the individual against the authority of King and State, and her courage, not in fighting against the enemy but in sacrificing her life for her beliefs. Joan does not change: the qualities that she showed in the first scene are still there, but the experiences she has been through have developed her character. This ability to develop character is very important both to the novelist and to the dramatist. If the main characters do not change at all throughout a play or a novel, we may lose interest in them; if they change so much that their actions in the latter part contradict those in the first part, we cannot believe in them. The skill lies in avoiding both these risks. The writer who does avoid them is reflecting life: experience does affect people's characters: as we get to know our friends better, we find out new things about them.

Saint Joan is a play without a villain. Shaw does not waken our sympathy for Joan by making those responsible for her death seem loathsome or contemptible. Cauchon does all he can to save Joan from the tragedy she has created for herself; the Inquisitor conducts the trial fairly; Warwick is serving his country and his fellow-nobles; the Dauphin understandably finds the task Joan has thrust upon him too great for him. This is not the obvious way to write such a play: a heroine seems to imply a villain. It is, however, completely convincing, for you can believe that the characters would react to their situation in this way. Joan's plight is all the more tragic because we see that honourable men with genuine good will for her cannot save her.

Joan's last speech, made when she has been offered perpetual imprisonment instead of burning at the stake if she will take back her heresy, is heroic and tragic, but in the voice there are still echoes of that first scene:

> You promised me my life; but you lied. You think that life is nothing but not being stone dead. It is not the bread and water I fear: I can live on bread: when have I asked for more? It is no hardship to drink water if the water be clean. Bread has no sorrow for me, and water no affliction. But to shut me from the light of the sky and the sight of the fields and flowers; to chain my feet so that I can never again ride with the soldiers nor climb the hills; to make me breathe foul damp darkness, and keep from me everything that brings me back to the love of God when your wickedness and foolishness tempt me to hate Him: all this is worse than the furnace in the Bible that was heated seven times. I could do without my warhorse; I could drag about in a skirt; I could let the banners and the trumpets and the knights and soldiers pass me and leave me behind as they leave the other women, if only I could still hear the wind in the trees, the larks in the sunshine, the young lambs crying through the healthy frost, and the blessed blessed church bells that send my angel voices floating to me on the wind. But without these things I cannot live; and by your wanting to take them away from me, or from any human creature, I know that your counsel is of the devil, and that mine is of God.

Where will you find finer prose than this?

Joseph Conrad

IN 1878 a twenty-year-old Polish seaman, scarcely able to speak a word of English, first set foot on English soil at Lowestoft. He died, a naturalised British citizen, at Bishopsbourne, near Canterbury in Kent, in 1924, celebrated as one of the outstanding British novelists of the century under his pen-name of JOSEPH CONRAD.

He was born in 1857 at Berdichev, a town in the Polish Ukraine, then under the government of the Russians. His father, who translated works by Victor Hugo and Shakespeare into Polish, was arrested by the Russians as a leader in the struggle for Polish independence and sent to a concentration-camp in North Russia. Although her health was never robust, Conrad's mother asked to accompany her husband, with the result that she died three years later. Conrad's father returned to Poland dispirited and weakened by his hardships, and he also died when Conrad was eleven years old. Conrad was placed in the care of his uncle for the next six years, during which time he read widely in French and German. He knew nothing about the sea or France beyond what he had read—there was no tradition of seafaring in the family—yet he left for Marseilles in 1874, just before his seventeenth birthday, to become a sailor.

Conrad's early experiences settled the pattern of his life and provided themes which often occurred in the books he later wrote. Like many of his heroes he was lonely and was seeking independence. His father's life had taught him that men have to make hard decisions and take risks for the things they believe in, and that heroism often leads to tragedy and death. His ideas at that time about life at sea were probably romantic and false, but they shaped his life: many characters in his stories sacrifice their happiness or even their lives for ideals or people they have not understood. Once Conrad had taken his decision to go to sea, he would not turn back. He cut himself off from Poland, a country that offered him little happiness or hope of freedom, but he could never become wholly French or English. He remained throughout the rest of his life a man apart. His novels are about men who are set apart from their fellows.

From Marseilles Conrad engaged in several gun-running expeditions on behalf of the pretender to the Spanish throne, Don Carlos, and he used these experiences as the basis of *The Arrow of Gold*, published in 1919. This tells how the young hero, Monsieur George, passes from boyhood to manhood through his adventures as a gun-runner and his love for Rita, an older woman, who finances their expeditions.

After four years in the French merchant navy Conrad signed on for a trip on a British ship, the *Mavis*. When he landed at Lowestoft he had decided that if he was to be a sailor, he would be a British sailor. In eight years he obtained a third mate's ticket, then a mate's, and finally a master's. He made several voyages to Far Eastern waters, notably Singapore, Borneo and the Gulf of Siam, all of which served as material for his novels. One trip up the Congo led to the writing of one of his best shorter novels, *Heart of Darkness*. These places are more than backgrounds to his stories: they have characters of their own, and the placing of an island or a reef affects the course of action.

The Congo stirred Conrad's imagination, but it also made him a victim of malarial attacks. He returned to sea, but his health would not stand up to this life. Conrad had already begun to write, though he had not so far seriously considered becoming a writer by profession. With the encouragement of John Galsworthy he now turned to writing, and his first novel, *Almayer's Folly* was accepted for publication and appeared in 1895. His efforts to return to sea continued for a time, but Conrad soon devoted himself to writing with his usual determination and desire for self-improvement. His novels include *The Nigger of the 'Narcissus'* (1897), *Lord Jim* (1900), *Nostromo* (1904), *The Secret Agent* (1907), *Chance* (1914), his first popular success, and *The Rover* (1924). Some of his best works are shorter stories—*Heart of Darkness* and *Youth* (1902), *Typhoon* (1903), *Gaspar Ruiz* (1906) and *Freya of the Seven Isles* (1910).

If you read Conrad's novels and stories, and then think about them, sooner or later you will begin to ask yourself, 'What is a novel?' No one has found a complete answer to this question, but Conrad gives us some important parts of the answer. *Typhoon*, for instance, is an exciting story which creates suspense. You wonder whether the ship can survive, whether all the Chinese coolies below will be battered to death and how they can be saved, whether there will be a riot when all their savings in dollars which have been strewn around in the storm are distributed again. The story has a beginning, a description of the *Nan-Shan*, its crew, passengers and purpose; a middle, the storm; and an end in which the ship reaches its destination and the incident is closed. Most novels have a story. Just as important as the story is the character of Captain MacWhirr. In fact, he cannot be separated from the story. The events would have turned out differently if Captain MacWhirr had been a different kind of man: in the storm the Captain showed the mate and the chief engineer that they had a false and incomplete impression of his character. He might lack imagination, but he had great courage; he seemed unintelligent, but his good sense solved the problem of the dollars in the simplest way. Interesting characters often appear in good novels; very good novels show how events and characters act on each other.

A profound novel sometimes expresses part of the author's view of life. In *Typhoon* Conrad is telling us that the man who will not swerve from his duty in the face of danger will overcome difficulties, hardships and problems that daunt cleverer men. He never says this in so many words, but unless you see this you do not understand *Typhoon.*

Sometimes a novelist creates or isolates a world of his own. This is true, for example, of the novels of Jane Austen and Henry James; once you are immersed in these books, other times, other places, other classes and kinds of people, cease to exist. It may be a small world, but if it is seen clearly and in depth, it can tell us a great deal about human nature. The very best Western novels sometimes do this also, though theirs is a simple world. During the storm the *Nan-Shan* is a world on its own, in which ruthlessness may be kinder than gentleness, where doggedness counts for more than cleverness.

You can read *Typhoon* for the first time and enjoy it as an exciting sea-story. You can read it again and appreciate the character of Captain MacWhirr. You can read it for the third time and digest its lesson about man's conduct in a crisis. Most good books can be read several times, and every time you read them you find a new layer of meaning. *Typhoon* is a suitable choice to begin with, for it has an immediate appeal as a story, and its other attractions are not too difficult for an attentive reader to find.

After *Typhoon* you might read *Youth*, the story of a voyage to Bangkok, full of mishaps that culminate in a disastrous fire at sea, but told with humour and a young man's eye for romance; *The Rover*, a longer novel which tells how Jean Peyrol, a retired pirate, sacrifices his own life in an exciting chase at sea, thus serving his country, and a girl, Arlette, of whom he has grown fond, and her lover, Lieutenant Real; *The End of the Tether*, a story about the captain of a ship who dare not reveal that he is going blind; *The Nigger of the 'Narcissus'* which shows the effect of a dying coloured seaman on the crew of the *Narcissus*; this story also has a storm which shows the truth about the men who make up the crew; and, if you have a stomach for evil, *Heart of Darkness*, the study of a Congo trader who has gained such power over the natives with whom he deals that he is tempted to believe he is God.

If you ever become a connoisseur of Conrad—and a connoisseur is someone who knows and understands a good deal about a subject—you should read *Lord Jim*, *Nostromo* and *The Rescue*. These are not novels for readers who like rapid action: much happens in them, but it does not happen quickly, and Conrad is not interested primarily in the action. He is more concerned with uncovering the motives for action, why people behave in a crisis in the way they do, and with showing that their motives are not always what they seem to be. He shows that circumstances may force ill-suited combinations of men to act together with results that they had not expected. The principal characters are often men who have been set apart from their fellows and who are called upon to make hard decisions. The mood is often pessimistic: good men whose intentions are for the best are destroyed by a turn of events they could not have foreseen. In his earlier books the writing of English did not come easily to Conrad. Apart from some difficulty with 'shall' and 'will', his correctness is astonishing, his vocabulary is wide. But he chose long words of Latin derivation, such as 'motionless', instead of shorter words like 'still', with the result that the words do not always flow smoothly. Conrad is not easy reading, but what he has to tell us about the human condition makes the effort to read him worth while.

Nostromo is a good example of his methods as a novelist; it expresses his views on life, and it has a rich texture. Although the story contains a suicide, two murders, a double-pronged invasion, a riot, and hidden treasure, it is not primarily an adventure-story. The Golfo Placido—the Gulf of Calm—and the two islands set in it, the Isabels, provide the setting for an important incident in the novel, but *Nostromo* is not a sea-story either. It is a study of a number of men acting under stress during a rebellion and in the shadow of a civil war; it examines the motives which underlie men's actions at such a time; it explores the reasons which force men into strange alliances and shows that fate can twist men's plans into shapes they would not recognise. These men are pitched into a deadly crisis, cut off from outside help, with only their own courage, strength, cunning and skill to rely on. How they react in this situation is the theme of the book.

Captain Mitchell described to a visitor, some time after the events, Nostromo's journey which led to the relief of the town:

Monygham arranged it all. He went to the railway yards, and got admission to the engineer-in-chief, who, for the sake of the Goulds as much as for anything else, consented to let an engine make a dash down the line, one hundred and eighty miles, with Nostromo aboard. It was the only way to get him off. In the Construction Camp at the railhead, he obtained a horse, arms, some clothing, and started alone on that marvellous ride—four hundred miles in six days, through a disturbed country, ending by the feat of passing through the Monterist lines outside Cayta. The history of that ride, sir, would make a most exciting book. He carried all our lives in his pocket.

No doubt it would make a most exciting book, and no doubt Conrad was capable of writing that book, but *Nostromo* is not that adventure-story. Conrad does not tell the events in the same order as they happened: there are several flash-backs. His purpose is not to confuse the reader—with patience in reading the line of the story is clear enough—but to give readers the chance to see events from more than one viewpoint, to show the reactions of the characters to the incidents they lived through.

The story concerns a rebellion in the South American state of Costaguana, during which the President, Ribiera, flees to the town of Sulaco and with the help of the town's chief citizens is able to escape by sea. The San Tomé silver mine is the richest industrial establishment in the republic: the rebels are anxious to seize its wealth; the owner, Charles Gould, known as Don Carlos, is just as anxious to keep it out of their hands. Like many other people in the town he is sick of revolution and corruption in the state. Martin Decoud, a pleasure-loving, cynical young man, more at home in Paris than in Sulaco, proposes a plan to declare the province around the town an independent state, and wins general support. He and Nostromo, the foreman of the dock-workers, are given the task of smuggling out of the town by sea six months' production of silver, and bringing military help from the port of Cayta some four hundred miles away. Their boat is struck in the Golfo Placido by a rebel invasion ship, but they manage to reach the Isabels where they bury the treasure. Everyone believes their boat to have been sunk and the treasure to lie at the bottom of the Gulf. Martin Decoud is left alone on the Isabels whilst Nostromo returns to Sulaco, but the loneliness overwhelms him and he commits suicide. Nostromo alone now possesses the secret of the treasure which he decides to remove, a few nuggets at a time. His ride to Cayta saves the town and leads to the establishment of the republic. He is regarded as a national hero, but he has been corrupted by his knowledge of the treasure. Eventually he is shot and killed as an intruder when he is making one of his periodic visits to the Isabels to remove part of the treasure.

In these events the characters reveal themselves. Martin Decoud has no faith in the plan he puts forward. He is in love with Antonia Avellanos who, like her father, believes she is a passionate supporter of liberty, and Decoud hopes that his proposal will win her favour for him. In the end he commits suicide for an idea in which he does not believe. Charles Gould is obsessed by the mine and supports the plan as the only means of protecting the men and preserving his control. His wife, Donna Emilia, acts out of love for her husband, and Dr Monygham, a man made bitter by failure, helps towards its success because he admires Donna Emilia. Everyone in the town thinks that Nostromo takes part in two dangerous expeditions out of loyalty to his masters, but in fact he values above all his reputation as a man who will succeed in enterprises beyond the powers of other men. Prestige and self-esteem drive him on.

In the end, against all likelihood, the plan is successful, but its results are completely different from everyone's expectations. Decoud shoots himself; Nostromo is corrupted by the treasure; Don Carlos finds that when his workers become prosperous their loyalty can no longer be trusted; Antonia, the lover of liberty, wants to annex the rest of Costaguana; Dr Monygham, the outcast and failure, becomes a respectable chief medical officer of health; Hernandez, the bandit who co-operates with the plotters, is made Minister of War, a post he holds with great dignity; Mrs Gould in helping her husband finds she has barred herself from any part in his life; Viola, an Italian café-owner, shoots Nostromo, his friend. Men may try to manipulate events, but fate is too strong for them.

The novel displays human nature in variety—the hero, the coward, the idealist, the materialist, the bitter and the gentle, the man who lives in the past, the man who looks to the future. More than that, it shows the variety that can exist in one man. Nostromo himself has four names. First, Nostromo, 'our man', of whom Captain Mitchell said, 'Devotion, courage, fidelity, intelligence were not enough. Of course, he was perfectly fearless and incorruptible.' And the chief engineer said, 'I found the Capataz always a very shrewd and sensible fellow, absolutely fearless, and remarkably useful.' Dr Monygham's comment was, 'His prestige is his fortune.' To the dockers he led, he was the Capataz, bold, clever and always successful. To Viola and his family, he was Gian' Battista, the big man who always protected them. When he set himself up as owner of a coastal trading-vessel he became Captain Fidanza. Some of the truth about him was contained in each of these facets, but the whole truth was known only to himself. Like many of Conrad's heroes, Nostromo was a man set apart, in his case by his knowledge of the treasure. This secret, hidden from everyone else, finally killed him.

Conrad shows also that false beliefs influence men's actions as strongly as the truth. People trust Nostromo because they believe he is incorruptible, and he fulfils all their hopes though he has been corrupted. Viola shoots Nostromo, thinking he is Ramirez come to court his daughter, but Nostromo dies. He keeps the treasure secret, because he thinks that Decoud has stolen four nuggets, and Nostromo with his reputation for honesty could not hand back the treasure with four nuggets missing. Decoud had put the nuggets in his pockets to make sure that his body would sink when he had shot himself. Sotillo, one of the rebel leaders, helped to bring about the downfall of his cause and his own death by dragging the harbour for a treasure that was not there. People mislead themselves and each other, and the result is often tragedy and disillusion.

Once the independence plan is launched, all those taking part are pushed on by events they are unable to control. As Charles Gould says to his wife:

> 'There were things to be done. We have done them; we have gone on doing them. There is no going back now. I don't suppose that, even from the first, there was really any possible way back. And, what's more, we can't even afford to stand still.'
>
> 'Ah, if only one knew how far you mean to go,' said his wife, inwardly trembling, but in an almost playful tone.
>
> 'Any distance, any length, of course,' was the answer, in a matter-of-fact tone, which caused Mrs Gould to make another effort to repress a shudder.
>
> She stood up, smiling graciously, and her little figure seemed to be diminished still more by the heavy mass of her hair and the long train of her gown.
>
> 'But always to success,' she said persuasively.
>
> Charles Gould, enveloping her in the steely blue glance of his attentive eyes, answered without hesitation—
>
> 'Oh, there is no alternative.'

This dialogue contains much of Conrad's philosophy. In this book he makes us see that human nature is very complicated and that men's characters can be twisted into strange patterns by the pressure of circumstances. This is a novel worth reading slowly and worth reading more than once. When you know it well, you will have some understanding of Conrad and, perhaps, some new ideas about the ways of men.

H. G. Wells

IF you wanted to show that talent and hard work would lead to success despite all the obstacles in the path, you could hardly choose a better example than H. G. Wells's career as an author. His birth, his education, the career chosen for him could hardly have been more obstructive to his ambitions. HERBERT GEORGE WELLS was born in 1866, the son of a professional cricketer, then a much more lowly occupation than it is now. After leaving the cricket field, his father tried unsuccessfully to run a hardware shop at Bromley in Kent. Wells's mother had been a lady's maid in a family which owned a large house and estate in Kent. When the hardware business failed, she returned to this kind of work. Both in *Bealby*, a farcical novel, and *Tono-Bungay*, there are echoes of the days Wells spent in these surroundings.

Wells was sent to (rather than educated at) Moreley's Academy in Bromley, and in *The History of Mr Polly* he describes his experiences there:

When he was about twelve, he was jerked by his parents to 'finish off' in a private school of dingy aspect and still dingier pretensions, where there were no object lessons, and the studies of book-keeping and French were pursued (but never effectually overtaken) under the guidance of an elderly gentleman, who wore a nondescript gown and took snuff, wrote copperplate, explained nothing, and used a cane with remarkable dexterity and gusto.

Mr Polly went into the National School at six, and he left the private school at fourteen, and by that time his mind was in much the same state that you would be in, dear reader, if you were operated upon for appendicitis by a well-meaning, boldly enterprising, but rather overworked and underpaid butcher boy, who was superseded towards the climax of the operation by a left-handed clerk of high principles but intemperate habits—that is to say, it was in a thorough mess. The nice little curiosities and willingness of a child were in a jumbled and thwarted condition, hacked and cut about—the operators had left, so to speak, all their sponges and ligatures in the mangled confusion—and Mr Polly had lost much of his natural confidence, so far as figures and sciences and languages and the possibilities of learning things were concerned. He thought of the present world no longer as a wonderland of experiences, but as geography and history, as the repeating of names that were hard to pronounce, and lists of products and populations and heights and lengths, and as lists and dates—oh! and Boredom indescribable. . . . He was uncertain about the spelling and pronunciation of most of the words in our beautiful but abundant and perplexing tongue—that especially was a pity, because words attracted him, and under happier conditions he might have used them well—he was always doubtful whether it was eight sevens or nine eights that was sixty-three (he knew no method for settling the difficulty), and he thought the merit of a drawing consisted in the care with which it was 'lined in'. 'Lining in' bored him beyond measure. . . . Outside the regions devastated by the school curriculum he was still intensely curious. He had cheerful phases of enterprise, and about thirteen he suddenly discovered reading and its joys. He began to read stories voraciously, and books of travel, provided they were also adventurous. . . .

Wells's mother seems to have been anxious for the boy to be apprenticed to a respectable trade, preferably in a shop, so at the age of fourteen he was sent off to a draper in Windsor to learn the business. Wells was soon sent back as unsuitable and for a short time was a chemist's assistant at Midhurst in Sussex. This stage of his career is the basis of the Wimblehurst episode in *Tono-Bungay*. A second attempt at the drapery business, this time in Southsea, was no more successful than the first, though Wells used his experiences there as material for parts of *The History of Mr Polly*, *The Wheels of Chance* and *Kipps*.

By this time Wells was seventeen, with little systematic education and no qualifications for a career except a hearty dislike of drapers' shops. However, whilst he had been at Midhurst, he had struck the headmaster of Midhurst Grammar School as a lad of unusual intelligence, and he offered Wells a job as a student-teacher. From there Wells gained a scholarship to the Normal School of Science (now the Imperial College of Science) where he was fortunate enough to come under the influence of a great and inspiring man, Professor T. H. Huxley. After completing his studies there, Wells took a post as a teacher in North Wales.

Wells's early life was much like Dickens's—an unsuccessful father, a sketchy schooling, a job he hated, then a period of hard-won, hard-working education.

Then occurred the first of two apparent misfortunes which proved to be blessings. Wells was badly injured whilst playing football with his pupils and had to give up his post. He returned to London, obtained another post there, and resumed his studies of science, this time at London University. His efforts were rewarded with a first-class honours degree in Zoology.

Wells now became a tutor in science to a correspondence college until a haemorrhage of the lungs compelled him to rest for a long time. A number of the stories and articles he had written had been accepted by magazines, so he turned to authorship to occupy himself. Success came to him rapidly; for the second time Wells had been directed towards his *métier* by unfitness to carry on his normal employment.

Wells first attracted attention as an author by a number of scientific romances which included *The Time Machine* (1895), *The Invisible Man* (1897) and *The First Men in the Moon* (1901). Science fiction now flourishes, but Wells was one of its founders. Only Jules Verne preceded him. The French author prophesied with uncanny accuracy many later scientific developments such as the submarine. The basis of Wells's books was not mechanical, however; he started from fantastic ideas—the possibility of a man making himself invisible or travelling in time as freely as he travelled in three dimensions. In working out these ideas Wells created amusing and interesting characters like Cavor in *The First Men in the Moon* or strangely impressive beings like the Morlocks in *The Time Machine* or the Grand Lunar. He wrote also a number of short stories on scientific themes, including the amusing *The Truth about Pyecraft*, which told of the embarrassing consequences for a fat man of the discovery of a formula for losing weight.

The next group of novels Wells wrote were semi-autobiographical with a background of late Victorian social life. *Kipps* (1905) was among the earlier ones, the story of a draper's assistant who came into a fortune and tried to adapt himself to a life of comfort, leisure and culture. Kipps was the first of Wells's simple young men who sought more from life than a monotonous job and a dull existence, who longed for travel, art, poetry, romance, but did not know how to put their desires into words or where to find the things they wanted. These books have a background of shop life, of people struggling to keep up an appearance of respectability despite lack of money.

There are strong likenesses between *Kipps* and *The History of Mr Polly* (1910). Like Kipps, Mr Polly comes into money, loses it, and finds contentment in a simple way of life. Although Kipps has some amusing experiences, notably in a London hotel which is much too grand for him, Mr Polly is the richer comic character with his love of high-sounding words ('eloquacious verboojuice'), his grandiose plans which usually fail because he is too timid to carry them through, his knack of emerging triumphant through sheer luck from the wreck of his plans, as he did after the great Fishbourne fire. Perhaps this reflected a wish planted in Wells's mind during his youth when he had been compelled to surmount the obstacles in his path by persistence and hard work.

We sometimes feel sorry for Mr Polly in the frustrations caused by his miserable marriage and his bankrupt business, but this story is the most comic and happy-go-lucky of Wells's novels in its mood. Into Mr Polly's life come a succession of amusing characters—Parsons, the over-enthusiastic shop-assistant; Uncle Pentstemon anticipating with relish all the disasters that may befall his relatives; Mr Rumbold's deaf mother-in-law enjoying the excitement of her rescue from the fire. Mr Polly has several hilarious encounters with Uncle Jim during his strenuous, but unintelligent, efforts to turn Mr Polly out of the comforts of the Potwell Inn.

The History of Mr Polly is a good-natured novel. In it Wells shows that inside the ordinary little shop-assistant there lived an extraordinary character who took charge of the ordinary man when the circumstances favoured him. Wells did not use Mr Polly's experiences to prove anything; he merely recorded them affectionately and tolerantly.

But inside this affectionate and tolerant writer there was an earnest instructor who eventually gained control. The two had wrestled in *Tono-Bungay*. This was also a story about a young man who came into money, this time through the sale of a patent medicine, lost his fortune, and became an inventor. Uncle Ponderevo is a lively, amusing character, and the story contains some funny scenes. Wells, however, often warns us about the Bladesover influence, the stranglehold of rich landowners on the lives of their countrymen. His view of life is often sour. The high spirits of Uncle Ponderevo and this gloomy philosophy do not mix.

As a young man Wells had been a Socialist and a member of the Fabian Society. Throughout his life he was convinced that he could see what was wrong with society and that he knew how to put it right. Like many people with strongly held views, he found it difficult to persuade other people to accept them. He disagreed with his fellow-Socialists and came to resent openly the stupidity of people who did not share his views. He used his later novels to express his ideas on the short-sighted follies of men and women and the treatment that this short-sightedness required. As he grew older, Wells became convinced that man would destroy himself by his own stupidity and he felt all the bitterness of a rejected prophet. This bitterness came out in his later work, which lacks the warmth and humour of his early novels.

During this period Wells was far more successful when he set out to teach directly. In such books as *The Outline of History*, *A Short History of the World*, *The Work, Wealth and Happiness of Mankind* and *The Shape of Things to Come*, he showed that he could explain history and economics clearly and interestingly for the general reader. He also wrote an unusual and frank autobiography called *Experiment in Autobiography*, which is well worth reading. He died in 1946, just after his country had survived a war which he had thought likely to destroy civilisation. He was embittered by the conviction that he had failed to show mankind the way to salvation. When he told a story and observed people, he convinced his readers. When he analysed modern life and prophesied doom for man, his books were read, but his message was not believed.

Arnold Bennett

THE lives of ARNOLD BENNETT (1867–1931) and John Galsworthy covered almost exactly the same span of years. Both are celebrated chiefly for their novels, although they also wrote plays. Their novels describe in detail two very different sections of English society. In almost every other way their lives and books are in strong contrast.

Arnold Bennett is best known for his stories of the Five Towns, the name he gave to the pottery towns of Staffordshire now joined in the borough of Stoke-on-Trent. The real names of the towns are Burslem, Hanley, Stoke, Tunstall and Longton; the names Bennett gave them were Bursley, Hanbridge, Knype, Turnhill and Longshaw. The neighbouring town of Newcastle-under-Lyme was called Oldcastle. Most of Bennett's finest novels are full of the scenes, incidents and characters that he had known during his boyhood in the Five Towns. He was born in Hanley, the son of a solicitor, and lived at the rear of a draper's shop which he used as the model for the Baines's shop in *The Old Wives' Tale*. After an education at Ashton-under-Lyme Grammar School he entered his father's office at the age of sixteen, but five years later he left to live in London where he became a journalist. He became assistant editor, and later editor, of *Woman*, a magazine for which he wrote a column under the pen-name of Gwendolen. His work on this paper gave him an unusual insight into the hopes and feelings of women, which he subsequently used to great effect in his novels. Most male novelists are more successful in describing men than women, and female novelists have a greater understanding of the feelings and actions of their women characters. Many of Bennett's most striking and most convincing characters, however, are women—Constance and Sophia Baines in *The Old Wives' Tale*, Anna Tellwright in *Anna of the Five Towns* and Hilda Lessways in the Clayhanger books.

His first novel, *The Man from the North*, was published in 1898; Bennett said that his net income from this work was £1. His work as a reviewer and as a writer of serial stories was more profitable, and he decided to resign from his post as editor, and become a professional writer. From 1898 until 1930 he wrote steadily and rapidly, though his claim to have written half a million words in a year was probably exaggerated. Like many famous authors, including Trollope and Shaw, he did not wait for inspiration: he sat at his desk every day and wrote. Bennett spent as freely as he wrote; he enjoyed luxury, he bought a yacht, he loved to dine with rich people and he lived in expensive flats and hotels. No matter how much his pen earned for him, he always needed more money, and in the end his efforts wore him out.

Bennett's novels of the Five Towns include *Anna of the Five Towns* (1902), *The Old Wives' Tale* (1908), *Clayhanger* (1910) and *The Card* (1911). The last of these is a loosely connected series of stories of the exploits of Edward Henry ('Denry' for short) Machin, who begins his rise to celebrity by inserting his own name in the list of guests invited to the Mayoress's ball which he is asked to write out, and becomes by sheer impudence and luck the youngest Mayor Bursley has ever had. If you read these comic episodes you will find out how Denry came to dance with the Countess of Chells, how he drove that lady to the official opening of the Police Institute in a mule-cart, how he evicted his mother from her cottage for her own good, and how he obtained the transfer of Callear, the international centre-forward, to Bursley Football Club.

The other novels, though they contain humorous incidents such as Samuel Povey's purchase of a dog in *The Old Wives' Tale*, present a more realistic picture of the harsh, vigorous, smoke-filled, narrow but cheerful life of the Five Towns. There are three dimensions in these novels—people, place and time. The background is lower middle-class; the main characters are shopkeepers, men with their own prosperous little printing and pottery businesses and their families. The older people, like Ephraim Tellwright, father of Anna, and Darius Clayhanger, are often mean, narrow-minded and tyrannical in their attitude to their children, but there are other families like the Suttons and the Orgreaves who spend money freely, entertain visitors generously, and are interested in music, architecture, books and furniture. Around these families gather their relatives such as the Clayhangers' Auntie Hamps, often frank and generous, occasionally sly; their workmen, notably Big James Yarlett, foreman printer and the finest bass singer in the Five Towns; their servants, such as Maggie, the Baines' household drudge, who astonishes the family when she finally marries after having been engaged twelve times; their friends, their business acquaintances and rivals. Their lives have both foreground and background, for Bennett shows great interest in houses, workshops, factories and drapery stores. The Tellwrights' kitchen, the Suttons' drawing-room, the Clayhangers' new house, the Orgreaves' friendly home and garden, Denry Machin's labour-saving creation—these are not only described in detail, but each has its own atmosphere derived from the lives lived there. Anna tours Henry Mynors' pottery works and Edwin shows Hilda the Clayhanger printing works.

Behind these we feel the bustle of life in the Five Towns—the steam cars puffing up and down the steep hills, the Bursley Theatre, nicknamed the Blood Tub, Saint Luke's Square, where the public houses call themselves vaults, Duck Bank, the railway stations, the processions through the streets. The novels are set just as firmly in time: we know the month and the year, the weather and the state of trade. Outside, Gladstone has made a speech on the Irish question or the Siege of Paris is taking place. It is a wonderfully solid world in which the people have friends, families, work, holidays, houses, furniture, gardens, clothes and books that seem almost as real as our own. And the wonder is that Bennett had left this world when he was twenty-one and reconstructed it from his boyhood memories. As a man he lived for years in France, but these years seem to have left no such vivid impression on his imagination, though his experiences in luxurious hotels provide the background for two accomplished entertainments, *The Grand Babylon Hotel* and *Imperial Palace*, written, one at the beginning, the other at the end of his career.

Perhaps his secret was that he was interested in everything that concerned people. Like Chirac, a character in *The Old Wives' Tale*, he believed that 'whatever existed might be admitted and examined by serious persons interested in the study of human nature'. Bennett does not seem to have thought of people as lovable or hateful, of events as important or trivial, of scenes as beautiful or ugly, but of all life as fascinating. He accepts the facts of existence without rapture and without complaint: he describes illness and death as strange and compelling sights as, for instance, when Edwin Clayhanger watches his father's last struggles against the enemy, but he admires the high spirits and youthful vigour of Sophia Baines. He sympathises with the efforts of Anna, Edwin and Sophia to break out of the narrow life they are used to, but he understands also the feelings of the miser, Ephraim Tellwright, the former workhouse boy, Darius Clayhanger, and the stay-at-home sister, Constance Baines, who marries her father's chief assistant and carries on the family business.

This effective use of contrast runs through most of Bennett's novels. The brisk, business-like Henry Mynors is an admirable man, but it is gawky, unsuccessful Willie Price who makes Anna realise that to admire a man is not the same as to love him. Anna comes back from a glorious holiday to find that she is responsible for the ruin and suicide of Titus Price; Edwin Clayhanger returns from the banquet to his father's deathbed, and Mr Baines has his fatal seizure whilst Sophia is flirting with Gerald Scales and the rest of the family have gone to see the elephant. *Riceyman Steps* (1923), the story of a miser who starves himself and his wife to death in their shop in Clerkenwell, is perhaps an exception in this respect: this powerful novel, regarded by some people as Bennett's best work, offers only occasional relief from its prevailing mood of tragedy.

This extract from *Anna of the Five Towns* describes the departure of Anna Tellwright for the Isle of Man on her first holiday. She is going with the Sutton family and Henry Mynors; Agnes, her young sister, is seeing her off—Bennett's novels contain many attractive children:

Agnes, far more excited than any of the rest, seized her straw hat, and slipping the elastic under her small chin, sprang into the cab, and found a haven between Mr. Sutton's short, fat legs. The driver drew his whip smartly across the aged neck of the cream mare. They were off. What a rumbling, jolting, delicious journey, down the first hill, up Duck Bank, through the market-place, and down the steep declivity of Oldcastle Street! Silent and shy, Agnes smiled ecstatically at the others. Anna answered remarks in a dream. She was conscious only of present happiness and happy expectation. All bitterness had disappeared. At least thirty thousand Bursley folk were not going to the Isle of Man that day—their preoccupied and cheerless faces swam in a continuous stream past the cab window—and Anna sympathised with every unit of them. Her spirit overflowed with universal compassion. What haste and exquisite confusion at the station! The train was signalled, and the porter, crossing the line with the luggage, ran his truck perilously under the very buffers of the incoming engine. Mynors was awaiting them, admirably attired as a tourist. He had got the tickets, and secured a private compartment in the through-coach for Liverpool; and he found time to arrange with the cabman to drive Agnes home on the box-seat. Certainly there was none like Mynors. From the footboard of the carriage Anna bent down to kiss Agnes. The child had been laughing and chattering. Suddenly, as Anna's lips touched hers, she burst into tears, sobbed passionately as though overtaken by some terrible and unexpected misfortune. Tears stood also in Anna's eyes. The sisters had never been parted before.

'Poor little thing!' Mrs. Sutton murmured; and Beatrice told her father to give Agnes a shilling to buy chocolates at Stevenson's in St. Luke's Square, that being the best shop. The shilling fell between the footboard and the platform. A scream from Beatrice! The attendant porter promised to rescue the shilling in due course. The engine whistled, the silver-mounted guard asserted his authority, Mynors leaped in, and amid laughter and tears the brief and unique joy of Anna's life began.

John Galsworthy

JOHN GALSWORTHY (1867–1933) was born in Surrey, educated at Harrow and Oxford, and qualified as a barrister. He never practised law, however, but decided to travel and write. Like Bennett, he published his first novel, *Jocelyn*, in 1898, but he did not achieve any success until his first novel about the Forsyte family, *The Man of Property*, appeared in 1906. Together with *In Chancery* (1920) and *To Let* (1921), this book formed the first part of *The Forsyte Saga*. The second part, entitled *A Modern Comedy*, consists of *The White Monkey* (1924), *The Silver Spoon* (1926) and *Swan Song* (1928).

Just as readers go to Arnold Bennett for a picture of lower middle-class life in a smoky, provincial town, they read Galsworthy for his detailed description of upper middle-class life in London at the turn of the century. The Forsytes are not only wealthy; they are intent above all things on preserving their wealth. Whilst many of Bennett's characters are trying to break out from the pattern of their lives, the main aim of the Forsytes is to stop outsiders breaking into their lives and threatening their possessions. They value everything in terms of money, and they do not completely trust each other. Soames Forsyte is 'The Man of Property'. He regards his wife, Irene, as one of his possessions, a most desirable property but nevertheless a property. Irene seeks freedom from her stifling life, but Soames refuses to grant it. She plans to run away with Bosinney, the architect, who had designed Soames's new house. Soames won a lawsuit against Bosinney, ruining him. Bosinney walked in front of a cab and was killed. Irene returned reluctantly for a time to Soames.

Soames is the key character—proud, avaricious, selfish, unimaginative but pathetic, because his wife, for all her weakness, can wound him with her indifference as deeply as he hurts her by his claim to own her body and soul. In the later books Soames becomes more sympathetic with age and loneliness. Unfortunately Irene remains a lifeless character, and the novel lacks the sharp conflict it needed. The younger Forsytes are also unconvincing, Galsworthy excelling in the portrayal of men, especially old men. Old Jolyon, Soames's uncle, is perhaps the finest of these characters. The Forsytes live in a world of their own by design, but even their servants seem unreal. With their love of property they have fine houses, sometimes effectively described by Galsworthy, but outside their own family and their own property they have only a shadowy existence. Their relationships with each other are complicated and subtle. The following extract from *The Man of Property* gives the flavour of the Forsytes:

He (James) raised his head as old Jolyon came in, and muttered: 'How are you, Jolyon? Haven't seen you for an age. You've been to Switzerland, they tell me. This young Bosinney, he's got himself into a mess. I knew how it would be!' He held out the papers, regarding his elder brother with nervous gloom.

Old Jolyon read them in silence, and while he read them James looked at the floor, biting his fingers the while.

Old Jolyon pitched them down at last, and they fell with a thump amongst a mass of affidavits in 're Buncombe, deceased,' one of the many branches of that parent and profitable tree, 'Fryer v. Forsyte.'

'I don't know what Soames is about,' he said, 'to make a fuss over a few hundred pounds. I thought he was a man of property.'

James's long upper lip twitched angrily; he could not bear his son to be attacked in such a spot. 'It's not the money—' he began, but meeting his brother's glance, direct, shrewd, judicial, he stopped.

There was a silence.

'I've come in for my Will,' said old Jolyon at last, tugging at his moustache.

James's curiosity was roused at once. Perhaps nothing in this life was more stimulating to him than a Will; it was the supreme deal with property, the final inventory of a man's belongings, the last word on what he was worth. He sounded the bell.

'Bring in Mr. Jolyon's Will,' he said to an anxious, dark-haired clerk.

'You going to make some alterations?' And through his mind there flashed the thought: 'Now, am I worth as much as he?'

Old Jolyon put the Will in his breast pocket, and James twisted his long legs regretfully.

'You've made some nice purchases lately, they tell me,' he said.

'I don't know where you get your information from,' answered old Jolyon sharply. 'When's this action coming on? Next month? I can't tell what you've got in your minds. You must manage your own affairs; but if you take my advice, you'll settle it out of Court. Goodbye!' With a cold handshake he was gone.

Here is seen the Forsytes' concern with money and property as the most significant facts about anyone, even a brother. They envy each other, they do not trust each other; but when there is any threat to the family's solidity from outside, they close together to protect themselves.

The Forsyte Saga deals with a small, enclosed group, the conflicts mostly internal. Galsworthy's plays are quite different in theme and mood. He sets one class or group against another—employers against workers in *Strife*; the poor and the rich in *The Silver Box* with a different kind of justice for each; the aristocratic land-owner against the rich upstart in *The Skin Game*; Gentiles and a Jew in *Loyalties*. Justice is the theme that runs through most of his plays with Galsworthy always on the side of the underdog. The situations which Galsworthy created to illustrate the theme of injustice have, unfortunately, dated, and the plays have lost their topical appeal. The dialogue is not sharp enough to make up for this; consequently the plays are not often acted now, nor are they as stimulating to read as Shaw's. Both *Strife* and *The Silver Box* show something of the conditions and social problems of their time, and the characters of Roberts, the strike leader, and Anthony, the chairman of the company, form a contrast of attitudes though the two men are similar in their temperaments.

Hilaire Belloc and G. K. Chesterton

WELLS and Shaw were fond of controversy both in speech and in print, their most frequent opponents being Hilaire Belloc and G. K. Chesterton. Shaw and Wells as Socialists believed that the future would bring greater prosperity and happiness to man, whilst Belloc and Chesterton, as Catholics and individualists, believed that the golden age for Europe had passed and that things were getting steadily worse.

These two writers were so closely associated with each other that Shaw imagined a creature, the Chester-belloc, that was a composite of the two. When a University don severely criticised Chesterton, Belloc wrote a poem in his friend's defence that began:

> Remote and ineffectual Don
> That dared attack my Chesterton. . . .

In fact, apart from their joint campaigning on behalf of Catholicism, the two men were very different. JOSEPH HILAIRE PIERRE BELLOC (1870–1953) was born a Frenchman and a Catholic, and died as a British citizen and a Catholic: Chesterton was born an English Protestant and died an English Catholic. Belloc's father was a French barrister who had married an Englishwoman. Their son was born at St Cloud on the outskirts of Paris, but the family moved to England in boyhood and he was educated at Oratory School, Birmingham, and at Balliol, Oxford, where he obtained a first-class degree in History. Between school and university, Belloc as a French citizen, served for six months in the Army at Toul. GILBERT KEITH CHESTERTON (1874–1936) was born in Kensington, London, and educated in the capital at St Paul's School and at the Slade School, where he studied Art.

Belloc became a naturalised British citizen in 1903, and sat in Parliament as a Liberal M.P. from 1906 to 1910, when he retired disillusioned from political life. Chesterton became a journalist, achieving success rapidly, and remained a journalist throughout his life. He was received into the Catholic Church in 1922, although it had been obvious for some years that he would take this step. Chesterton was a huge man with abundant, untidy hair, and a fondness for dressing picturesquely. Belloc was a smaller man who dressed like a French priest in a black cloak and a black hat with a low crown.

Both men were versatile writers and obviously very talented. When we look at their work, however, it is disappointing to realise how little of what they wrote is likely to survive. By training a historian, Belloc wrote several biographies, including *Marie Antoinette*, *Richelieu*, *Wolsey* and *Napoleon*. He also wrote a *History of England* in four volumes. The style is lively, the material interesting, but Belloc wrote history as one expression of his Catholic faith, and his work is neglected these days because scholars think that in his ardour he sometimes distorted facts, and often placed the emphasis wrongly. *The Servile State*, another book with a historical background, criticised modern life and recommended a return to the medieval guild system as a cure for our ills.

Belloc's comic verse is still enjoyed, however, in *The Bad Child's Book of Beasts* (1896) and *Cautionary Tales* (1907). In the latter book he recounted the fates that befell such people as Henry King, whose 'chief defect was chewing little bits of string'; of Lord Lundy, who 'from his earliest years was far too freely moved to tears'; of Matilda, a dreadful little girl who was constantly raising false fire alarms; and Godolphin Horne, who 'was Nobly Born, and held the Human Race in Scorn'. Belloc's good-natured callousness is shown in these rhymes:

> Lord Finchley tried to mend the Electric Light
> Himself. It struck him dead: And serve him right!
> It is the business of the wealthy man
> To give employment to the artisan.

Belloc also wrote *The Path to Rome* (1902), a description of a walk from Toul in the north-east of France, through Switzerland and Northern Italy to Rome, in fulfilment of a vow. Belloc had returned to his birthplace of St Cloud, where he was greatly impressed by the rebuilding of the Catholic church, formerly 'tumble-down and gaping', now 'noble and new'. In gratitude he vowed to walk all the way from Toul, where he had performed his military service, to Rome as a pilgrimage. He tells of his setbacks when he tried to cross the Alps, of the people he met, some helpful and kind, others suspicious; of those who welcomed him and those who overcharged him for food and shelter, and of one town where he was arrested and put in gaol; he describes the meals he ate and the wines he drank, the beds and other places where he slept. All these experiences are accompanied by a brisk commentary on the events, mostly expressing his devotion to the Catholic Church. The book invites comparison with R. L. Stevenson's *Travels with a Donkey*, and, although many people prefer Stevenson, Belloc stands up to the comparison.

Stevenson's reflections on his bivouac and his relations with his temperamental donkey, Modestine, are more to some people's taste than Belloc's commentary on his journey, but if you enjoyed *Travels with a Donkey* you will find much that you like in *The Path to Rome*.

Later in life Belloc lived quietly in Sussex, about which he wrote one or two poems that express his love of the countryside, notably 'The South Country':

> If I ever become a rich man,
> Or if I ever grow to be old,
> I will build a house with deep thatch
> To shelter me from the cold,
> And there shall the Sussex songs be sung
> And the story of Sussex told.

He did not write much as he grew older, and it is still not certain that his ambition will be fulfilled:

> When I am dead, I hope it may be said:
> 'His sins were scarlet, but his books were read.'

Chesterton, as has been said, became a journalist as a young man, and much of his life and energy was taken up by journalism. He reviewed books; he wrote articles and essays; he composed verses for newspapers and magazines. Ideas and the words in which to express them came to him readily, perhaps too readily; he wrote abundantly and he wrote rapidly. Much of his work was done to order, the demand for his work finally draining him of the vitality that had flowed so freely for many years. He wrote comic, religious, and patriotic verse; biographies of Browning, Dickens and St Francis of Assisi; several novels including *The Napoleon of Notting Hill* (1904), *The Man who was Thursday* (1908) and *The Flying Inn* (1914); short stories about Father Brown, the priest who, by his insight into the human soul, solved mysterious crimes; innumerable essays; *A Short History of England*; books on religion in which he wittily proclaimed his faith; and one play, *Magic*, which was successful, but which he never followed up. Few men have written so many different kinds of book, all with some degree of success, but none of which has certainly passed into a permanent place in our literature.

As a poet, he showed himself a master of rhythm: a swinging, marching rhythm in 'The Rolling English Road':

> Before the Roman came to Rye or out to Severn strode,
> The rolling English drunkard made the rolling English road.
> A reeling road, a rolling road, that rambles round the shire,
> And after him the parson ran, the sexton and the squire;

A merry road, a mazy road, and such as we did tread
The night we went to Birmingham by way of Beachy Head.

This poem expresses Chesterton's love for old things, for human oddity rather than inhuman efficiency, for the enjoyment that comes from good food and drink. His zest for life is not only in the ideas and the words, but in the rhythm of the verse. The same qualities come out in his comic verse, notably 'The Song against Grocers':

God made the wicked Grocer
For a mystery and a sign,
That men might shun the awful shops
And go to inns to dine;
Where the bacon's on the rafter
And the wine is in the wood,
And God that made good laughter
Has seen that they are good.

The righteous minds of innkeepers
Induce them now and then
To crack a bottle with a friend
Or treat unmoneyed men,
But who hath seen the Grocer
Treat housemaids to his teas
Or crack a bottle of fish-sauce
Or stand a man a cheese?

Chesterton was an anti-Puritan; he believed that God gave man many pleasures to enjoy, and he despised the man who rejected pleasure from his life.

Not all his poetry was light and comic verse. 'Lepanto' praises Don John of Austria, who commanded the fleet which won the great naval battle of Lepanto against the Turks to save Christendom from being overrun by Mohammedans. This poem is full of vivid pictures and splendid sounds:

Dim drums throbbing, in the hills half heard,
Where only on a nameless throne a crownless prince has stirred,
Where risen from a doubtful seat and half-attainted stall,
The last knight of Europe takes weapons from the wall,
The last and lingering troubadour to whom the bird has sung,
That once went singing southward when all the world was young.
In that enormous silence, tiny and unafraid,
Comes up along a winding road the noise of the Crusade.

Strong gongs groaning as the guns boom far,
Don John of Austria is going to the war,
Stiff flags straining in the night-blasts cold,
In the gloom black-purple, in the glint old gold,
Torchlight crimson on the copper kettle-drums,
Then the tuckets, then the trumpets, then the cannon, and he comes.
Don John laughing in the brave beard curled,
Spurning of his stirrups like the thrones of all the world.

These lines have a clear, invigorating note that has not often been heard in English poetry since the time of Macaulay.

He wrote also patriotic verse like the 'Ballad of the White Horse', religious poems such as 'The Donkey', whimsical poems like 'The Song of Quoodle' and scornful poems like 'The Logical Vegetarian' and 'The Pessimist'. These are all worth seeking out and reading in the Chestertonian spirit—for sheer enjoyment and the wisdom that comes with enjoyment as a bonus.

Chesterton's longer books and poems are not wholly successful—they contain fine passages, but his talent did not lie in arrangement and organisation. *The Napoleon of Notting Hill* is the best of his novels, telling of Adam Wayne, the Provost of Pump Street, who defends Notting Hill by clever ruses against commercial invasion by the Provost of North Kensington and the property magnates of the day. In the story London is divided into little principalities based on the suburbs, and Adam Wayne is a relic of chivalry in the twentieth-century metropolis. The idea is an amusing one, but it goes on rather too long with tedious patches amongst the excitement. Like *The Man who was Thursday* and *The Flying Inn* some parts of it are much better than the whole, and the book is a series of loosely connected short stories rather than a novel.

The Father Brown stories show Chesterton to much greater advantage. Father Brown is a quiet, insignificant-looking, diffident priest, whose presence attracts crime. Like all detectives in stories he solves the mysteries which baffle others. Father Brown might have been created as a contrast to Conan Doyle's Sherlock Holmes. Holmes with his deer-stalker, curled pipe, dressing-gown, violin, hypodermic needle, aquiline features and his Baker Street flat is a striking, picturesque figure; no one would notice Father Brown. Holmes makes a great show of his test-tubes, microscope and magnifying glass, but Father Brown uses no apparatus in his detection. Holmes is an imperious, active man, who solves his cases by rushing to the scene of the crime and vigorously stirring up people and action. Father Brown watches unnoticed, and penetrates to the mystery by his insight into human nature, by his knowledge of human wickedness and folly. Despite a lack of all the properties with which Conan Doyle equips himself, Chesterton can arouse interest:

First there came a long rush of rapid little steps, such as a light man might make in winning a walking race. At a certain point they stopped and changed to a sort of slow, swinging stamp, numbering not a quarter of the steps, but occupying about the same time. The moment the last echoing stamp had died away would come again the run or ripple of light, hurrying feet, and then again the thud of the heavier walking. It was certainly the same pair of boots, partly because (as has been said) there were no other boots about, and partly because they had a small but unmistakable creak in them. Father Brown had the kind of head that cannot help asking questions; and on this apparently trivial question his head almost split. He had seen men run in order to jump. He had seen men run in order to slide. But why on earth should a man run in order to walk? Or, again, why should he walk in order to run?

Father Brown finds the explanation in the case of 'The Queer Feet' from *The Innocence of Father Brown.* The interest of the Father Brown stories lies in the ideas and the writing: dramatic versions of the stories have never gripped audiences, whilst plays and films and radio versions of Conan Doyle's Sherlock Holmes stories seem always to grip.

Chesterton also wrote many, many short essays, most of them as a regular part of his journalistic work. These often have titles that arouse curiosity: *On Running after one's Hat*; *The Extraordinary Cabman*; *The Advantages of having one Leg*; *The Shop of Ghosts: A Good Dream*; *On Pigs as Pets*; *On Logic and Lunacy.* They begin with odd statements that lure the reader on:

Lying in bed would be an altogether perfect and supreme experience if only one had a coloured pencil long enough to draw on the ceiling.

If a prosperous modern man, with a high hat and a frock-coat, were to solemnly pledge himself before all his clerks and friends to count the leaves on every third tree in Holland Walk, to hop up to the City on one leg every Thursday, to repeat the whole of Mill's 'Liberty' seventy-six times, to collect three hundred dandelions in fields belonging to any one of the name of Brown, to remain for thirty-one hours holding his left ear in his right hand, to sing the names of all his aunts in order of age on the top of an omnibus, or make any such unusual undertaking, we should immediately conclude that the man was mad, or, as it is sometimes expressed, was 'an artist in life.'

No reader can doubt the ready flow of words and ideas, his wit, his vitality. He wrote much that gives immediate pleasure, little apart from a few poems that remains long in the memory. Perhaps there is something self-contradictory in backward-looking prophets like Belloc and Chesterton. Perhaps a writer limits himself if he spends much of his time writing to order, and part of the rest replying to the arguments of his opponents. Chesterton would have been the last to resent a statement that his writings had given many readers entertainment and enjoyment.

E. C. Bentley

ONE of Chesterton's friends, EDMUND CLERIHEW BENTLEY (1875–1956), had the rare distinction of giving his name to a new literary form, though a minor one. The clerihew is a four-line biographical poem in two rhyming couplets. The lines do not scan, the rhymes are often odd, and the verse gives one important biographical fact in irreverent fashion. Most people know the clerihews about Sir Christopher Wren and Humphry Davy. Bentley himself explained how his verses got their name:

When first it dawned on mankind
'Biography for beginners' was signed
(For reasons with which I will not weary you)
With the name of E. Clerihew.

I am not without a claim
To the use of that honourable name,
Which those who happened to be listening
Heard bestowed on me at my christening.

But (for reasons which would only bore you)
The name on the collection before you
Has been changed—I hope not detrimentally
—To E. Clerihew Bentley.

Here are two more examples of his work:

When their lordships asked Bacon
How many bribes he had taken
He had at least the grace
To get very red in the face.

Mr H. G. Wells
Was composed of cells.
He thought the human race
Was a perfect disgrace.

Max Beerbohm

CHESTERTON and MAX BEERBOHM (1872–1956) were amongst the last writers who looked upon the essay as a branch of belles-lettres. Subsequent essayists, George Orwell for instance, have written essays because they had something to say on a topic which interested them, and the essay was a convenient form of the right length. They have used the essay to inform their readers, or to persuade them, hoping to please them at the same time. Usually for Chesterton and Beerbohm the desire to say something was not their principal motive for writing an essay; it was often a means of providing exercise for their style. With Beerbohm it is difficult to avoid the word 'exquisite', for he wrote essays whose slightness of content was concealed by their elegance of form. He was also an accomplished parodist and caricaturist, modes which enabled him to concentrate on style as he used material provided for him by his victims. His best-known work is a novel of Oxford life, called after its principal character, *Zuleika Dobson* (1911). He tells with mock gravity how Zuleika's beauty so captivates the students that they commit suicide en masse for her sake. Beerbohm's inspiration exhausted itself early and he retired to live in Rapallo, Italy. Late in life he made a reputation as a broadcaster in talks and readings. If recorded talk ever becomes a recognised literary form, he will be amongst the outstanding exponents of its early days.

J. M. Synge

IN 1904 the Abbey Theatre, Dublin, was constructed from the old Mechanics' Institute and the morgue, and was opened with John Millington Synge as director. An Englishwoman, Miss Annie Elizabeth Horniman, had paid for the conversion, so giving the Irish National Theatre Association the opportunity to fulfil its aim of encouraging the writing and production of plays by Irish dramatists. Amongst the most prominent members of the Society were William Butler Yeats, the outstanding figure in the revival of Irish literature, and Lady Gregory, who not only wrote and translated plays for the Theatre, but also managed the Theatre and mothered the playwrights. Miss Horniman had formerly been secretary to Yeats, but in 1909 she withdrew the grant she had been making to the Theatre because she disagreed with its policy. Until the building was destroyed by fire in 1951, the Theatre had a history of achievement and disturbance. Its most famous writers, Yeats, Synge, Lennox Robinson, Sean O'Casey, Paul Vincent Carroll, and Denis Johnston, attracted great attention to the Theatre, and it was equally celebrated for the standard of its acting. From time to time, however, the plays produced there outraged the feelings of the public, who often showed skill equal to that of the company in expressing their feelings.

In the early years of the Theatre, the production of *The Playboy of the Western World* by Synge in 1907 caused riots every night for a week. JOHN MILLINGTON SYNGE was born in 1871, the son of a Dublin barrister. After his education at Trinity College, Dublin, he travelled, like Goldsmith, for some time on the continent to further his knowledge of music. He settled for a time in Paris, until Yeats told him: 'Give up Paris. . . . Go to the Aran Islands. Live there as if you were one of the people themselves; express a life that has never found expression'. Surprisingly Synge obeyed this command, and his experiences there inspired him to write stories and plays about life in the Aran Islands and in the remote west of Ireland. His best-known plays were *Riders to the Sea* (1904), *The Playboy of the Western World* (1907) and *Deirdre of the Sorrows*, which was produced in 1910, a year after his death at the age of thirty-eight in 1909. He also wrote *Stories of the Aran Islands* and *Poems and Translations*.

Riders to the Sea is a one-act play in which Maurya, an old Irishwoman, mourns the death of her last two sons, drowned in the sea off the western coast of Ireland. Earlier she had lost in the same way her husband, her husband's father, and four other sons. Brief though the play is, it is a memorable portrait of sorrow and pride:

MAURYA (*raising her head and speaking as if she did not see the people around her*): They're all gone now, and there isn't anything more the sea can do to me. . . . I'll have no call now to be up crying and praying when the wind breaks from the south, and you can hear the surf is in the east, and the surf is in the west, making a great stir with the two noises, and they hitting one on the other. I'll have no call now to be going down and getting Holy Water in the dark nights after Samhain, and I won't care what way the sea is when the other women will be keening. (*To* NORA) Give me the Holy Water, Nora; there's a small sup still on the dresser.

The strongly rhythmical language expresses the mother's grief with great intensity. In his preface to *The Playboy* Synge wrote:

In a good play every speech should be as fully flavoured as a nut or apple, and such speeches cannot be written by any one who works among people who have shut their lips on poetry. In Ireland, for a few years more, we have a popular imagination that is fiery, and magnificent, and tender; . . .

Although *The Playboy of the Western World* is a three-act play, it has little plot; it develops a situation. Christy Mahon seeks shelter and protection at a country public-house in a remote part of County Mayo, saying that he has killed his bullying father by hitting him on the head with a spade. The play explores the effect of his arrival and confession on the publican and his friends, who are proud of their tradition of helping wrong-doers to outwit the law; on the publican's daughter who sees Christy as a desperate and romantic criminal; on the Widow Quin, who schemes to get a man who will lift the burden of widowhood from her; on Shawn Keogh, engaged to Pegeen, the publican's daughter, and terrified of Christy's imagined ruthlessness. The situation is complicated by the return of Christy's father, half resentful and half delighted at his son's belated show of spirit. Meantime, Christy has confirmed his reputation for strength and skill by sweeping the board at the country sports held in the village. Pegeen spurns Christy as an impostor, but when he goes off driving his father before him, satisfied with his new-found independence, she laments the loss of a lad of spirit:

Oh, my grief, I've lost him surely. I've lost the only Playboy of the Western World.

The play pokes fun at many of the illusions the Irish had about themselves and shows that they share many of the weaknesses of the rest of mankind. Pegeen Mike and the Widow Quin plot and struggle against each other for Christy; the publican and his friends are determined that nothing shall interfere with their attendance at a wake and with their drinking; they are full of religious sentiment and outrageous moral beliefs; one young man is a braggart, the other a coward. The first audiences resented these unflattering comments on the national character; later audiences have enjoyed the humour of the situations and the characters, and above all the darting, gleaming phrases in which the dialogue is written:

PEGEEN: A soft lad the like of you wouldn't slit the windpipe of a screeching sow.

CHRISTY (*offended*): You're not speaking the truth.

PEGEEN (*in mock rage*): Not speaking the truth, is it? Would you have me knock the head of you with the butt of the broom?

CHRISTY (*twisting round on her with a sharp cry of horror*): Don't strike me. I killed my poor father, Tuesday was a week, for doing the like of that.

PEGEEN (*with blank amazement*): Is it killed your father?

CHRISTY (*subsiding*): With the help of God, I did, surely, and that the Holy Immaculate Mother may intercede for his soul.

PHILLY (*retreating with Jimmy*): There's a daring fellow.

JIMMY: Oh, glory be to God!

MICHAEL (*with great respect*): That was a hanging crime, mister honey. You should have had good reason for doing the like of that.

CHRISTY (*in a very reasonable tone*): He was a dirty man, God forgive him, and he getting old and crusty, the way I couldn't put up with him at all.

PEGEEN: And you shot him dead?

CHRISTY (*shaking his head*): I never used weapons. I've no licence, and I'm a law-fearing man.

MICHAEL: It was with a hilted knife maybe? I'm told, in the big world, it's bloody knives they use.

CHRISTY (*loudly, scandalised*): Do you take me for a slaughter-boy?

PEGEEN: You never hanged him, the way Jimmy Farrell hanged his dog from the licence, and had it screeching and wriggling three hours at the butt of a string, and himself swearing it was a dead dog, and the peelers swearing it had life?

CHRISTY: I did not, then. I just riz the loy and let fall the edge of it on the ridge of his skull, and he went down at my feet like an empty sack, and never let a grunt or groan from him at all.

After this explanation, Pegeen's father offers him a job as pot-boy in the public-house. As they depart for the wake, Jimmy, one of his friends, says:

> Now, by the grace of God, herself will be safe this night, with a man killed his father holding danger from the door, and let you come on, Michael James, or they'll have the best stuff drunk at the wake.

Though much of the play is comical, there is pathos in the situation of Pegeen, isolated in this village with no hope of finding a man with a spirit that matches her own. There is also shrewd comment on the human character. Christy finds in the end that if everyone thinks him a bold, desperate rogue, then he is a bold, desperate rogue, and not a worm after all. His father, who has hitherto bullied Christy, accepts with delight the change in his son by which he himself is now bullied. The play tells only part of the truth about man, but there are some piercing hits amongst its shots, and the talk is always lively and amusing. It no longer arouses riots: we have meantime heard many truths that are much more distasteful than anything in *The Playboy*.

Synge's other well-known play, *Deirdre of the Sorrows*, is an Irish legend of the elopement of Deirdre with Naisi and the revenge of Conchubor, High King of Ulster, who had planned to marry Deirdre. It has much more plot than *The Playboy* and shows that Synge's gift was in the writing of dialogue and the effective handling of a situation. He has not the same ability to keep the story moving. The pace of the play is monotonous, with the story brought out by characters asking and answering each other's questions. Although many of the speeches are strikingly expressed, the play lacks light and shade, especially light. It is all staged in a dim, grey light with little variation of mood or pace.

Synge's death was untimely. He had a rare vein of poetic comedy. His gift of words and his eye for absurdity were shared by a later writer for the Abbey Theatre, Sean O'Casey, who added a fierceness that Synge did not possess.

PART TWO: 1914-1945

Georgian Poetry

IN 1911 Edward Marsh, a civil servant with excellent taste, ample leisure, and a wide acquaintance with young poets, had a discussion with Rupert Brooke. As a result of that discussion the first volume of *Georgian Poetry*, a collection of work written by young poets during 1911 and 1912, was published, to be followed by four other volumes published at intervals until 1922. Marsh chose the title because the accession of George V to the throne in 1910 seemed to mark the beginning of a new age, and the time seemed ripe for a revival of English poetry after twenty feeble years. Among the poets whose work was included in the first volume were Rupert Brooke, G. K. Chesterton, W. H. Davies, Walter de la Mare, W. W. Gibson, D. H. Lawrence, John Masefield and James Stephens. Some of these poets, Lawrence and Masefield, for instance, dropped out of the later volumes and went their own way, but their place was taken by others, including Edmund Blunden, John Freeman, Robert Graves, Ralph Hodgson, Siegfried Sassoon, Edward Thomas and W. J. Turner. All the volumes sold many thousands of copies, and they introduced a number of younger poets to a wide audience for the first time.

Although Georgian poetry is still read, mainly in anthologies, it is not fashionable: a liking for Georgian poetry has to be explained away, rather apologetically. Why should its achievements be accepted only in this grudging manner? In the first place, its name proved to be an unfortunate choice. The Victorian age, Victorian furniture, the Victorian family; Edwardian elegance and wit, the Edwardian musical-comedy, Edwardian clothing: these phrases have a meaning. 'Georgian', as in Georgian architecture, means belonging to the period of the first four Georges. We do not think of the reign of George V as a distinct period with its own individuality. The First World War and the changes it brought were too great; the world of 1910 had disappeared by 1920.

The Georgian poets are compared with the poets of the 1920s and 1930s, not with the poets of the 1890s and 1900s. None of them changed the course of poetry as did T. S. Eliot. Consequently, they are regarded as minor, but pleasant, writers, who had little that was striking to say, but who had the knack of expressing this very neatly. This criticism is not altogether true: Siegfried Sassoon had much to say, and though many of his poems are very short, they bite to the bone. Both by his friendship and by his example Sassoon did much to encourage the work of Wilfred Owen, the outstanding poet of the First World War. Apart from this, Georgian poetry was a revival, ushering in a period of new vitality in the writing of poetry, and a new interest in the reading. The novel and the drama had flourished during the Edwardian period, but, except for Thomas Hardy, the poetical scene had been empty and lifeless.

Rupert Brooke

RUPERT BROOKE (1887–1915) has become a legendary figure, an ideal picture of the young poet. Handsome, intelligent, athletic, popular with all who knew him, Brooke expressed this personality in much of his poetry. It was fresh, direct, vigorous, idealistic, the voice of youth. He died at the age of twenty-eight whilst serving as an officer in the Navy, having foreshadowed his own death in the sonnets he wrote at the beginning of the war. He was a story-book hero, and his own fate came to be regarded as typical of a generation of young men who gave their lives for their country.

Brooke, the son of a housemaster, attended Rugby School, from where he went on to King's College, Cambridge. After leaving Cambridge, he travelled both in Europe and in America, staying at the Old Vicarage, Grantchester, during an interval in his travels. The memory of this English village came back to him when he was in Berlin in 1912 and he wrote 'The Old Vicarage, Grantchester', recalling the contentment he had experienced there:

> But Grantchester! ah, Grantchester!
> There's peace and holy quiet there,
> Great clouds along pacific skies,
> And men and women with straight eyes,
> Lithe children lovelier than a dream,
> A bosky wood, a slumbrous stream,
> And little kindly winds that creep
> Round twilight corners, half asleep.

The mixture of nostalgia and fanciful humour, expressed in smooth verse, has appealed to the young and the sentimental in every generation since it was written.

In the early part of 1914 Brooke was in Tahiti, where he wrote 'Tiare Tahiti' and 'The Great Lover'. These lines from 'Tiare Tahiti' give a romantic description of the island:

> Crown the hair, and come away!
> Hear the calling of the moon,
> And the whispering scents that stray
> About the idle warm lagoon.

Hasten, hand in human hand,
Down the dark, the flowered way,
Along the whiteness of the sand,
And in the water's soft caress,
Wash the mind of foolishness,
Mamua, until the day.
Spend the glittering moonlight there
Pursuing down the soundless deep
Limbs that gleam and shadowy hair,
Or floating lazy, half-asleep.

In 'The Great Lover' he gives thanks for all the things in life that have given him pleasure:

The benison of hot water; furs to touch;
The good smell of old clothes; and other such—

Already, in this poem, he seems to hear the approach of Death, and he is anxious to set down all that he has enjoyed before it is too late.

The humour of 'Grantchester' appears again in 'Heaven', a fish's vision of the perfection that awaits it in the next life:

We darkly know, by Faith we cry,
The future is not Wholly Dry.
Mud unto mud!—Death eddies near—
Not here the appointed End, not here!
But somewhere, beyond Space and Time,
Is wetter water, slimier slime!

In June 1914, just before the outbreak of the war, Brooke returned to England. He joined the Royal Naval Division and took part in the unsuccessful expedition to save Antwerp. Early in 1915 he embarked for the Dardanelles, but he was taken ill on the way and died of blood-poisoning on the island of Skyros in April. Between the two expeditions Brooke had written five sonnets which he called *1914*. In them Brooke welcomes the prospect of serving in the war as a release from the pettiness and shame of life. War, death even, brings a sense of security to men who feel they are fulfilling a purpose. In recompense war brings back into men's lives Holiness, Love, Honour and Nobleness. Though they surrender the delights they knew in life, death gives them a perfect beauty:

. . . a white
Unbroken glory, a gathered radiance,
A width, a shining peace, under the night.

In the last, and most famous, of the sonnets, 'The Soldier', beginning 'If I should die, think only this of me', Brooke recalls the joys he had known in England, earlier celebrated in 'Grantchester', and asserts that these will remain with him even after death.

The sonnets are inspired, not by the experience of war, but by the prospect of war and death. The war proved to be not the gallant adventure, the young man's chance to express his idealism, that Brook expected. If he had known the long nightmare of the trenches, he might have written with the fierce concentration of Siegfried Sassoon or Wilfred Owen. If he had survived the war, he might have looked back full of pity as Edmund Blunden did. But before he had learned to live intimately with the shadow of death, he expressed the ardour of youth, the vision that he had, in bright, ringing words.

Siegfried Sassoon

No one knows whether Rupert Brooke, if he had lived, would have become one of the outstanding poets of the twentieth century. A comparison of his life with that of Siegfried Sassoon (1886–1967) shows what might have been, not what would have been. Sassoon was born a year earlier than Brooke and outlived him by more than fifty years. If he had died at the same age as Brooke, his name would hardly be remembered today. His war experiences shattered many of his beliefs, but made him into a poet. Only through poetry could he express the intense emotions of horror, disgust, pity and hatred that war aroused in him.

Sassoon enlisted in the army on 3 August 1914, the day before war was declared. Until then he had lived a quiet life in Sussex and Kent, his life filled with the pleasures of rural sports—hunting, village cricket, point-to-point racing. He describes his life as a boy and as a young man in *Memoirs of a Fox-Hunting Man*, the first of three books in which he reconstructs his experiences. The incidents are all true; details of place and time accurate; only the names of the characters are changed. The only invented character is Aunt Evelyn, who represents Sassoon's family.

Although talented, Sassoon had accomplished little by the outbreak of war. A sensitive, rather lonely young man, he felt dissatisfied with his life so far, and he almost welcomed the coming of war as a release from self-questioning. He did not come face to face with trench-warfare until the end of 1915, and some of his early war poems show the same kind of idealism as Brooke's sonnets:

> War is our scourge; yet war has made us wise,
> And, fighting for our freedom, we are free.

Sassoon's war experiences are set down in *Memoirs of an Infantry Officer* and in two volumes of poetry, *The Old Huntsman* and *Counter-Attack*. The memoirs give a continuous narrative account; the poems isolate moments and scenes. The war-poems are short and terse. The incidents speak for themselves; there is no need for emphasis or elaboration. Many of them deal with everyday incidents of the war, but common though the events described were, Sassoon's eye for odd detail makes them real and striking, not general. The titles tell you the themes—

'Stretcher-Case', 'The Death-Bed', 'Wirers', 'Trench Duty', 'Break of Day'—but despite your expectations they still shock, as in this poem, 'The Rear-Guard' (Hindenburg Line, April 1917):

> Groping along the tunnel, step by step,
> He winked his prying torch with patching glare
> From side to side, and sniffed the unwholesome air.
>
> Tins, boxes, bottles, shapes too vague to know;
> A mirror smashed, the mattress from a bed;
> And he, exploring fifty feet below
> The rosy gloom of battle overhead.
>
> Tripping, he grabbed the wall; saw some one lie
> Humped at his feet, half-hidden by a rug,
> And stooped to give the sleeper's arm a tug.
> 'I'm looking for headquarters.' No reply.
> 'God blast your neck!' (For days he'd had no sleep,)
> 'Get up and guide me through this stinking place.'
>
> Savage, he kicked a soft, unanswering heap,
> And flashed his beam across the livid face
> Terribly glaring up, whose eyes yet wore
> Agony dying hard ten days before;
> And fists of fingers clutched a blackening wound.
>
> Alone he staggered on until he found
> Dawn's ghost that filtered down a shafted stair
> To the dazed, muttering creatures underground
> Who hear the boom of shells in muffled sound.
> At last, with sweat of horror in his hair,
> He climbed through darkness to the twilight air,
> Unloading hell behind him step by step.

The same incident is narrated in *Memoirs of an Infantry Officer*, Part Eight: The Second Battalion (Section V).

The war-poems are full of the sight of death, often described in gruesome detail. Sassoon wanted to drive home the squalor and horror of war to everyone not fighting in the front line. Those back home who expressed their admiration of our gallant fighting-men had no idea of the conditions in which they fought; the staff-officers who planned the offensives had no personal knowledge of the men on whom they inflicted filth and death. This bitterness against staff-officers is expressed in 'Base Details':

If I were fierce and bald and short of breath,
  I'd live with scarlet Majors at the Base,
And speed glum heroes up the line to death.
  You'd see me with my puffy petulant face,
Guzzling and gulping in the best hotel,
  Reading the Roll of Honour. 'Poor young chap,'
I'd say—'I used to know his father well;
  Yes, we've lost heavily in this last scrap.'
And when the war is done and youth stone dead
I'd toddle safely home and die—in bed.

and in 'The General':

'Good-morning; good-morning!' the General said
When we met him last week on our way to the line.
Now the soldiers he smiled at are most of 'em dead,
And we're cursing his staff for incompetent swine.
'He's a cheery old card,' grunted Harry to Jack
As they slogged up to Arras with rifle and pack.

. . . . .

But he did for them both with his plan of attack.

He writes with contempt of the ignorant admirers back home in England: 'The Fathers', 'Gross, goggle-eyed and full of chat': 'Glory of Women':

You love us when we're heroes, home on leave,
Or wounded in a mentionable place.

the war-reporters in 'Editorial Impressions':

He seemed so certain 'all was going well',
As he discussed the glorious time he'd had
While visiting the trenches.

the music-hall audience enjoying jokes about the war:

I'd like to see a Tank come down the stalls,
Lurching to rag-time tunes, or 'Home, sweet Home',
And there'd be no more jokes in Music-halls
To mock the riddled corpses round Bapaume.

Despite his disillusion with the war and his bitter criticism of those responsible for the slaughter, Sassoon was a brave soldier who was awarded the Military Cross for rescuing the wounded under fire. He tells of one of his exploits in *Memoirs of an Infantry Officer*, when he took an enemy trench single-handed. He was incensed by the death from a sniper's bullet of his lance-corporal:

But after blank awareness that he was killed, all feelings tightened and contracted to a single intention—to 'settle that sniper' on the other side of the valley. If I had stopped to think, I shouldn't have gone at all. As it was, I discarded my tin hat and equipment, slung a bag of bombs across my shoulder, abruptly informed Fernby that I was going to find out who was there, and set off at a downhill double. While I was running I pulled the safety-pin out of a Mills' bomb; my right hand being loaded, I did the same for my left. I mention this because I was obliged to extract the second safety-pin with my teeth, and the grating sensation reminded me that I was half way across and not so reckless as I had been when I started. I was even a little out of breath as I trotted up the opposite slope. Just before I arrived at the top I slowed up and threw my two bombs. Then I rushed at the bank, vaguely expecting some sort of scuffle with my imagined enemy. I had lost my temper with the man who had shot Kendle; quite unexpectedly, I found myself looking down into a well-conducted trench with a great many Germans in it. Fortunately for me, they were already retreating. It had not occurred to them that they were being attacked by a single fool; and Fernby, with presence of mind which probably saved me, had covered my advance by traversing the top of the trench with his Lewis gun. I slung a few more bombs, but they fell short of the clumsy field-grey figures, some of whom half turned to fire their rifles over the left shoulder as they ran across the open toward the wood, while a crowd of jostling helmets vanished along the trench. Idiotically elated, I stood there with my finger in my right ear and emitted a series of 'view-holloas' (a gesture which ought to win the approval of people who still regard war as a form of outdoor sport). Having thus failed to commit suicide, I proceeded to occupy the trench—that is to say, I sat down on the firestep, very much out of breath, and hoped to God the Germans wouldn't come back again.

In 1917, whilst recovering in this country from a wound he had received in the Battle of Arras, Sassoon felt compelled to make a protest against the continued slaughter. When asked to explain why he had overstayed his leave, he posted a statement to his commanding officer which began: 'I am making this statement as an act of wilful defiance of military authority, because I believe that the War is being deliberately prolonged by those who have the power to end it.' He also threw the ribbon of his Military Cross into the River Mersey. The Army was unwilling to make a martyr of an officer with a distinguished record, and eventually Robert Graves, a fellow-poet and officer, persuaded Sassoon to appear before a medical board which decided that he was suffering from shell-shock.

After a spell in a military hospital Sassoon asked to be returned to duty. He never reached the front line again, for he was wounded in 1918 and did not return to battle. In 'Banishment', written at the time he gave up his protest, he tells how his gesture to help his comrades had failed:

> Their wrongs were mine; and ever in my sight
> They went arrayed in honour. But they died, —
> Not one by one: and mutinous I cried
> To those who sent them out into the night.
>
> The darkness tells how vainly I have striven
> To free them from the pit where they must dwell
> In outcast gloom convulsed and jagged and riven
> By grappling guns. Love drove me to rebel.
> Love drives me back to grope with them through hell;
> And in their tortured eyes I stand forgiven.

After the war Sassoon completed his memoirs with *Sherston's Progress*. George Sherston represented a generation of men, most of whom were sacrificed in a holocaust they had not foreseen. Sassoon continued to write poetry, though never again with the same intensity. He wrote quiet, reflective poems about the passing of time, youth and age, and the changes they bring, the identity of man amongst these changes:

> 'When I'm alone'—the words tripped off his tongue
> As though to be alone were nothing strange.
> 'When I was young,' he said; 'when I was young. . . .'
>
> I thought of age, and loneliness, and change.
> I thought how strange we grow when we're alone,
> And how unlike the selves that meet, and talk,
> And blow the candles out, and say good-night.
> *Alone*. . . . The word is life endured and known.
> It is the stillness where our spirits walk
> And all but inmost faith is overthrown.

Wilfred Owen

WHILST he was in Craiglockhart Hospital, Edinburgh, where he was sent to recover from his nervous breakdown, Sassoon met WILFRED OWEN (1893-1918), also a patient there. Owen later wrote to Sassoon of the changes the four months they spent together in hospital wrought in his life and in his development as a poet: 'You have fixed my Life—however short. You did not light me: I was always a mad comet; but you have fixed me. I spun round you like a satellite for a month, but I shall swing out soon, a dark star in the orbit where you will blaze.' The year 1917 was a decisive one for Wilfred Owen for two reasons: in January he had been sent out to France for the first time to fight in the front line, and in August he met Sassoon. His experiences as a soldier went far beyond any horror he had imagined. When he had first arrived in France, he had written in a letter, 'There is a fine heroic feeling about being in France, and I am in perfect spirits.' After a short time in the front line he described the scene as 'Hideous landscapes, vile noises, foul language, and nothing but foul, even from one's own mouth (for all are devil-ridden)—everything unnatural, broken, blasted; the distortion of the dead, whose unburiable bodies sit outside the dug-outs all day, all night, the most execrable sights on earth'. Owen felt compelled to tell others what he had seen and express the emotions that these sights had aroused in him. At this point he read and admired Sassoon's collection of war-poems, *The Old Huntsman*, then met their author. Owen had been writing poetry since boyhood, much of it under the influence of Keats, his favourite poet. Much of this had been ornate and slow-moving in a style which Owen knew to be quite inadequate for what he now wanted to say. He was interested in Sassoon's terse, colloquial style and spent hours discussing with him the technique of writing poetry. Under Sassoon's influence Owen shed some of the decoration of his earlier verse, but his ear for music would not allow him to copy Sassoon's style. In May 1914 he had written, 'I certainly believe I could make a better musician than many who profess to be, and are accepted as such. . . . I love Music, with such *strength* that I have had to conceal the passion, for fear it be thought weakness.'

Owen was killed by German fire whilst trying to force a canal crossing a week before the Armistice, on 4 November 1918. During the year that had passed since he had left Craiglockhart he had written two or three of the finest war-poems in English. In the Preface he wrote for his poems he said:

> Above all I am not concerned with Poetry.
> My subject is War, and the pity of War.
> The Poetry is in the pity.

Until 1917 he had been deeply concerned with Poetry—the choice of words and the form he used. Now he was concerned to describe what he had seen and the pity he had felt. This called for passionate utterance; for that reason 'The Poetry is in the pity'.

For all that, Owen revised his work carefully, altering words, and changing their order to heighten their effect. 'Greater Love' compares the love shown for a man by a woman with the love shown by a soldier in dying for his country. The theme has some resemblance to Sassoon's 'The Kiss', though Sassoon's 'Brother Lead and Sister Steel' have echoes of Saint Francis, whilst Owen's comparisons are sensual:

> Red lips are not so red
> As the stained stones kissed by the English dead.
> Kindness of wooed and wooer
> Seems shame to their love pure.
> O Love, your eyes lose lure
> When I behold eyes blinded in my stead!
>
> Your slender attitude
> Trembles not exquisite like limbs knife-skewed,
> Rolling and rolling there
> Where God seems not to care;
> Till the fierce love they bear
> Cramps them in death's extreme decrepitude.
>
> Your voice sings not so soft—
> Though even as wind murmuring through raftered loft,—
> Your dear voice is not dear,
> Gentle, and evening clear,
> As theirs whom none now hear,
> Now earth has stopped their piteous mouths that coughed.
>
> Heart, you were never hot,
> Nor large, nor full like hearts made great with shot;
> And though your hands be pale,
> Paler are all which trail
> Your cross through flame and hail:
> Weep, you may weep, for you may touch them not.

Here the words are often simple, but the effect is never that of everyday speech as it often is in Sassoon. 'O love, your eyes lose lure' and 'Weep, you may weep, for you may touch them not' are lines written by a poet conscious of verbal beauty.

'Anthem for Doomed Youth' depends as much on the pattern of contrasting rhythms as on the meaning of the words; rhythm and meaning cannot in fact be separated:

> What passing-bells for these who die as cattle?
>   Only the monstrous anger of the guns.
>   Only the stuttering rifles' rapid rattle
> Can patter out their hasty orisons.
> No mockeries for them; no prayers or bells,
>   Nor any voice of mourning save the choirs,—
> The shrill demented choirs of wailing shells;
>   And bugles calling for them from sad shires.
>
> What candles may be held to speed them all?
>   Not in the hands of boys, but in their eyes
> Shall shine the holy glimmers of good-byes.
>   The pallor of girls' brows shall be their pall;
> Their flowers the tenderness of silent minds,
> And each slow dusk a drawing-down of blinds.

Owen's last poem, 'Strange Meeting', though unfinished, is his best-known work. In it he begins with much the same situation as that which Sassoon described in 'The Rear-Guard', a descent into a tunnel where the poet sees the body of his enemy. In Owen's poem the place is Hell, not the Hindenburg Line, and instead of kicking the body aside, the poet enters into conversation with the other:

> 'Strange friend,' I said, 'Here is no cause to mourn.'
> 'None,' said the other, 'save the undone years,
> The hopelessness. Whatever hope is yours,
> Was my life also; I went hunting wild
> After the wildest beauty in the world,
> Which lies not calm in eyes, or braided hair,
> But mocks the steady running of the hour,
> And if it grieves, grieves richlier than here.
> For by my glee might many men have laughed,
> And of my weeping something had been left,
> Which must die now. I mean the truth untold,
> The pity of war, the pity war distilled.
> Now men will go content with what we spoiled.
> Or, discontent, boil bloody, and be spilled.'

The two men had the same purpose: to reveal to others the richness of life in joy, sorrow and in pity. Without their guidance men would accept something less from life—obedience, regimentation, the prison of their own limited minds and imaginations from which the poet could set them free. The dead man concludes:

> I am the enemy you killed, my friend.
> I knew you in this dark; for so you frowned
> Yesterday through me as you jabbed and killed.
> I parried; but my hands were loath and cold.
> Let us sleep now. . . .

The poet has destroyed what he valued in life, and made possible the triumph of everything to which he was opposed.

Sassoon's 'The Rear-Guard' excites horror and disgust; 'Strange Meeting', sadness, pity, a sense of loss. Sassoon is often condemning those who cause suffering, Owen sympathising with those who suffer.

In this poem, as in some of his earlier work, Owen uses assonance ('Friend-frowned, Killed-cold'), not rhyme. This device was copied by some poets of the thirties when Owen's deep compassion and his metrical skill were fully recognised.

Edmund Blunden

SASSOON seemed the obvious man to collect and edit Owen's work after his death, but in fact EDMUND BLUNDEN (born 1896) was chosen. Blunden, a Sussex man, went almost straight from Oxford to France. Like Sassoon he saw much bitter fighting and won the Military Cross. He also set down his war experiences in an autobiographical work, *Undertones of War* and in his war-poetry. There the resemblance ends, for Blunden was a patient, reflective man whose nature would not allow him to condemn. In *Undertones of War*, an entirely appropriate title, he notes the signs of the changing seasons or the discovery of a fine collection of books in a dignified house. His poetry was for the most part written after the war and the tone is quiet and musing. His best poetry describes and reflects upon the countryside, its characters, and its lasting traditions.

Names are vanished, save the few
In the old brown Bible scrawled;
These were men of pith and thew,
  Whom the city never called;
Scarce could read or hold a quill,
Built the barn, the forge, the mill.
('Forefathers')

Today's house makes tomorrow's road;
  I knew these heaps of stone
When they were walls of grace and might,
The country's honour, art's delight
That over fountained silence showed
  Fame's final bastion.
('The Survival')

The same love of English country life is shown in *Cricket Country*, again a title that describes the book perfectly. It is odd that with this enduring affection Blunden should have spent much of his life in Tokyo and Hong Kong teaching English at the Universities there. Apart from his lectures he will have informed the students of the English character and of English tastes by being the man he is.

Walter de la Mare

A KNOWLEDGE of some writers' lives is necessary for a full understanding of their work. Sometimes, like Wilfred Owen, they write about their current experiences; others, including Arnold Bennett, often recall the scenes of their boyhood; D. H. Lawrence used in his novels his own experiences, his travels, and people he knew in life, who became characters in the stories. The work of other writers can be enjoyed and understood without knowing much about their lives. Such a writer is WALTER DE LA MARE (1873–1956).

His life appears to have been free from crises, and there are few identifiable places, characters, or times in his work. Although many of his poems are recollections of childhood, they are recollections of moods and fancies, not of particular scenes and incidents. The title of one of his poems—'Echo (A Memory of Childhood)'—tells us something of the distinctive qualities of his work.

'Who called?' I said, and the words
  Through the whispering glades,
Hither, thither, baffled the birds—
  'Who called? Who called?'

The leafy boughs on high
  Hissed in the sun;
The dark air carries my cry
  Faintingly on.

Eyes in the green, in the shade,
  In the motionless brake,
Voices that said what I said
  For mockery's sake:

'Who cares?' I bawled through my tears;
  The wind fell low:
In the silence, 'Who cares? Who cares?'
  Wailed to and fro.

His poems are full of wondering children, of unanswered questions, echoes, silent listeners, woods that seem to whisper and watch. The child alone is a common enough situation, but de la Mare hints at the menace barely concealed in everyday events.

He also wrote jolly poems that quite young children enjoy for their lively stories and quaint characters: 'Three Jolly Farmers', 'Jim Jay', who got stuck fast in Yesterday, 'The Corner', about old Mister Jones who in his illness has turned the corner and is now growing younger and younger. These are amusing fancies, but below the surface is the callousness found in many children: Farmer Turvey is drowned in his determination to win the bet; poor Jim Jay—what happens to him as time and the world leave him behind? having eluded death, old Mister Jones is faced with the inevitability of birth. Sometimes the fancy takes a macabre turn as in 'John Mouldy', who sits silent and smiling in his dripping cellar while the rats clamber over him. Generally, however, the first words of 'Miss T.' describe the situation in these poems of fancy:

It's a very odd thing—
  As odd as can be—

The passage of time is a theme that recurs. Even 'Jim Jay' and 'The Corner' approach this theme from unusual angles. In 'All that's Past' de la Mare says that a sense of antiquity is part of the beauty of the woods, the brooks, and of mankind. In 'Fare Well' he regrets that time will ultimately deprive him of all the beautiful things he has enjoyed in the world:

Look thy last on all things lovely,
Every hour. Let no night
Seal thy sense in deathly slumber
        Till to delight
Thou hast paid thy utmost blessing;
Since that all things thou wouldst praise
Beauty took from those who loved them
        In other days.

He gives thanks also in 'The Scribe' for the lovely things God has created.

The poems are things of a moment, short, simple, catching a mood or a fancy. His imagination lit up quickly and often, but the light was not a steady, lasting glow. Many of the poems are written in short, rhyming lines with a simple vocabulary, so that the reader is often reminded of nursery rhymes. But, though simple, they are not artless: in 'The Listeners', lines like

And his horse in the silence champed the grasses
  Of the forest's ferny floor:

  The silence surged softly backward,
When the plunging hoofs were gone.

show great sensitivity in the choice of words and the effective use of sound. The light is often subdued in his poems ('Nod', 'Shadow', 'Dawn', 'Winter') and the music of the verse is quiet and delicate:

Speak not—whisper not;
Here bloweth thyme and bergamot.

This is a poetry of suggestion, not statement: a poetry where the reader is not told what he should think or feel, but is given a brief view of something strange and makes of it whatever he pleases to imagine about it. De la Mare is not a major poet; he is no philosopher or reformer. He preserves a child's sense of wonder in a world that is full of strange things.

James Stephens

ANOTHER poet who had the eye and imagination of a child was JAMES STEPHENS (1882–1950), an Irishman. To hear him read his own poems, crooning and with a strong Irish accent, was an unforgettable experience. His poetry was perhaps a little more vigorous, less delicate, more direct, less suggestive, than de la Mare's, but the two had much in common. Here are two of his poems:

Check

The Night was creeping on the ground!
She crept, and did not make a sound

Until she reached the tree: And then
She covered it, and stole again

Along the grass beside the wall!
I heard the rustling of her shawl

As she threw blackness everywhere
Along the sky, the ground, the air,

And in the room where I was hid!
But, no matter what she did

To everything that was without,
She could not put my candle out!

So I stared at the Night! And she
Stared back solemnly at me!

A Visit from Abroad

A speck went blowing up against the sky
   As little as a leaf: then it drew near
And broadened.—'It's a bird,' said I,
   And fetched my bows and arrows. It was queer!

It grew from up a speck into a blot,
  And squattered past a cloud; then it flew down
All crumply, and waggled such a lot
  I thought the thing would fall.—It was a brown
Old carpet where a man was sitting snug
  Who, when he reached the ground, began to sew
A big hole in the middle of the rug,
  And kept on peeping everywhere to know
Who might be coming—then he gave a twist
  And flew away. . . . I fired at him but missed.

Gerard Manley Hopkins

ALTHOUGH Robert Bridges was Poet Laureate from the death of his forgotten predecessor, Alfred Austin, in 1913, until his own death in 1930, all the short lyrics by which he is best known were written in the nineteenth century. In 1929, at the age of eighty-five, he published a long philosophical poem, 'The Testament of Beauty', which showed his skill in the handling of a difficult metre, twelve-syllable lines with the stresses varied to avoid monotony. The poem fails to sustain interest because the philosophical ideas are neither clear nor compelling, and he will remain known for his earlier charming lyrics such as 'I heard a linnet courting', 'A Passer-by', 'There is a hill beside the silver Thames', 'I love all beauteous things' and others.

Bridges' principal contribution to the development of English poetry during his laureateship lies not in his own work, but in the publication in 1918 of the poems of GERARD MANLEY HOPKINS, which he had edited. The two men were born in the same year, 1844, and became friends when they were at Oxford together. Hopkins was converted to Roman Catholicism in 1866 and became a Jesuit priest. In 1884 he was appointed Professor of Greek at Dublin University, dying of typhoid in that city in 1889. His poetry was confided to Bridges, who thought that readers of poetry were not ready to accept this strange and original work until almost thirty years after Hopkins' death.

Hopkins himself wrote:

> No doubt my poetry errs on the side of oddness. I hope in time to have a more balanced and Miltonic style. But as air, melody, is what strikes me most of all in music, and design in painting, so design, pattern, or what I call 'inscape' is what I above all aim at in poetry. Now it is the virtue of design, pattern, or inscape to be distinctive, and it is the vice of distinctiveness to become queer. This vice I cannot have escaped.

There is some truth in this opinion, but it takes no account of what Hopkins' distinctiveness enabled him to achieve.

Let us look at three of his poems in order to find a part of the answer. First, 'The Leaden Echo':

How to kéép—is there ány any, is there none such, nowhere known
some, bow or brooch or braid or brace, lace, latch or catch or key to keep
Back beauty, keep it, beauty, beauty, beauty, . . . from vanishing away?
Is there no frowning of these wrinkles, rankèd wrinkles deep,
Dówn? no waving off of these most mournful messengers, still
messengers, sad and stealing messengers of grey?
No there's none, there's none, O no there's none,
Nor can you long be, what you now are, called fair,
Do what you may do, what, do what you may,
And wisdom is early to despair:
Be beginning; since, no, nothing can be done
To keep at bay
Age and age's evils, hoar hair,
Ruck and wrinkle, drooping, dying, death's worst, winding sheets, tombs
  and worms and tumbling to decay;
So be beginning, be beginning to despair.
O there's none; no no no there's none:
Be beginning to despair, to despair,
Despair, despair, despair, despair.

In this poem Hopkins' interest in design or pattern shows itself in the complex arrangement of stresses in the lines. The idea behind the poem—that human beauty decays and there is no hope for those who wish to preserve it—is very simple, but the form of expression is very elaborate. Hopkins emphasises words that carry the main weight of his ideas, by repetition, by alliteration, by placing two, three strongly stressed words together. The order of words in sentences is bent to his purpose—'Do what you may do, what, do what you may'. Interjections like 'O' and purely emphatic words like 'no' are introduced or repeated. Words are sometimes chosen both for their strangeness and for their effect as sound—'rankèd wrinkles', 'ruck and wrinkle', 'be beginning'.

'God's Grandeur' says more, and says it in sonnet form which imposes some limit on Hopkins' freedom of expression, without, however, forcing him into strict regularity of form:

The world is charged with the grandeur of God.
It will flame out, like shining from shook foil;
It gathers to a greatness, like the ooze of oil
Crushed. Why do men then now not reck his rod?
Generations have trod, have trod, have trod;
  And all is seared with trade; bleared, smeared with toil;
  And wears man's smudge and shares man's smell: the soil
Is bare now, nor can foot feel, being shod.

And for all this, nature is never spent;
There lives the dearest freshness deep down things;
And though the last lights off the black West went,
Oh, morning, at the brown brink eastward springs—
Because the Holy Ghost over the bent
World broods with warm breast and with ah! bright wings.

Hopkins contrasts the grandeur of God with the pettiness and ugliness of man's achievements. God is always there to redeem man's errors and to renew hope. Again we have the repetition, the alliteration, the interjection, the placing together of strongly emphasised words, strange phrases like 'reck his rod', the setting of 'Crushed' as the last word of a sentence with a heavy stress as the first word in the line, making the full-stop seem particularly abrupt. There are the striking and unexpected comparisons of God's greatness with 'the ooze of oil crushed', and with 'the shining from shook foil'. The leaps in thought from the majesty of God to the grossness of man, and back to the mercy of God, are also characteristic of Hopkins.

Hopkins called 'The Windhover' 'the best thing I have ever done'. In the octave of the sonnet he admires the freedom and grace of the falcon in flight. In the sextet he asserts that the beauty of the falcon is nothing in comparison with Christ's sacrifice for man. The change in the poet's admiration of the falcon to his reverence for Christ is not stated; Hopkins leaps from one to the other, and the reader must follow him. The sonnet is not only about the falcon and Christ, however; it is also about Hopkins the poet with the soaring imagination and Hopkins the priest with an apparently humdrum round of religious duties, which are in fact far more splendid than his finest verse. The steady labour of the ploughman makes the furrows gleam, and when the dull ember falls from the fire on to the hearth, the sparks flash brightly.

I caught this morning morning's minion, king-
dom of daylight's dauphin, dapple-dawn-drawn Falcon, in his riding
Of the rolling level underneath him steady air, and striding
High there, how he rung upon the rein of a wimpling wing
In his ecstasy! then off, off forth on swing,
As a skate's heel sweeps smooth on a bow-bend: the hurl and gliding
Rebuffed the big wind. My heart in hiding
Stirred for a bird,—the achieve of, the mastery of the thing!

Brute beauty and valour and act, oh, air, pride, plume, here
Buckle! AND the fire that breaks from thee then, a billion
Times told lovelier, more dangerous, O my chevalier!

No wonder of it: shéer plōd makes plough down sillion
Shine, and blue-bleak embers, ah my dear,
Fall, gall themselves, and gash gold-vermilion.

The description of the falcon in flight is certainly distinctive, but not queer, for Hopkins uses his devices to recreate the joy he felt in watching the bird, and its mastery of the air. The words are often unexpected, but here they are right: 'morning's minion'—a royal morning and the falcon the beloved favourite; 'daylight's dauphin', inheriting the morning's majesty and joy; 'dapple-dawn-drawn', attracted by the rich, variegated colours of the dawn.

Towards the end of his life Hopkins' certainty in God's goodness was shaken, and he asked:

Comforter, where, where is your comforting?
Mary, mother of us, where is your relief?

But the last words of another of his poems on the 'Comfort of the Resurrection' state his faith:

In a flash, at a trumpet crash,
I am all at once what Christ is, / since he was what I am, and
This Jack, joke, poor potsherd, / patch, matchwood, immortal diamond,
Is immortal diamond.

John Masefield

TWO contributors to the first volume of *Georgian Poetry*, John Masefield and D. H. Lawrence, broke off their connection with the Georgian poets. Masefield was seven years older than Lawrence and already an established author when Marsh's first volume appeared. He had published two volumes of verse, a longer poem, two plays, a collection of short stories, two novels, and a biography of Shakespeare.

JOHN MASEFIELD (1878–1967) was born in Ledbury, a small market-town in Herefordshire. The rural scenes he had known as a boy form the background to much of his work. At thirteen he joined the training-ship *Conway* to train as an officer in the Merchant Navy. This romantic longing for the sea is reflected in many of Masefield's earlier poems, notably *Sea-Fever* and *Cargoes*. After ill-health had cut short his career in the Merchant Navy, Masefield worked in a New York bar, on a farm, and in a carpet-factory before his return to England in 1897. The exertion and lack of privacy of life at sea had given him little chance to read as widely as he had wished to do, and so when he returned to England he made up for the time he had lost.

He also began to write, his first book being *Salt Water Ballads* (1902), which was immediately compared with Kipling's *Barrack Room Ballads*. Many of them tell in a sailor's own language his reactions to the scenes and incidents of life at sea. In their use of everyday speech and in the free, swinging rhythms, Kipling and Masefield had something in common, though Kipling's soldiers are perhaps more realistic and more stoical than Masefield's sailors. 'Sea-Fever', 'The West Wind' and 'Tewkesbury Road' from this volume have appeared in many anthologies.

His next collection, *Ballads and Poems* (1903), includes 'Cargoes', 'Spanish Waters', 'Captain Stratton's Fancy', 'Beauty' and 'Laugh and be Merry', all of them very familiar poems now. Though the language is still simple and the rhythm strongly marked, these poems do not make the same use of the sailor's speech, and several of them express a simple philosophy, a capacity to see beauty and enjoyment in life.

After these two volumes Masefield wrote a number of longer poems. The first of these, 'The Everlasting Mercy' (1911), stirred up strong feelings when it was published. It tells how Saul Kane, a poacher, a jailbird, a ruffian, reaches a crisis in his life after defeating his best friend,

Billy Myers, in a grudge-fight over a poaching dispute. After a night's drinking Saul rouses the town by ringing the fire-bell, then runs naked through the streets with half the town in pursuit. Next day he accuses the parson in the street of hypocrisy and callousness to the sufferings of the poor. At times during the fight and in the inns Saul had felt disgust about his own life, the noise, smoke, stench, and coarseness in which he wallowed. That night Saul insults Miss Bourne, a Quaker, who toured the inns seeking to convert the depraved. He goes out into the air and feels that there is

> someone waiting to come in,
> A hand upon the door latch gropin'
> Knocking the man inside to open.

He is now converted and decides to break with his past and to work as a ploughman.

The controversy about the poem arose partly from the theme and partly from Masefield's choice of idiom and vocabulary. 'The Everlasting Mercy' is full of detailed, realistic descriptions of low life, which some readers thought unsuited to poetry:

> The room was full of men and stink
> Of bad cigars and heavy drink.
> Riley was nodding to the floor
> And gurgling as he wanted more,
> His mouth was wide, his face was pale,
> His swollen face was sweating ale.

The same charge of coarseness was brought against the language:

> From drunken man to drunken man
> The drunken madness raged and ran.
> 'I'm climber Joe who climbed the spire.'
> 'You're climber Joe the bloody liar.'
> 'Who says I lie?'
> 'I do.'
> 'You lie,
> I climbed the spire and had a fly.'
> 'I'm French Suzanne, the Circus Dancer,
> I'm going to dance a bloody Lancer.'

In fact, 'The Everlasting Mercy' is an uneven poem, containing some lively description, notably of the mad chase through the streets, an occasionally acute analysis of Saul Kane's feelings, a clear impression of the scum of a small country town, but also some embarrassing passages that ring false, notably an unconvincing denunciation of Saul by Mrs Jaggard, and the moment of conversion. It is, nevertheless, an interesting work as an early attempt at depicting low life realistically, a theme that has since been developed in the novel and in drama rather than in poetry.

In his narrative poem, 'Dauber' (1913), Masefield writes about the experiences at sea of a young man with a burning ambition to become a painter. He has to put up with the hardships of life on a sailing-ship rounding the Horn and with the sneers and malice of his ship-mates. He overcomes his sick fear of climbing aloft in a blizzard to win the grudging respect of his fellows, but in another, lesser storm he falls from the mast and is killed.

Masefield knew something of the experiences of a frustrated artist working on a sailing-ship, and the background of life aboard and the effects of changing weather sprang from his own experience. There are four elements in the poem: it is a story; it is a character-study; it is a description of life as a sailor; it embodies an idea, the artist's struggle to develop his powers of expression in an indifferent or a hostile world. Unfortunately the elements are not fused. A passage of narrative is followed by a few stanzas examining Dauber's character; then come some reflections on his ambitions as an artist. 'Dauber' might have maintained the interest more consistently if the line of development had been narrative, allowing the reader to make out for himself the motives, character and aspirations of Dauber from his actions. Equally, the theme of the artist, desperate to express himself but deficient in talent, would have offered a fascinating study to Browning. Rhyme royal is not the most helpful metre for narrative. The most memorable passage is the last four stanzas describing the ship's return to port after Dauber's death:

> Cheerly they rang her in, those beating bells,
> The new-come beauty stately from the sea,
> Whitening the blue heave of the drowsy swells,
> Treading the bubbles down. With three times three
> They cheered her moving beauty in, and she
> Came to her berth so noble, so superb;
> Swayed like a queen, and answered to the curb.

With 'Reynard the Fox' Masefield's narrative and descriptive gifts came to fruition. Masefield is very good at telling a tale about clearly visualised characters. The poem is in two parts, the first describing the scene as the hunt assembles, displaying a gallery of portraits from country life. The second part is the tale of the fox-hunt, in which Reynard is driven from cover, hunted across country, gains by his cunning short breathing-spaces, finds two earths stopped, and finally, when he seeks refuge in a copse, exhausted, he is saved when another fox is flushed into the open. Together, the two parts give a striking picture of English rural life in the first quarter of this century.

Masefield greatly admired Chaucer, and the first part of 'Reynard the Fox' constantly reminds the reader of Chaucer's Prologue. In his essay on *Fox-Hunting*, Masefield wrote: 'At a fox-hunt, and nowhere else in England, except perhaps at a funeral, can you see the whole of the land's society brought together, focused for the observer, as the Canterbury Pilgrims were for Chaucer.' Masefield makes the Parson and his wife, the Doctor's son, Pete Gurney, Tom Dansey, and the rest stand for England in his day as surely as the Squire and the Monk did in Chaucer's day:

Pete Gurney was a lusty cock
Turned sixty-three, but bright and hale,
A dairy-farmer in the vale,
Much like a robin in the face,
Much character in little space,
With little eyes like burning coal;
His mouth was like a slit or hole
In leather that was seamed and lined.
He had the russet-apple mind
That betters as the weather worsen.
He was a manly English person,
Kind to the core, brave, merry, true.

The second part keeps up a cracking pace, the occasional checks providing suspense. Here is a passage telling of the fox's attempt to reach the shelter of the copse with the hounds close behind him:

Three hundred yards and the worst was past,
The slope was gentler and shorter-grassed;
The fox saw the bulk of the woods grow tall
On the brae ahead, like a barrier-wall.
He saw the skeleton trees show sky
And the yew-trees darken to see him die,
And the line of the woods go reeling black:
There was hope in the woods—and behind, the pack.

Two hundred yards and the trees grew taller,
Blacker, blinder, as hope grew smaller;
Cry seemed nearer, the teeth seemed gripping,
Pulling him back; his pads seemed slipping.

He was all one ache, one gasp, one thirsting,
Heart on his chest-bones, beating, bursting;
The hounds were gaining like spotted pards,
And the wood hedge still was a hundred yards.

Out of the story comes a splendid picture of the English countryside—Ghost Heath Wood, Copsecote Larking, Tencombe Rings, Lark's Leybourne, Wan Dyke Hill, and the rest. 'Reynard the Fox' gives us Masefield's vigorous verse at its best.

He has also written a number of stories of adventure, mostly at sea, which are suitable for both boys and adults with a taste for tales of the sea. *Lost Endeavour* tells of the experiences of a kidnapped schoolboy and his villainous French master in Virginia and in South America. *Dead Ned* or *The Autobiography of a Corpse* is as strange and exciting as the title suggests. Ned Mansell, the hero, is sentenced to death, hanged, but cut down before life is quite extinct and revived. His adventures in West Africa among slave-traders, his eventual return, and the proof of his innocence of the crime for which he had been condemned form the subject of this book and its sequel, *Live and Kicking Ned.*

D. H. Lawrence

IN 1930 Masefield succeeded Robert Bridges as Poet Laureate. This was also the year of D. H. Lawrence's death. Lawrence, whose life and work was a protest against everything that society regarded as fixed and certain —materialism, obedience to the machine, the cult of the intellect and the neglect of the emotions—could no more have become Poet Laureate than Martin Luther could have become Pope. His birth, boyhood and youth largely account for his attitude of protest. DAVID HERBERT LAWRENCE was born at Eastwood, a colliery village in Nottinghamshire, in 1885. His father was a miner, virile, lively, pleasure-loving. Though these qualities had attracted Lawrence's mother, a former school-teacher, she found disillusion in the poverty and bickering of their married life. Lawrence describes in *Sons and Lovers* their married life as it appeared to him at the time, though he later came to think that he had been harsh to his good-natured, feckless father. Whilst he sought his enjoyment outside, Mrs Lawrence dominated the home and the family. She was determined that her sons should not follow their father into the mines and into the squalid life of a colliery village. An elder brother, Ernest, died young in London, just like William in *Sons and Lovers*, when he had a promising business career in front of him. David won a scholarship to Nottingham High School, a greater achievement at that time than it would now seem, where he stayed until he was fifteen. He left then to take a job, like Paul Morel, with a manufacturer of surgical goods in Nottingham. Illness forced Lawrence to give up this work, and he became a pupil-teacher. In 1904 he took the King's Scholarship examination and was bracketed equal first in the whole country. After qualifying as a teacher at Nottingham University College Teachers' Training Department, he took a post in a school in Croydon.

In 1909 some of his poems were accepted for publication in *The English Review*. Two years later his first novel, *The White Peacock*, was published, and was regarded by many critics as a promising performance, particularly for its descriptions of the East Midlands countryside. Although this work foreshadows much of Lawrence's later writing, the background of middle-class life in which he set it, and of which he knew little at the time, was unconvincing. The story is told in the first person by one of the characters, Cyril Beardsall, in many ways like Lawrence and with the same surname as his mother's maiden name.

A pre-publication copy of the novel was specially printed so that Mrs Lawrence could see it before she died of cancer, but she was too ill to do more than look at it. After an attack of pneumonia in 1911 Lawrence gave up teaching to become a professional writer. At this time he contributed to *Georgian Poetry*. When Lawrence visited Nottingham University College in 1912 to seek advice about his future from Professor Ernest Weekley, he met the Professor's wife, Frieda, the daughter of a German baron. Within a few weeks Frieda left her husband and three small children to run away with Lawrence to Germany. Frieda was five years older than Lawrence.

Lawrence now began to revise a novel he had written, *Sons and Lovers.* The central figure, Paul Morel, is of course Lawrence, and the novel is an account of his boyhood and youth. All the characters except Clara Dawes play much the same part in the story as they did in Lawrence's life. Mrs Morel despises her husband and seeks compensation in lavishing love on her children. In a letter about the book Lawrence wrote: 'But as her sons grow up, she selects them as lovers—first the eldest, then the second. . . . But when they come to manhood, they can't love, because their mother is the strongest power in their lives, and holds them.' Paul is held from his boyhood sweetheart, Miriam (in real life, Jessie Chambers) by his mother's corrosive love. When he turns away from Miriam to a married woman, Clara Dawes, he finds that the first rapture fades. Mrs Morel dies, another meeting with Miriam leads nowhere, and Paul turns his back on the past.

One of the main themes of *Sons and Lovers* runs through several of Lawrence's novels—the difficulty men and women have in establishing a completely satisfactory relationship. Whilst they have a deep need of each other, by making this need the focus of their whole lives, they often stifle each other's individuality. They should not be entirely submerged in each other:

> Then, we shall be two and distinct, we shall have each our
> separate being.
> And that will be pure existence, real liberty.
> Till then, we are confused, a mixture, unresolved,
> unextricated one from the other.
> It is in pure, unutterable resolvedness, distinction of
> being, that one is free,
> not in mixing, merging, not in similarity.

Lawrence's life was spent in a vain pursuit of this ideal.

In *Sons and Lovers* Lawrence re-creates with great poignancy his own feelings as a youth. He also re-creates vividly the scenes of his youth.

Throughout his career, this keen sense of place remained with Lawrence; the scenes are not a painted backcloth, but an element in the development of the action. Paul's feelings arise from his reactions not only to events, but also to the contrasting countryside and industrial dirt and mess in which he grows up. If you wish to understand Lawrence, this is certainly the novel to begin with.

In July 1914 Lawrence married Frieda, a month before the outbreak of the war. The following year *The Rainbow* was published, only to be banned as obscene. With his wife Lawrence went to live in a cottage at Zennor on the Cornish coast until they were expelled in 1917. Lawrence opposed the war, he was regarded as the immoral author of obscene books, his wife was German. They were therefore suspected of being German spies who signalled from the cliffs to enemy submarines.

When the war was over Lawrence travelled extensively in Italy and Sicily, Ceylon and Australia, U.S.A. and Mexico, returning to Italy in 1928. Here the tuberculosis that had been diagnosed in Mexico became worse, and in 1930 Lawrence died of the disease on the French Mediterranean coast. In these years he went from place to place seeking a refuge from industrial civilisation which he loathed and from his own problems. These last he took with him.

In the last ten years of his life Lawrence published *Women in Love*, in which some of the characters of *The Rainbow* reappear; *Kangaroo*, a novel with an Australian background, a study of a leader with Fascist characteristics; *The Plumed Serpent*, which transfers the theme of leadership to a Mexican setting; and *Lady Chatterley's Lover*, in which Lawrence glorifies sex as a liberating agent from the sterility of industrial civilisation. He also wrote much poetry, notably about birds, animals, reptiles and trees. Of these 'Kangaroo', 'Snake' and 'Cypresses' are found in many anthologies. He was a most prolific and versatile writer, and his output included also travel books with vivid descriptions of the countries he had visited, short stories, essays, plays, translations, a historical work and literary studies.

Certain ideas constantly recur in Lawrence's writing. He loathes the machine:

> New houses, new furniture, new streets, new clothes, new
> sheets
> everything new and machine-made sucks life out of us
> and makes us cold, makes us lifeless
> the more we have.

He associates the middle-class and the industrialist with their products:

> Isn't he handsome? isn't he healthy? Isn't he a fine
> specimen?
> doesn't he look the fresh clean englishman, outside?
> Isn't it God's own image? tramping his thirty miles a day
> after partridges, or a little rubber ball?
> wouldn't you like to be like that, well off, and quite the
> thing?
>
> Oh, but wait!
> Let him meet a new emotion, let him be faced with another
> man's need,
> let him come home to a bit of moral difficulty, let life
> face him with a new demand on his understanding
> and then watch him go soggy, like a wet meringue.
> Watch him turn into a mess, either a fool or a bully,
> Just watch the display of him, confronted with a new demand
> on his intelligence,
> a new life-demand.

This contempt is shown in the treatment of many of his characters, such as Tom Brangwen in *The Rainbow*, Gerald Crich in *Women in Love* and Sir Clifford Chatterley. They are all prosperous, they destroy the lives of those nearest to them. Lawrence hates also the emancipated, intelligent, cultured, apparently independent woman, whose life is hollow because she cannot accept an unselfconscious emotion. Winifred Ingmer is this type of woman, but the most clearly drawn is Hermione Roddice in *Women in Love*. She represents the supremacy of the intellect. Lawrence put his own belief in a letter he wrote in 1913: 'My great religion is a belief in the blood, the flesh, as being wiser than the intellect. We can go wrong in our minds. But what our blood feels and believes and says, is always true.'

One of the things that Lawrence's blood felt was man's kinship with nature, some power flowing into man even through the contact of his foot with the earth. When Anna in *The Rainbow* is awaiting the birth of her child, she becomes part of the growth that is going on everywhere around her:

> Day after day came shining through the door of Paradise, day after day she entered into the brightness. The child in her shone till she herself was a beam of sunshine; and how lovely was the sunshine that loitered and wandered out of doors, where the catkins on the big hazel bushes at the end of the garden hung in their shaken, floating aureole, where little fumes like fire burst out

from the black yew-trees as a bird settled clinging to the branches. One day bluebells were along the hedge-bottoms, then cowslips twinkled like manna, golden and evanescent on the meadows. She was full of a rich drowsiness and loneliness. How happy she was, how gorgeous it was to live: to have known herself, her husband, the passion of love and begetting; and to know that all this lived and waited and burned on around her, a terrible purifying fire, through which she had passed for once to come to this peace of golden radiance, when she was with child, and innocent, and in love with her husband and with all the many angels hand in hand. She lifted her throat to the breeze that came across the fields, and she felt it handling her like sisters fondling her, she drank it in perfume of cowslips and of apple-blossoms.

Lawrence also has favourite images and associations—the awakening of passion and the unfolding of a flower, most fully worked out in his poem, 'Snap-Dragon'; darkness and voluptuousness. The titles of his novels show his use of symbolism: *The White Peacock*, a symbol of a selfish woman; *The Rainbow*, in which Ursula Brangwen saw 'the earth's new architecture, the old, brittle corruption of houses and factories swept away, the world built up in a living fabric of Truth, fitting to the over-arching heaven'; in *The Plumed Serpent* Ursula's vision of the gigantic horses pursuing her and hemming her in; Birkin's stoning of the reflection of the moon in the lake in *Women in Love*; his wrestling-match with Gerald Crich: these incidents also embody an idea or a mood or a relationship.

Believing that what the blood told him was more trustworthy than what his mind told him, Lawrence was both a sensual and a sensuous writer. He had an acute visual sense as his natural descriptions show, but it was the sense of touch that aroused him emotionally.

The great virtue of his poetry is its spontaneity. His later poetry does not rhyme and is irregular in form, though not haphazard. Many of the poems have a natural eloquence that speaks straight to the reader; this is not the lumbering free verse of Whitman. Lawrence is an instinctive poet, and 'Snake', 'Kangaroo' and 'Bats' have an immediate appeal. 'Bavarian Gentians' is his most highly-wrought poem; 'The Ship of Death', in which he prepares for his own death, is his most profound:

> We are dying, we are dying, so all we can do
> is now to be willing to die, and to build the ship
> of death to carry the soul on the longest journey.

Lawrence had certain things that he wanted to say intensely. He is often accused of having no sense of humour, but such scenes as the wedding of Anna and Will Brangwen in *The Rainbow* disprove this. The first third of that book has much the same humour and earthiness that Thomas Hardy's rustic scenes and characters had. But humour was of little use to Lawrence in what he most wanted to say. His range was narrow but he has made men look at the world in a different way. He has disturbed their belief in mechanical progress, in the virtue of possession; he showed that satisfaction is emotional, not material; he undermined the comfortable assumption that the relationship between man and woman should be a calm and reasonable one. His novels are novels of tension: tension between man and his environment, between man and woman, between man and man. His work had great influence on the next generation of novelists, and the world, the people and the objects in it have never looked the same to the writer and the reader since his day. What he had to say was not the whole truth, but much of it was a strange truth.

W. B. Yeats

THE position of WILLIAM BUTLER YEATS (1865–1939) amongst modern poets is as lonely and majestic as the course he chose for his spiritual evolution when still a young man. There is no trend that can assimilate, or even lay claim to a portion of his beliefs. Almost every other poet of this century has handled the medium tentatively, as though uncertain that poetry was really the right form for the times. T. S. Eliot questions and argues with the form in his *Four Quartets*: in a mock-grandiose passage he makes fun of the effects he relies on. W. H. Auden, always conscious of the contrived nature of poetry, exaggerates this contrivedness with verbal tricks. More recent poets have often seemed so apologetic for writing in verse that they have struggled for prose effects which detract from both forms. Yeats was at odds with his generation in being a lover of certainties not of questions: he accepted poetry on its old terms:

> . . . with a mind
> That nobleness made simple as a fire,
> With beauty like a tightened bow, a kind
> That is not natural in an age like this,
> Being high and solitary and most stern.

These lines from 'No Second Troy' refer to the woman, Maud Gonne, whom Yeats loved, but the terms are ones that he might equally have applied to his poetry. He had an arrogance which never doubts poetry, and which the practice of poetry assumes: other poets, lacking this arrogance, have often lacked the strength that goes with it.

Arrogance and genius, however, are not the only factors which make a poet write with assurance. Much depends upon his position in his times, upon the relationship he can make with contemporary life. In this Yeats, being Irish, was more fortunate than the English poets of the day. He had divided his boyhood and youth between homes in London and Ireland: in the process he assimilated much of the thought and way of life of each country. Each was rich in a different way. England had the literary tradition that Ireland lacked, and Yeats found friends among the young poets of the eighteen-nineties, who met at a London pub called *The Cheshire Cheese*. Many years after the group had disintegrated, he celebrated their companionship in a long poem, 'The Grey Rock'; in his prose writings he describes how they helped his artistic development.

Their single-minded devotion to poetry made him feel that his theorising and arguing was somehow 'not quite well-bred'; they made him concentrate primarily on the poem as a thing. But there was much in England that Yeats could not accept, for everything that was essential in him was Irish.

Yeats believed that in Ireland, which, unlike England and the other countries of Europe, had not been corrupted by commerce and industry, a spiritual revolution would be possible. In Ireland as he saw it, the old values had not quite vanished: the medieval, even the pre-Christian civilisations seemed to linger on. In the country areas that make up most of Ireland belief in the supernatural was still unquestioned, and the myths and legends of the old heroes who ruled Ireland long before St Patrick came to convert them, were still told. Yeats's first dream was to evoke by his poetry, even amongst the educated classes, a kind of collective national memory, so that the Irish could converse in terms of their legends and history, and a literary tradition be founded on them. His plan was to write what he called a *Légende des Siècles* of Ireland, and 'show something of every century' so that the Irish might know their history and respect it. Although he later changed his mind, the first works in this series were written: they were the long poem, *The Wanderings of Oisin*, and the play, *The Countess Cathleen.*

In the story, Oisin was the son of Finn, who was the poet of an old heroic clan called the Fianna, to which incredible exploits were attributed. Oisin was loved by a faery woman, Niamh, who seduced him from his world and carried him off on her horse to the land of faery eternity over the sea. He lived with her there for what seemed a short time, and then old memories made him long to return to the real world and his friends. When he returned, he found that he had been away for three centuries. Christianity had come to Ireland, and those who lived there now remembered Finn and the Fianna only vaguely, as an old legend. Back in the mortal world, Oisin's three hundred years fell upon him, and in the hours before his death, St Patrick came to baptise him and try to save his soul by teaching him about the Christian heaven and hell. But the Christian heaven was a poor consolation to Oisin for the loss of his immortal bride on her faery horse, or for the passing away of Finn and the Fianna for whose sake he had rejected even her. In her later version of the story, Lady Gregory gives him these words: 'I will cry my fill, but not for God, but because Finn and the Fianna are not living'.

Yeats used the story of Oisin to evoke the vision of faeryland which he expanded into three separate islands, at the expense of the violent heroes of the Fianna, and the characters of Oisin, Niamh and St Patrick. At the time of *The Wanderings of Oisin*, Yeats, in his early twenties, was writing an intense, melancholy verse inspired by a dream world into which he fitted the story of Oisin. This dream world was peopled with powerful images: strange symbolic animals, supernatural landscapes, and sad, noble, inbred faery beings who might have stepped out of a painting by Burne–Jones:

> We galloped over the glossy sea:
> I know not if days passed or hours,
> And Niamh sang continually
> Danaan songs, and their dewy showers
> Of pensive laughter, unhuman sound,
> Lulled weariness, and softly round
> My human sorrow her white arms wound.
>
> We galloped; now a hornless deer
> Passed by us, chased by a phantom hound
> All pearly white, save one red ear;
> And now a lady rode like the wind
> With an apple of gold in her tossing hand;
> And a beautiful young man followed behind
> With quenchless gaze and fluttering hair.

The poems in Yeats's first books are nearly all written in this dreamy, somnolent, richly evocative style. In them, Yeats was trying to celebrate the eerie beauty and the splendour of Irish history. There is much that is enchanting in these poems, but they are enchanting because they are unreal: what we are shown is not the true Irish history, but a secret hiding-place in Yeats's mind, a compilation of all that he found attractive in Irish history, that he had set up against all he despised in contemporary life.

It was the publication of *The Wanderings of Oisin* that introduced Yeats to Maud Gonne. She read the poem, and admired it, and the motives that had led Yeats to write it, so much that she called on the young poet in London. Yeats had always dreamed of a legendary beauty:

> All dreams of the soul
> End in a beautiful man's or woman's body.

Maud Gonne was that, but she was also a brilliant and strong-minded woman whose whole heart was dedicated to the cause of Irish nationalism. Yeats fell desperately in love with her beauty, but always resented the political passion which in his view marred it. Many years later, in 'Michael Robartes and the Dancer', he elucidated what he had always felt about the minds of beautiful women:

> HE: . . . bear in mind your lover's wage
> Is what your looking-glass can show,
> And that he will turn green with rage
> At all that is not pictured there.

SHE: May I not put myself to college?
HE: Go pluck Athene by the hair;
For what mere book can grant a knowledge
With an impassioned gravity
Appropriate to that beating breast,
That vigorous thigh, that dreaming eye?
And may the Devil take the rest.

But although she did not return his love, and although their views came to diverge more widely in time, at the beginning of their friendship Yeats admired the selflessness of Maud Gonne's devotion to Irish freedom enough to write a play for her on the theme. When *The Countess Cathleen* was performed, with Maud in the title role, it stirred up considerable nationalist feeling.

The story of *The Countess Cathleen* comes from a west-of-Ireland folk-tale. In a time of famine, the Countess Cathleen sold her soul to the devil to save her tenants from starvation, and to save their souls, which they had exchanged for food. The people were saved, but so was the Countess, although devils and angels battled for her soul, because her motive in committing the mortal sin was charity, which can never send a soul to hell. The play is well constructed, and the poetry fine and suited to the stage, but as there is no real struggle, and the Countess's salvation a foregone conclusion, it lacks power. In his old age, Yeats wrote of it: 'It was not, nor is it now more than a piece of tapestry. The Countess sells her soul, but she is not transformed. If I were to think out that scene today, she would, the moment her hand has signed, burst into loud laughter, mock at all she has held holy, horrify the peasants in the midst of their temptations.'

When he was a young man, Yeats, no less than Maud Gonne, was eager to see the end of English rule, and freedom for Ireland.

Two of the nationalist leaders had caught his imagination: John O'Leary and Parnell. Yeats was a romantic, and he could well believe the salvation of Ireland might spring from these two great men, whom he saw as heroes of the old kind: modern versions of Finn and his Fianna. But O'Leary died, and Parnell was shamed into obscurity by the mean morals of his ungrateful countrymen, who raised an uproar when he was cited as the co-respondent in a divorce case. Maud Gonne's enthusiasm for the Irish cause continued, but Yeats was shocked and disillusioned. The dreams he had had about noble Ireland fell in pieces; he looked at his countrymen with dismay and anger; the whole tone of his poetry changed. *Responsibilities*, the book of poems he published in 1914, is furiously realistic. Not a vestige of daydream is left; his themes are often political; he speaks now of living men and women, often with scorn and disillusion. Although his old heroic values remain, he has hammered them into a modern context. For example, in the introductory rhymes he describes his own ancestors in terms that he would earlier, and reverently, have set aside for the remote heroes of myth:

> Merchant and scholar who have left me blood
> That has not passed through any huckster's loin,
> Soldiers that gave, whatever die was cast:
> A Butler or an Armstrong that withstood
> Beside the brackish waters of the Boyne
> James and his Irish when the Dutchman crossed;
> Old merchant skipper that leaped overboard
> After a ragged hat in Biscay Bay;
> You most of all, silent and fierce old man,
> Because the daily spectacle that stirred
> My fancy, and set my boyish lips to say,
> 'Only the wasteful virtues earn the sun'; . . . .'

He had learnt to recognise in modern life the extravagance that had touched his imagination in the more obviously flamboyant exploits of Finn and his like. That sailor who leapt overboard after a ragged hat displayed the same absurd magnificence as the old Irish king Cuchulain when for three days and nights he battled fruitlessly with the waves of the sea. In 'September 1913' in the same book, Yeats pays homage to the heroes of recent Irish history, and laments the moralising pettiness that has sapped away the insane souls of his own generation:

> What need you, being come to sense,
> But fumble in a greasy till
> And add the halfpence to the pence
> And prayer to shivering prayer, until
> You have dried the marrow from the bone?
> For men were born to pray and save:
> Romantic Ireland's dead and gone,
> It's with O'Leary in the grave.
>
> Yet they were of a different kind,
> The names that stilled your childish play,
> They have gone about the world like wind,
> But little time had they to pray
> For whom the hangman's rope was spun,
> And what, God help us, could they save?
> Romantic Ireland's dead and gone,
> It's with O'Leary in the grave.

Was it for this the wild geese spread
The grey wing upon every tide;
For this that all that blood was shed,
For this Edward Fitzgerald died,
And Robert Emmet and Wolfe Tone,
All that delirium of the brave?
Romantic Ireland's dead and gone,
It's with O'Leary in the grave.

In this vehement rebuke, Yeats decries all those whom he believed to have betrayed the patriots who gave their lives for them. All the passion of his early romance had gone into outrage, and he withdrew for a time from the political scene, hoping to find peace of mind, and a way of life that he could respect in place of the sordid quarrels of public life: 'For they are at their old tricks yet'.

It was at this time that Yeats came most to appreciate a friend of many years' standing, Lady Gregory, and to formulate in his mind exactly what her aristocratic way of life meant to him.

Lady Gregory, herself a writer of talent, had given Yeats the freedom of her country house, Coole Park, and for many years had provided a respite from the troubles of the nationalist movement, or his unsatisfactory relationship with Maud Gonne, who had married an old enemy of his, Sean MacBride. Lady Gregory shared his enthusiasm for an Irish literary revival, and helped him to found the Abbey Theatre, where his own plays and those of John Synge were, amongst others, performed. She also helped to ease him out of the dream world of his early poems, and it is this that he praises her for in these lines from the poem, 'Friends':

. . . her hand
Had strength that could unbind
What none can understand,
What none can have and thrive,
Youth's dreamy load, till she
So changed me that I live
Labouring in ecstasy.

Yeats wrote a very personal elegy when Lady Gregory's son was killed in the First World War. 'In Memory of Major Robert Gregory' shows that the poet was beginning to realise not only that Major Gregory represented another in that saga of extravagant heroes, but also a model of courtesy and propriety. He is certainly described as outrageous and romantic in the old heroic image:

When with the Galway foxhounds he would ride
From Castle Taylor to the Roxborough side
Or Esserkelly plain, few kept his pace;
At Mooneen he had leaped a place
So perilous that half the astonished meet
Had shut their eyes; and where was it
He rode a race without a bit?
And yet his mind outran the horses' feet.

But a new quality has entered Yeats' admiration. He has grown a certain reserve, not in his admiration, but in his grief, and this has been aroused by the quality he particularly admires in both the Gregorys: their aristocratic good taste and breeding. When he spoke of death in 'September 1913', the death which swept O'Leary and 'all that delirium of the brave' away with it, it was a violent hungry force with little time to wait for good manners. But that death was in its way splendid. The death of Major Robert Gregory is shocking because unnecessary (nothing, as Yeats points out in 'An Irish Airman Foresees his Death', forced him to fight for the English) and Yeats describes it as an offence against the proper order of things:

I am accustomed to their lack of breath,
But not that my dear friend's dear son,
Our Sidney and our perfect man,
Could share in that discourtesy of death.

At about this time Yeats, who had long given up hope of Maud Gonne, married a much younger woman, Georgie Hyde-Lees. Established in a family, and with a home of his own (he had bought an old tower near Coole Park) he was able to work out exactly what it was that he believed to be the proper order of things. And all his admiration went to the ceremony and orderliness, the old customs that still left room for eccentricity and extravagance, that he saw personified in the Irish land-owning classes. These beliefs inspire a very fine later poem, 'A Prayer for my Daughter', written calmly and with assurance out of yet more disillusion and destruction in Ireland:

I have walked and prayed for this young child an hour
And heard the sea-wind scream upon the tower,
And under the arches of the bridge, and scream
In the elms above the flooded stream;
Imagining in excited reverie
That the future years had come,

Dancing to a frenzied drum,
Out of the murderous innocence of the sea.

. . . . .

In courtesy I'd have her chiefly learned;
Hearts are not had as a gift but hearts are earned
By those that are not entirely beautiful;
Yet many, that have played the fool
For beauty's very self, has charm made wise,
And many a poor man that has roved,
Loved and thought himself beloved,
From a glad kindness cannot take his eyes.

May she become a flourishing hidden tree
That all her thoughts may like the linnet be,
And have no business but dispensing round
Their magnanimities of sound,
Nor but in merriment begin a chase,
Nor but in merriment a quarrel.
O may she live like some green laurel
Rooted in one dear perpetual place.

. . . . .

And may her bridegroom bring her to a house
Where all's accustomed, ceremonious;
For arrogance and hatred are the wares
Peddled in the thoroughfares.
How but in custom and in ceremony
Are innocence and beauty born?
Ceremony's a name for the rich horn,
And custom for the spreading laurel tree.

But before this poem was written, Yeats had been shocked and shocked again by political developments in Ireland. The Nationalist cause that he had rejected as squalid, suddenly reared up again: where Yeats had thought it impossible, new heroes had died and a new myth risen up: he was forced to pay homage, though his new-found tranquillity could not approve the violence. The Easter Rising of 1916 was doomed from the outset. Those who participated were only a handful of passionate rebels against the whole British Army. But they died deliberately, knowing they had no hope of success, in order to make a gesture towards Irish freedom, and to commit future generations to winning that freedom, or betraying these patriots' deaths. Yeats commemorated them in 'Easter 1916': those who died included Sean MacBride, Maud Gonne's husband, whom he had always hated, but was now forced to accept as a hero:

I have met them at close of day
Coming with vivid faces
From counter or desk among grey
Eighteenth-century houses.
I have passed with a nod of the head
Or polite meaningless words,
Or have lingered awhile and said
Polite meaningless words,
And thought before I had done
Of a mocking tale or a gibe
To please a companion
Around the fire at the club,
Being certain that they and I
But lived where motley is worn:
All changed, changed utterly:
A terrible beauty is born.

This concrete Dublin that he describes is amazingly remote from the visionary landscapes of his first poems, but the events that are enacted there are no less legendary. Yeats is staggered to have missed the heroic quality in these conspirators in the days before the rebellion:

I write it out in a verse—
MacDonagh and MacBride
And Connolly and Pearse
Now and in time to be,
Wherever green is worn,
Are changed, changed utterly:
A terrible beauty is born.

A final shock awaited Yeats in the political world. In 1919 civil war broke out in Ireland: the glory of the Easter Rising had perhaps provoked a thirst for bloodshed which resulted in these meaningless and callous killings. Yeats can be assured, at this price, that his own image of a gentler greatness was the right one. In 'Nineteen Hundred and Nineteen', his most bitter poem, he writes:

Now days are dragon-ridden, the nightmare
Rides upon sleep: a drunken soldiery
Can leave the mother murdered at her door,
To crawl in her own blood, and go scot-free;
The night can sweat with terror as before
We pieced our thoughts into philosophy,
And planned to bring the world under a rule,
Who are but weasels fighting in a hole.

Here he writes with Shakespearean violence, sneering at the dream he had entertained as a young man, of Ireland, the country uncorrupted by commerce and industry, leading the world in a cultural revolution:

> . . . but now
> The winds of winter blow
> Learn that we were crack-pated when we dreamed.

It can be seen through this that Yeats, unlike any other poet of the century, possessed the epic vision: even in his own times he could register the importance of public events and turn them into legends for the future. In this he resembled another of his heroes, Homer, who created Troy and the course of Western literature in the same book. Yeats made a living legend of the heroes of his day, and also created an Irish tradition, in which James Joyce, Sean O'Casey and Samuel Beckett amongst others have succeeded him. He came to write in a style powerful because stripped of all the poetic fantasy that had adorned his verse when he was young: he wrote almost in common speech, and yet a speech so passionate that it becomes poetry without forcing. In one of his last poems, all his greatest qualities are shown: the simple speech, the faculty that could make myths out of his friends, and the respect for human beings above all other things, that had remained with him since Oisin preferred Finn and the Fianna to God and Heaven, that had kept him a hero-worshipper even in the times of his deepest disillusionment:

Beautiful Lofty Things

> Beautiful lofty things: O'Leary's noble head;
> My father upon the Abbey stage, before him a raging crowd:
> 'This Land of Saints', and then as the applause died out,
> 'Of plaster Saints'; his beautiful mischievous head thrown back.
> Standish O'Grady supporting himself between the tables
> Speaking to a drunken audience high nonsensical words;
> Augusta Gregory seated at her great ormolu table,
> Her eightieth winter approaching: 'Yesterday he threatened my life.
> I told him that nightly from six to seven I sat at this table,
> The blinds drawn up'; Maud Gonne at Howth station waiting a train,
> Pallas Athene in that straight back and arrogant head:
> All the Olympians; a thing never known again.

T. S. Eliot

THE life of THOMAS STEARNS ELIOT (1888–1965) followed a general pattern very like that of Henry James, but with an interval of forty-five years between them. He was born in St Louis, Missouri, where his father was president of the Hydraulic Press Brick Company. His mother wrote a dramatic poem on the life of Savonarola. His education, much more formal than Henry James's, took him in turn to Harvard, where he studied under Bertrand Russell, to the Sorbonne in Paris, and to Merton College, Oxford. In 1916 he settled in London, the persuasion of Ezra Pound reinforcing the fondness for London he had already developed. In 1927 he took British citizenship, and was also baptised into the Church of England. From this time onwards he described himself as 'an Anglo-Catholic in religion, a classicist in literature and a royalist in politics'. He won the Nobel Prize for literature in 1948, a year in which he was also admitted to the Order of Merit. No man could have taken on more fully the characteristics of an adopted country—reserve, reticence, a dislike of over-emphasis, conservatism.

Henry James lived on a private income and his earnings as a writer; Eliot, at first from necessity, later from choice, took employment. In 1916 he taught in the junior department of Highgate School, where one of his pupils was John Betjeman, who, in his verse autobiography, *Summoned by Bells*, recalls showing his juvenile poems to him:

> To one who, I was told, liked poetry—
> The American master, Mr Eliot.
> That dear good man, with Prufrock in his head
> And Sweeney waiting to be agonized,
> I wonder what he thought? He never says
> When now we meet, across the port and cheese.
> He looks the same as then, long, lean and pale,
> Still with the slow deliberating speech
> And enigmatic answers. At the time
> A boy called Jelly said 'He thinks they're bad'—
> But he himself is still too kind to say.

Eliot himself gives another impression of this subject:

How unpleasant to meet Mr Eliot!
With his features of clerical cut,
And his brow so grim
And his mouth so prim
And his conversation, so nicely
Restricted to What Precisely
And If and Perhaps and But.
How unpleasant to meet Mr Eliot!

Later he worked for a time in Lloyd's Bank, and in 1923 he founded a quarterly review, *The Criterion*, which he ran until 1939. Probably in no other age has there been a magazine so indispensable to an understanding of the thought and opinions of its age. For many years until his death Eliot was a director of the publishing house of Faber and Faber, where by his selection of poetry for publication he did much to form the taste of the reading public.

Eliot's early poems are about the emptiness, the feelings of frustration, the round of petty, pointless activities of upper-class social life in Boston and New England. 'The Love Song of J. Alfred Prufrock' portrays the representative figure of this kind of life, a middle-aged bachelor who is different from his contemporaries only in his awareness of his own meaningless life and insignificance:

No! I am not Prince Hamlet, nor was meant to be;
Am an attendant lord, one that will do
To swell a progress, start a scene or two,
Advise the prince; no doubt, an easy tool,
Deferential, glad to be of use,
Politic, cautious, and meticulous;
Full of high sentence, but a bit obtuse;
At times, indeed, almost ridiculous—
Almost, at times, the Fool.

In this early poem some of the distinctive qualities of Eliot's poetry may be seen. He is commenting on urban life, social activity. The phrasing is terse and unemphatic, the tone self-deprecatory. The memorable phrases and images are there:

. . . the yellow smoke that slides along the street
Rubbing its back upon the window-panes

I have measured out my life with coffee spoons.

. . . as if a magic lantern threw the nerves in patterns on a screen.

I grow old. . . . I grow old. . . .
I shall wear the bottom of my trousers rolled.

We see also the effective contrast reached by placing together the splendid romantic notion and the commonplace or squalid:

I have heard the mermaids singing each to each.
I do not think that they will sing to me.

Even at this stage Eliot is concerned with the problem of being understood, of the imperfection of words as a means of communication, a problem that remained with him right through to the *Four Quartets*:

It is impossible to say just what I mean!

And would it have been worth it, after all,
. . . .
If one, settling a pillow by her head,
  Should say: 'That is not what I meant at all.
  That is not it, at all.'

With the appearance of *The Waste Land* in 1922 it became clear that Eliot was not only a major poet, but wrote poetry of a new kind. The 'Waste Land' was twentieth-century civilisation, a world of sterile lust. Eliot describes both the parched world awaiting the rain that can bring back life, and the corruptness of sexual behaviour not only in modern London, but through the centuries. In doing this he seeks to show the universality of the disease that is now afflicting man. The parched land is a symbol of the shrivelled soul of man. In the last section, 'What the Thunder said', a possible means of salvation is indicated; after the prolonged drought a thunderstorm would bring relief. The thunder is heard, uttering a message from the Hindu scriptures: 'Give, sympathise, control'. The poem ends with the hope that something may be saved from the desolation:

I sat upon the shore
Fishing, with the arid plain behind me
Shall I at least set my lands in order?

The poem expresses the mood of the age—disgust, disillusion, despair. It points to the need for a spiritual revival without prophesying that this will necessarily follow. For many people *The Waste Land* put into words their own feelings, but both the message and the form of expression aroused resentment in others. The poem, just over four hundred lines long, is notable for its compression. Eliot achieves this compression by omitting links between scenes and by a rapid succession of literary and religious allusions which are not explained. The range of his own reading shown in *The Waste Land*—Dante, Goldsmith, Shakespeare, Spenser, Ovid, Marvell, Wagner, Sanskrit texts—is vast; since few readers can match Eliot's erudition, the effect on the reader is often obscurity. Some of them thought that the obscurity was deliberate and the learning ostentatious. Eliot in fact intended that these references and allusions would make his theme eternal and universal.

Some of the scenes, like the conversation in the public-house in Section II and the seduction of the typist in Section III, are clear enough. It is also clear that certain ideas, images and symbols recur in the poem—lust without tenderness; rocks, heat and dust as symbols of sterility; water as the means of redemption; crowds of moving people in search of something unspecified; allusions to rats and bones and bells. The poem's unity comes from the repetition and varied relationships of these symbols and images, but it is a unity that can be only dimly discerned at first. The approach to *The Waste Land* should be intuitive, not analytical in the first place. Instead of trying to work out the significance of each allusion or image or symbol, it is better to recognise the principal themes, allowing the more explicit passages to provide a framework for the fuller understanding that can come only with several readings. Once the general shape of the poem has been apprehended, the detailed analyses by Dr Leavis, Cleanth Brooks and others will assist towards this fuller understanding.

In *The Hollow Men* (1925) Eliot depicts twentieth-century man as a scarecrow. Here it is not man's rottenness he is exposing, but his spiritual emptiness. Extinction faces him, but there will be neither dignity nor drama in his doom:

> This is the way the world ends
> This is the way the world ends
> This is the way the world ends
> Not with a bang but a whimper.

After 1925 Eliot's mind turned towards the problems of religious faith and towards dramatic form. He was received into the Church of England in 1927, and *Ash Wednesday* (1930) has for its theme the struggle towards a faith. Ash Wednesday, the first day of Lent, signifies the beginning of a spiritual progress in which Eliot turns his back on the world and its ambitions and seeks to climb a stairway that will lead him to God. The poem ends with questioning and pleading, for he recognises his need for help. It is, however, a self-examination in which hope persists:

> Teach us to sit still
> Even among these rocks,
> Our peace in His will
> And even among these rocks
> Sister, mother
> And spirit of the river, spirit of the sea,
> Suffer me not to be separated
>
> And let my cry come unto Thee.

In the Choruses from *The Rock* (1934), a pageant play, Eliot confidently affirms his faith; although the world is not ready to accept the message of the Church, the work of building the Church must continue:

> What life have you if you have not life together?
> There is no life that is not in community,
> And no community not lived in praise of God.

Man's thoughts are occupied with business, materialism, pleasure, and he will not heed. All that he has built will be destroyed by time:

> And the wind shall say: 'Here were decent godless people:
> Their only monument the asphalt road
> And a thousand lost golf balls'.

Eliot finds the images that pitilessly expose man's pretensions:

> Will you build me a house of plaster, with corrugated roofing,
> To be filled with a litter of Sunday newspapers?

Although the Church cannot hope to overcome the world's apathy in one generation, and although the building of one church may seem an unimportant contribution, man must be satisfied with what he can accomplish, taking one step at a time:

> Be not too curious of Good and Evil;
> Seek not to count the future waves of Time;
> But be ye satisfied that you have light
> Enough to take your step and find your foothold.

In this pageant, which was written on behalf of a fund to preserve the old churches of London, the Choruses are sometimes spoken in unison, sometimes by individuals, sometimes divided between groups. From this *Murder in the Cathedral*, written for the Canterbury Festival of 1935, followed naturally enough. It tells of the return of Thomas à Becket, Archbishop of Canterbury, from France where he had been forced to flee by the King, to a death he knows to be certain. He is tempted by four Tempters who try to play upon his past frailties until he rejects them. Between the two parts of the play the Archbishop preaches a sermon on martyrdom. In the second part he is killed by four knights who later justify the murder to the audience. There is a Chorus consisting of women of Canterbury who want only peace and freedom from oppression. The interest lies neither in the story, which is slight, nor in the characters, who personify one quality or motive like the characters in the old mystery plays, but in the examination of Becket's ideals and motives and in the effective contrasts between the Archbishop on the one hand and the priests, the Tempters, and the Knights who murder him on the other.

In his next play, *The Family Reunion* (1939), Eliot transfers to a modern English country-house the Greek tragedy of Orestes. The play contains a number of effective situations as the central figure, Harry, Lord Monchensey, learns the truth about his mother's use of his father to achieve her own ends, his father's plot to murder her, and his aunt's love for and renunciation of his father. The characters are varied, and their interplay as they are involved in Harry's crisis maintains interest. Surprisingly, Eliot succeeds much better with the setting and characters he takes from conventional drawing-room comedy than he does with the Eumenides, whose appearance is embarrassingly unconvincing. He also went part of the way towards solving the problem of writing a modern play in verse. The dialogue keeps the play moving, though sometimes a little cumbrously. When the characters reflect on their situation, the verse adds to the impact, but it is not yet flexible enough to allow the rapid exchange that the dramatist sometimes needs.

After the war Eliot wrote three plays which were produced at the Edinburgh International Festival: *The Cocktail Party* (1949), *The Confidential Clerk* (1953) and *The Elder Statesman* (1958). Like the earlier plays *The Cocktail Party* presents us with the moment of decisive choice, but this time the choice is not of one man only to whom the other characters and the whole of the action are subordinated. Peter Quilp, Edward and Lavinia Chamberlayne and Celia Coplestone have all reached a crisis in their lives, and for all of them the crisis has arisen because of their relationships with each other. None of their characters or crises or choices are comprehensible without reference to the others. For that reason the play is both more complex and more compact in structure than any of Eliot's other plays, much more satisfying, and much more successful on the stage.

Characters and themes are taken from the stock of fashionable drama—successful barrister, his wife and mistress, ambitious young film-maker, fashionable psychiatrist; adultery, marital quarrels and a reunion, departure overseas of a disappointed lover, imminent nervous breakdowns, elegant drawing-room and consulting-room. What goes on beneath the surface, the significance of the events, is, however, much more subtle and much more profound. The play is both comic and deeply serious, yet the comedy of Reilly's drinking-scene with Edward does not impair the seriousness of the scene in which he counsels Celia. Eliot reaches a workable solution of the main problem of verse drama: how to carry on trivial conversations, how to stage a quarrel, how to exchange the commonplaces of existence without seeming either ludicrous or pompous. The bickering between Edward and Lavinia, the bright empty chatter at the party, are successfully brought off, the loose rhythms of the verse pointing the dialogue, not distracting attention from it. There is nothing artificial in Celia's confession to Reilly:

> Well, my bringing up was pretty conventional—
> I had always been taught to disbelieve in sin.
> Oh, I don't mean that it was ever mentioned!
> But anything wrong, from our point of view,
> Was either bad form, or was psychological.
> And bad form always led to disaster
> Because the people one knew disapproved of it.

Reilly's speech to Celia shows that the verse is flexible enough to bear more weight than that: he is speaking about those who are persuaded to content themselves with the give-and-take of an ordinary marriage that is neither happy nor unhappy:

> . . . They do not repine;
> Are contented with the morning that separates
> And with the evening that brings together
> For casual talk before the fire
> Two people who know they do not understand each other,
> Breeding children whom they do not understand
> And who will never understand them.
>
> CELIA: Is that the best life?

REILLY: It is a good life. Though you will not know how good
Till you come to the end. But you will want nothing else,
And the other life will be only like a book
You have read once, and lost. . . .

The later plays are slighter in structure, looser in texture, and less taut in dialogue than *The Cocktail Party.*

Between 1935 and 1942 Eliot wrote the *Four Quartets*: 'Burnt Norton', 'East Coker', 'The Dry Salvages' and 'Little Gidding'. Each of the four places from which the Quartets took their titles had some association for Eliot—Burnt Norton was a manor in Gloucestershire; East Coker, the village in Somerset from which his family had emigrated to America; the Dry Salvages, a small group of rocks off the Massachusetts coast which Eliot knew well as a boy; Little Gidding, the Huntingdonshire home of a religious community with which two religious poets, George Herbert and Crashaw, were associated.

The form of the *Four Quartets* has a close affinity with musical compositions. Each is in five sections corresponding to the movements of a quartet or symphony. Like a composer, Eliot introduces a theme, develops it, follows with another theme, recapitulates them and then integrates them. There is a balance between the movements: the first and last are reflective, the second and fourth lyrical, the latter being much shorter and more intense, and the third is more active than the others, usually containing the idea of passengers in motion. All the time one hears echoes and variations of themes that occurred earlier, not only in the Quartets, but also in Eliot's poems and plays that came before the Quartets. So closely linked are they that it is a mistake to think of them as four poems; together they form a definitive statement of Eliot's beliefs.

It is much easier to say that than it is to define the beliefs. The poet several times insists that his words are inadequate to express his meaning:

So here I am in the middle way, having had twenty years—
Twenty years largely wasted, the years of l'entre deux guerres—
Trying to learn to use words, and every attempt
Is a wholly new start, and a different kind of failure
Because one has only learnt to get the better of words
For the thing one no longer has to say, or the way in which
One is no longer disposed to say it.

And again:

. . . The poetry does not matter.
It was not (to start again) what one had expected.

Man cannot acquire from life the equipment that Eliot feels he needs for understanding:

> . . . There is, it seems to us,
> At best, only a limited value
> In the knowledge derived from experience.
>
> The only wisdom we can hope to acquire
> Is the wisdom of humility: humility is endless.

The activities of life lack a meaning. Of the fishermen in 'The Dry Salvages' he says:

> We have to think of them as forever bailing,
> Sitting and hauling while the North East lowers,
> Over shallow banks unchanging and erosionless
> Or drawing their money drying sails at dockage;
> Not as making a trip that will be unpayable
> For a haul that will not bear examination.

The philosophy of the Quartets, however, is not one of despair. Eliot is greatly concerned with the nature of experience. Although most human experience is meaningless, most activity empty, there are moments that are different. These moments he identifies with 'the still point'.

> . . . at the still point, there the dance is,
> But neither arrest nor movement. And do not call it fixity,
> Where past and future are gathered. Neither movement from
> nor towards,
> Neither ascent nor decline. Except for the point, the
> still point,
> There would be no dance, and there is only the dance.

In circular motion, the centre of the circle is still, but it is the hub of movement. In life there are moments of intense experience: whilst these are enjoyed, one part of the consciousness can abstract the experience and can make it permanent. These moments take place in time, but they have a reality, a value, that goes beyond the moment. Even when they are attained, these experiences are difficult to recognise and evaluate:

> The moments of happiness. . . .
> We had the experience but missed the meaning.

For a few recognition is possible:

. . . But to apprehend
The point of intersection of the timeless
With time, is an occupation for the saint.

For most of us, there is only the unattended
Moment, the moment in and out of time.
The distraction fit, lost in a shaft of sunlight,
The wild thyme unseen, or the winter lightning
Or the waterfall or the music heard so deeply
That it is not heard at all, but you are the music
While the music lasts. These are only hints and guesses;
Hints followed by guesses; and the rest
Is prayer, observance, discipline, thought and action,
The hint half guessed, the gift half understood is Incarnation.
Here the impossible union
Of spheres of existence is actual,
Here the past and the future
Are conquered and reconciled,
. . . .

These comments only indicate one or two of the themes of the Quartets. A guide to the thought of the poems is contained in the last chapter of *The Art of T. S. Eliot* by Helen Gardner. The Quartets are difficult to understand, not because Eliot's language is obscure, but because the ideas are profound, and much of the meaning lies in the connections he sensed between his experiences, his memories, his beliefs, his reading, his speculations. Inevitably these associations cannot be expressed in plain statements.

Eliot is beyond doubt one of the outstanding poets of the century, a man with a profound and sensitive mind who used symbol and imagery in a manner that was entirely his own to project his thoughts and feelings. His plays will continue to be read and acted; his critical prose is clear and elegant, his comment penetrating; but it is as a poet that he extended the range of literary technique. At one time it seemed that his reputation and his influence would both rest on *The Waste Land*, which had a shattering impact in the 1920s. Now it appears possible that the cool analysis of the *Quartets* will come to be regarded as his most distinctive work.

Ezra Pound

WITH Eliot for many years was associated EZRA POUND (born 1885). He also was an American who, after his formal education was completed, elected to settle in Europe, though Pound has spent most of these years in Italy. When he saw the draft of *The Waste Land*, he helped Eliot to shorten it and insisted that he should have it published. Pound himself has always been a scholar and an aesthete with a wide knowledge of other languages and literatures. Amongst his poetry are many translations from Italian, Provençal, Chinese, Japanese, and Old English; of these 'The Seafarer' is one of his finest poems.

Pound's early poetry was imagist—that is, he created a sharply defined image to convey a feeling. Since then, he has passed through a number of influences, though he has been too cool and detached to surrender completely to any of them. Irony marks some of his best work, for example 'Portrait d'une Femme':

> You are a person of some interest, one comes to you
> And takes strange gain away:
> Trophies fished up; some curious suggestion;
> Fact that leads nowhere; and a tale or two,
> Pregnant with mandrakes, or with something else
> That might prove useful and yet never proves,
> That never fits a corner or shows use,
> Or finds its hour upon the loom of days.

This is a charming, quite unsentimental portrait.

In 'Hugh Selwyn Mauberley' (1920) he applied these qualities of detachment and irony to himself, his own work, and its relation to the insensitive age in which he lived.

> He strove to resuscitate the dead art
> Of poetry; to maintain 'the sublime'
> In the old sense. Wrong from the start—
>
> No, hardly, but seeing he had been born
> In a half-savage country, out of date. . . .
>
> The age demanded an image
> Of its accelerated grimace.
> . . . .
> No, not certainly, the obscure reveries
> Of the inward gaze.

Mauberley with his aestheticism ('His true Penelope was Flaubert') is completely out of touch with the mechanistic age in which he lives:

All things are a flowing,
Sage Heraclitus says;
But a tawdry cheapness
Shall outlast our days.

In the fourth of these poems he deplores the young men who had died in the war, 'believing in old men's lies':

There died a myriad,
And of the best, among them,
For an old bitch gone in the teeth,
For a botched civilisation.

Pound has a considerable talent for comic characterisation in verse that is shown also in 'Mr Nixon' and 'Mœurs Contemporaines'.

For forty years he has been engaged on a sequence of Cantos and Pisan Cantos. In these he draws on his extensive knowledge of literature, especially Italian, for allusions that sometimes baffle. There are also, however, piercing rays of light in lines like these:

Nothing matters but the quality of the affection—
in the end—that has carved the trace in the mind
what thou lovest well is thy true heritage
what thou lovest well shall not be reft from thee.

The Cantos are a summation of his experience. Many of the Pisan Cantos were written when he was in an American army prison after the Second World War on a charge of helping Mussolini's propaganda during the war, a charge which was finally dismissed in 1958.

Pound will certainly be remembered for the help and advice he gave to Eliot and Joyce amongst others. His own talents were perhaps too various, his attitude to the age in which he lived too detached, for his voice to be distinctive of the twentieth century. There is much truth in the acute self-criticism of 'Mauberley'. His poetry is not likely, however, to be affected by the passage of time to the same extent as the work of other poets that had a direct relevance to the events and the ideas of the age.

James Joyce

THE history of English literature is full of Irishmen who left their native country to live elsewhere, either permanently or for considerable periods. JAMES JOYCE (1882–1941), born in Dublin, quit his native city in 1904 to live in Switzerland, Italy and France for the rest of his life, but Dublin and the experiences of his youth filled his imagination throughout that period. One would have to search minutely through his work to discover that he had lived for many years in Zurich, Trieste and Paris, but the fascination, half-love, half-hate, that Dublin held for him is on every page he wrote.

The story of Joyce's boyhood and youth is to be found in *A Portrait of the Artist as a Young Man*. It is not intended as a detailed and accurate record of fact, but it traces the development of Joyce's awareness of the world around him as a child, as a boy, and as a young man, and of his own relationship to that world. An earlier, uncompleted draft of this work, published after his death as *Stephen Hero*, shows that Joyce abandoned a factual approach for one which brought into perspective the steps in his own moral, emotional and artistic growth. In *Dubliners*, a collection of fifteen short stories, he gives his own view of the city in which he had grown up.

Joyce himself said of *Dubliners*: 'My intention was to write a chapter of the moral history of my country and I chose Dublin for the scene because that city seemed to me the centre of paralysis. I have tried to present it to the indifferent public under four of its aspects: childhood, adolescence, maturity and public life. The stories are arranged in this order. I have written it for the most part in a style of scrupulous meanness'. There is no doubt that Joyce thought such a style appropriate to the subject. It is a debilitated city he describes, its typical figure Mr Duffy in *A Painful Case*, an 'outcast from life's feast'. He had in fact cast himself out by rejecting the affection of Mrs Sinico, causing also the suicide of that lady. These are not short stories in any conventional sense of the word, that is, neat plots with a twist at the end, but door-crack glimpses of the Dublin life Joyce had known. In them he is persuading both himself and the reader that his decision to leave the city was inevitable, that this was no climate in which a talent like his could flower. In the last and longest of the stories, *The Dead*, Gabriel Conway probably represents the kind of man Joyce feared he would have grown into if he had remained.

Joyce had some trouble in getting *Dubliners* published: he mentioned people and places by their real names, he used the word 'bloody', and in a frank, but not unfriendly way attributed to King Edward VII a share of human frailty. This difficulty with censors, official and unofficial, persisted through his career, and has perhaps obscured his real gifts.

In 1916 *A Portrait of the Artist as a Young Man* was published. In this book Joyce tells how he came to be the man he was, an artist. The originality of Joyce is that he is not merely a writer—in one sense his books are almost by-products of his struggle to achieve a greater sensibility and to set down what he had achieved. He is interested not in people, objects, incidents, for their own sake, but for the sensations which they produce in him—after all, those sensations are the only things of which we have experience. In the *Portrait* we find Joyce, clothed in his fictional personality of Stephen Dedalus, passing through a succession of influences which exert claims upon his conscience and personality: family, academic learning, sex, the Catholic faith. The ambition to become a priest was the hardest to resist, for it offered him 'secret knowledge and secret power. . . . He would know obscure things, hidden from others. . . . He would know the sins, the sinful longings and sinful thoughts and sinful acts, of others. . . .' This prospect touched something deep in Joyce's personality, but he was able to satisfy this longing to know the hidden truths about life by becoming an artist. His final affirmation was:

> I will tell you what I will do and what I will not do. I will not serve that in which I no longer believe, whether it call itself my home, my fatherland, or my church: and I will try to express myself in some mode of life or art as freely as I can and as wholly as I can, using for my defence the only arms I allow myself to use—silence, exile and cunning.

On the way to this discovery of himself, he has realised at school the existence of injustice when he is punished for not doing work which he has been excused because his glasses are broken. He has recognised that his father is a feckless man driven from house to house by debt because he spends his money on drink. At the Christmas dinner he hears his elders reviving the empty arguments about Parnell and loses faith in the salvation of his country. The Church tries to fill him with fears of hell-fire and he himself throws fuel on the flames by his early sexual experiences. The incidents are chosen so that each relates a stage in his development towards self-knowledge. This development is revealed not only in the incidents and discussions, but also by the change in style in the course of the book; the account of his childhood is written in a sensuous, imagistic, self-indulgent style, the boy obviously savouring the experience:

How pale the light was at the window! But that was nice. The fire rose and fell on the wall. It was like waves. Someone had put coal on and he heard voices. They were talking. It was the noise of the waves. Or the waves were talking among themselves as they rose and fell.

He saw the sea of waves, long dark waves rising and falling, dark under the moonless night. A tiny light twinkled at the pierhead where the ship was entering: and he saw a multitude of people gathered by the waters' edge to see the ship that was entering their harbour. A tall man stood on the deck, looking out towards the flat dark land: and by the light at the pierhead he saw his face, the sorrowful face of Brother Michael.

He saw him lift his hand towards the people and heard him say in a loud voice of sorrow over the waters:

—He is dead. We saw him lying upon the catafalque.

A wail of sorrow went up from the people.

—Parnell! Parnell! He is dead!

They fell upon their knees, moaning in sorrow.

And he saw Dante in a maroon velvet dress and with a green velvet mantle hanging from her shoulders walking proudly and silently past the people who knelt by the waters' edge.

As he grows older the self-indulgence disappears and both language and thought contract and harden.

Joyce worked for eight years from 1914 to 1922 on *Ulysses*, the book for which he is best known, and one which, in the opinion of many, is the most important work in English prose of the twentieth century. By the time he began *Ulysses* Joyce had decided what kind of man he was and what work he had to do. He turned now to the traditional subjects of the novelist: the nature of man and the kind of world he lived in. His approach was highly individual. He chose the events of one day, 16 June 1904, in the lives of two men, Leopold Bloom and Stephen Dedalus, and one woman, Molly Bloom, in Dublin. The city he had left and the year in which he had departed from it continued to haunt Joyce. He also draws a parallel—which accounts for the title—between the three principal characters and Ulysses, Telemachus and Penelope; the eighteen incidents in *Ulysses* each have counterparts in incidents in *The Odyssey*. Thus, when Leopold Bloom goes down to the sea-shore and sees a girl called Gerty MacDowell playing with some children, Joyce is recalling Ulysses' meeting with Nausicaa by the sea-shore in *The Odyssey*. The effect of these parallels is of course intended to be satirical by showing how the nobility of Ulysses has been degraded in the twentieth century to squalor, hypocrisy and despair.

Bloom is a Jew, a canvasser for an advertising-agency, betrayed by his unfaithful wife, an outsider in the society where he has to live. Dedalus is of course Joyce himself, a young artist seeking fulfilment. The two move in and out of Dublin scenes on this day, not meeting until midnight and then parting after a discussion on art, philosophy and the problems of the Jews and the Irish. Each represents what the other is seeking: Bloom's son, Rudy, had died as a baby and in his loneliness he needs a son. Stephen is cut off from his family and he needs a father. Bloom represents experience; Stephen is seeking experience. Bloom's failures have not embittered him, but have made him able to bear disappointment philosophically; Stephen has youth, a capacity for new experience, but not the temperament to assimilate it.

The method Joyce uses is the 'stream of consciousness' technique, of which the following passage is an example. In it Bloom is attending the funeral of his friend, Paddy Dignam:

> They halted by the bier and the priest began to read out of his book with a fluent croak.
>
> Father Coffey. I knew his name was like a coffin. *Dominenamine.* Bully about the muzzle he looks. Bosses the show. Muscular christian. Woe betide anyone that looks crooked at him: priest. Thou art Peter. Burst sideways like a sheep in clover Dedalus says he will. With a belly on him like a poisoned pup. Most amusing expressions that man finds. Hhhn: burst sideways.
>
> *Non intres in judicio cum servo tuo, Domine.*
>
> Makes them feel more important to be prayed over in Latin. Requiem mass. Crape weepers. Blackedged notepaper. Your name on the altarlist. Chilly place this. Want to feed well, sitting in there all the morning in the gloom kicking his heels waiting for the next please. Eyes of a toad too. What swells him up that way? Molly gets swelled after cabbage. Air of the place maybe. Looks full of bad gas. Must be an infernal lot of bad gas round the place. Butchers for instance: they get like raw beef-steaks. Who was telling me? Mervyn Brown. Down in the vaults of saint Werburgh's lovely old organ hundred and fifty they have to bore a hole in the coffins sometimes to let out the bad gas and burn it. Out it rushes: blue. One whiff of that and you're a goner.
>
> My kneecap is hurting me. Ow. That's better.

Here it is not difficult to follow the stream of sensations and thoughts that pass through Bloom's mind.

Joyce referred to the moments when these sensations were most acute as 'epiphanies': 'Remember your epiphanies on green, oval leaves, deeply deep, copies to be sent if you died to all the great libraries of the world, including Alexandria?'

The Epiphany was the day on which Christ was manifested to the wise men of the East; to Joyce it was an occasion, a moment when through some apparently trivial event or circumstance he caught a glimpse of the nature and glory of the world, apprehended something about the reality of life. The kind of experience is best described by Marguerite Duras in the prelude to her novel, *The Afternoon of Monsieur Andesmas*, when she speaks of a time of day when the sun shines brightly and clearly on everything, yet seems to concentrate its beams on a particular object, so that the radiance of the afternoon seems to stem from that small object. Joyce was eager to make his readers understand that if the nature of those moments was understood, then by concentration on every detail, the whole of life could be made up of them. In *Ulysses* he is seeking to show that every action, buying a bar of soap, cooking a kidney even, has something very real and revelatory about it.

There are all kinds of questions to ask about *Ulysses*. Is it a novel or is it an epic poem? Do the parallels with the *Odyssey* contribute enough to the effect of the book to justify all the ingenuity Joyce expended on them? Does this account of the events of a single day in the life of three people tell us enough that is new and true about man and his life to repay the effort involved in the writing and the lesser effort of concentration required in the reading? However the reader answers these questions, *Ulysses* remains a work of great originality, and one that has profoundly influenced other writers such as Henry Miller, Jack Kerouac, and George Orwell in *Down and Out in London and Paris*.

Joyce spent even longer, seventeen years from 1922 to 1939, on his last work, *Finnegans Wake*. During that period extracts from it appeared in periodicals under the title *Work in Progress*. It is the most ambitious work attempted in the whole of English literature; the theme has certain similarities to *Paradise Lost*, for it deals with man's original sin, his fall and redemption. In conception, however, it is much more complex than Milton, for it attempts to present the experiences, dreams, thoughts and sensations of Humphrey Chimpden Earwicker, the keeper of a public-house in Dublin. His initials also stand for 'Here Comes Everybody', for he is a representative of the whole human race, just as his wife, Anna Livia Plurabelle, represents all women. Their story—and 'story' is certainly the wrong word, for the right word does not exist—is the story of the whole of mankind. Dublin, the background, is a microcosm. The book is indeed much more complicated than even this suggests, for places (Howth Castle) and rivers (the Liffey) are identified with the characters and Joyce expounds philosophies about history, anthropology, man's sexual behaviour and religious belief. Several books have been written to identify the main themes and the way in which they are connected, but this remains a book which few people can hope to understand.

The difficulties are further increased by Joyce's rejection of conventional English vocabulary and syntax as inadequate to his purpose. The language is full of portmanteau words and assimilations, some of them like Lewis Carroll's 'Jabberwocky' and just as funny. There are also puns, allusions, snatches from newspaper headlines, advertisements and popular songs, and every other imaginable source. The most famous section, 'Anna Livia Plurabelle' is supposed to have taken Joyce 1,600 hours to compose. Joyce claimed that if it was read aloud, the difficulties disappeared and that the comic effect was obvious, as it is in these brief snatches:

But toms will till. I know he well. Temp untamed will hist for no man. As you spring so shall you neap. O, the roughty old rappe! Minxing marrage and making loof. . . .

Who blocksmitt her saft anvil or yelled lep to her pail? Was her banns never loosened in Adam and Eve's or were him and her but captain spliced? For mine ether duck I thee drake. And by my wildgaze I thee gander.

Ezra Pound put into words the reactions of many people when he said of *Finnegans Wake* in its *Work in Progress* state, 'Nothing would be worth plowing through like this, except the Divine Vision—and I gather it's not that sort of thing'. It is, however, a vision.

Among Joyce's outstanding characteristics were his faith in the sufficiency of his work as an artist; his sensibility; his mastery of the English language. Throughout his life his eyesight was very poor, and this made him particularly sensitive to the effects of words—most of his work is best read aloud. This passage from *A Portrait of the Artist as a Young Man* tells a good deal about his gifts, his personality, his achievements:

He drew forth a phrase from his treasure and spoke it softly to himself:

A day of dappled seaborne clouds.

The phrase and the day and the scene harmonised in a chord. Words. Was it their colours? He allowed them to glow and fade, hue after hue: sunrise gold, the russet and green of apple orchards, azure of waves, the grey-fringed fleece of clouds. No, it was not their colours: it was the poise and balance of the period itself. Did he then love the rhythmic rise and fall of words better than their associations of legend and colour? Or was it that, being as weak of sight as he was shy of mind, he drew less pleasure from the reflection of the glowing sensible world through the prism of a language manycoloured and richly storied than from the contemplation of an inner world of individual emotions mirrored perfectly in a lucid supple periodic prose?

Sean O'Casey

LIKE several other Irish writers, SEAN O'CASEY (1880–1964), the dramatist, left his own country and settled abroad. He was born in Dublin and died in Devon—these two facts provide a clue to his work. Whilst he was living in Ireland the plays he wrote depicted Irish characters set against a background of Dublin tenement life with the Easter Rebellion of 1916 and the Irish troubles having some part in the action. In these plays O'Casey was putting on the stage people, incidents and a manner of life that he knew at first hand. They were not in a strict sense realistic plays, for he heightened eccentricity of character and picturesqueness of speech, but the people he put on the stage, their actions, their ideas, their speech were, if the audience was willing to accept some exaggeration, recognisable. The exaggeration was easily accepted too, for it made the plays more effective on the stage.

In his autobiography O'Casey says that he was educated in the streets of Dublin and that he did not learn to read and write until he was twelve years old. As a young man he worked as a plasterer, a ganger on the railway and a general labourer; his pictures of working-class life in Dublin are therefore authentic. He also helped to organise the Irish Citizen Army which took part in the Easter Rebellion in 1916, an event which cast its shadow over his early plays.

His first three plays were *Shadow of a Gunman* (1923), *Juno and the Paycock* (1924) and *The Plough and the Stars* (1926). The two finest Irish plays of the first half of the century are Synge's *Playboy of the Western World*, with a background of rural Ireland, and *Juno and the Paycock*, a play of city life. Both plays mingle broad humour and tragedy; they present striking comic characters and women with strong wills; both writers delight in vivid speech. In O'Casey's play the outstanding characters are 'Captain' Boyle, a boastful, feckless, work-shy labourer; his long-suffering wife, Juno, who faces the improvidence of her husband, the death of her son executed for treachery by his former comrades in the Irish Citizen Army, and the ruin of her daughter, with dignity and courage; and Joxer Daly, who encourages the 'Captain' when he sees the prospect of a free drink, and reviles him when the prospect fades. Here is a passage of dialogue between the Paycock, Captain Boyle, and Joxer Daly which gives some idea of the comic flavour of their scenes:

JOXER: God be with the young days when you were steppin' the deck of a manly ship, with the win' blowin' a hurricane through the masts, an' the only sound you'd hear was, 'Port your helm!' an' the only answer, 'Port it is, sir!'

BOYLE: Them was days, Joxer, them was days. Nothin' was too hot or too heavy for me then. Sailin' from the Gulf o' Mexico to the Antanarctic Ocean. I seen things, I seen things, Joxer, that no mortal man should speak about that knows his Catechism. Ofen, an' ofen, when I was fixed to the wheel with a marlin-spike, an' the wins blowin' fierce an' the waves lashin' an' lashin', till you'd think every minute was goin' to be your last, an' it blowed an' blowed—blew is the right word, Joxer, but blowed is what the sailors use. . . .

JOXER: Aw, it's a darlin' word, a daarlin' word.

BOYLE: An', as it blowed an' blowed, I ofen looked up at the sky an' assed myself the question—what is the stars, what is the stars?

VOICE OF COAL VENDOR: Any blocks, coal-blocks; blocks, coal-blocks!

JOXER: Ah, that's the question, that's the question—what is the stars?

BOYLE: An' then I'd have another look, an' I'd ass myself—what is the moon?

JOXER: Ah, that's the question—what is the moon, what is the moon?

In the end, with her family broken, Juno decides that the Paycock will always be an empty fraud, and with Mary she leaves him. In the last scene, Boyle and Joxer, drunk and ignorant of the family tragedy, are still flattering each other and boasting in a room from which the furniture has been taken away for debt. Although the mixture of broad comedy and tragedy is a dangerous one, O'Casey brings it off in this play, perhaps because Boyle's childish love of showing off and his neglect of his duty towards his family are the roots of the tragedy, though comic in themselves.

The Plough and the Stars repeats the mixture, not quite so successfully. In this play some of the devices O'Casey had used in *Juno and the Paycock* are worked a little too hard and begin to look like tricks. Joxer Daly and Boyle had had their own characteristic phrases—'it's a darlin' word' and 'a terrible state of chassis', but Fluther Good's fondness for 'derogatory' and 'vice versa' is overdone. O'Casey becomes proud of the bright verbal colours of his dialogue, using alliteration, self-consciously poetic prose and lavish adjectives to make his effects:

> There's th' men marchin' out into th' dhread dimness o' danger, while th' lice is crawlin' about feedin' on the fatness o' the land! But yous'll not escape from th' arrow that flieth be night, or th' sickness that wasteth be day. . . . An' ladyship an' all, as some o' them may be, they'll be scattered abroad, like th' dust in th' darkness.

> . . . in dhread any minute that he might come staggerin' in covered with bandages, splashed all over with th' red of his own blood, an' givin' us

barely time to bring th' priest to hear th' last whisper of his final confession, as his soul was passin' through th' dark doorway o' death into th' way o' th' wondherin' dead.

These speeches read extravagantly no doubt, but on the stage an Irish actor can make them sound impressive and convincing. The play has amusing scenes, pathetic scenes, and comic characters, though there is no one as fine as Juno to balance the comedy, so that in the end the effect is pathos rather than tragedy. It is not quite another *Juno and the Paycock* as the writer intended, but it is still a good play.

In *The Summing Up* Somerset Maugham says that the greatest danger that besets the professional author is success, for

It may very well deprive him of that force which has brought him success. His individuality has been formed by his experiences, his struggles, his frustrated hopes, his efforts to adapt himself to a hostile world; it must be very stubborn if it is not modified by the softening influences of success.

Success besides often bears within itself the seed of destruction, for it may very well cut the author off from the material that was its occasion. . . . The new world into which his success has brought him excites his imagination and he writes about it; but he sees it from the outside and can never so penetrate it as to become a part of it.

The success of O'Casey's Dublin tenement plays aroused in him the ambition to write plays with a social or a political message. In these he got away from the world he had grown up in, the people he had known and the events of which he had had experience. As time went on, he mistook the nature of his own gifts: he had excelled as a dramatist of low life with a keen eye for oddity of character and a sharp ear for the lilt and humour of common speech. Now he saw himself as a reformer and a philosopher with a talent for writing splendid prose. The change is best illustrated in *The Silver Tassie* (1929). The first act shows Mr and Mrs Heegan with their friends and neighbours awaiting the return of their son, Harry, from the football cup-final in which he has been playing for Avondale. The characters and dialogue are spirited, and the scene is enlivened by a quarrel between Teddy Foran and his wife from the upstairs tenement. Harry returns, a hero, with the cup, 'The Silver Tassie', which his goals have won for the club. They celebrate the victory, then Harry with his friend and a neighbour, all of them on leave from the Army, depart to sail back to the fighting front. O'Casey has given us a taste of his comedy of character and incident with the implication that tragedy will follow. The second act, as we have foreseen, does present the tragedy of war, but in a symbolic form. Only one character from the first act re-appears, a minor one, Harry's friend, who is recognisable only because of his name. The other characters are not individuals, but representatives, types — soldiers worn out by their sufferings, a falsely genial visitor to the troops, a staff-wallah who proclaims orders, then departs. The soldiers express their feelings in chants and passages of free verse. O'Casey has abandoned his natural idiom for a far more pretentious style that is unsuited to him, and is quite irreconcilable with the warm individuality of the first act.

Within the Gates (1933) is an attack on social injustice, hypocrisy and poverty shown in a series of interviews a Bishop holds in a London park with typical figures like a Salvation Army Officer, a Guardsman, several down-and-outs and a Young Whore who proves to be the Bishop's own illegitimate daughter. There are again several chants and songs, and again a feeling that this is a picture of humanity in the abstract rather than men and women. *The Star Turns Red* (1940) shows a struggle between Fascism and Communism with O'Casey's sympathies wholly on the side of the Communists.

In his later plays O'Casey allowed his fondness for fine words to swamp what he wanted to say. *Red Roses for Me* (1946) is a study of impatience and intolerance in which are portrayed Catholic bigots, Protestant bigots and an atheistic bigot. Like the Police Sergeant who is responsible for the death of the hero by ordering his men to charge the strikers, all these intolerant men and women are willing to destroy opinions they do not share and those who hold beliefs that they dislike. O'Casey's power of comic characterisation is still to be seen in a sly old man, Brennan o' the Moor, and there is an amusing scene in which the verger exasperates the Rector by the long-winded, sanctimonious way in which he tells the story of the daffodils and the cross. But these are only glimpses, and the development of the play is often halted by the characters' fondness for embroidering their speeches in this manner:

> Time's a perjured jade, an' ever he moans a man must die. Who through every inch of life weaves a patthern of vigour an' elation can never taste death, but goes to sleep among th' stars, his withered arms outstretched to greet th' echo of his own shout. It will be for them left behind to sigh for an hour, an' then to sing their own odd songs, an' do their own odd dances, to give a lonely God a little company, till they, too, pass by on their bare way out. When a true man dies, he is buried in th' birth of a thousand worlds.

He splashes colours extravagantly too:

> Th' sky has thrown a gleaming green mantle over her bare shoulders, bordhered with crimson, an' with a hood of gentle magenta over her handsome head—look! . . . Look! Th' vans an' lorries rattling down the quays, turned to bronze an' purple by the sun, look like chariots forging forward to th' battle-front.

When O'Casey moved to England to live, he left behind him the places, the people, the rough life that had inspired his early plays, and in a land that was foreign to him he found nothing that would take their place. His head was in the clouds, but his feet had left the ground.

Eugene O'Neill

EUGENE O'NEILL (1888–1953) told the story of his family and of his own youth in *Long Day's Journey into Night*, written in 1940–1 but not produced until 1956. In this play Edmund Tyrone, who represents O'Neill, recalls his experiences as a sailor and faces the prospect of entering a sanatorium because of tuberculosis. His father, James Tyrone, like O'Neill's father, James O'Neill, is a popular actor who has played one part for so many years that he cannot get away from it:

'That God-damned play I bought for a song and made such a great success in—a great money success—it ruined me with its promise of an easy fortune. I didn't want to do anything else, and by the time I woke up to the fact I'd become a slave to the damned thing and did try other plays, it was too late. They had identified me with that one part, and didn't want me in anything else.'

For James O'Neill the part was the Count of Monte Cristo.

Since O'Neill had been born into the theatre, it was natural that when he was recovering in the sanatorium he should pass the time by writing plays, and that he should find the material for them in his life as a sailor. Of these early plays the best-known is *Anna Christie* (1922); in this Anna's father blames all his misfortunes on to 'dat ol' devil sea', and determines to keep his daughter away from it. She, however, drifts eventually into a waterside dive where she falls in love with a tough Irish seaman. Her love for him brings her back to a decent life, and eventually she is reconciled with her father. At intervals O'Neill had lived as a down-and-out on the waterfront in New York and Buenos Aires, so the picture of life and the dialogue in this play are strikingly authentic.

It was characteristic of O'Neill that, having succeeded with a realistic play about the kind of life he knew well, he should turn to other themes and experiment with new techniques instead of exploiting his success. In *The Great God Brown* (1925) the characters wore masks which symbolised their personalities. He employs the same device in the choruses of *Lazarus Laughed* (1927), in which Lazarus, after being raised from the dead by Jesus, expresses his faith in love and life by laughing at whatever and whomever he meets. Although this play has been highly praised by critics for its audacity of technique, few producers have been bold enough to present it. In *Desire under the Elms*, a more conventional play, O'Neill submits himself to the discipline of time, place, character and plot in a study of the human desire for possession. Although he was always a ready victim to the temptation of a new theory about human behaviour or dramatic representation, O'Neill's strength lay not in the originality of his ideas, but in his ability to portray powerful emotions.

Strange Interlude (1928) reached a length of nine acts largely because the characters not only spoke openly to each other, but voiced their inner thoughts which often ran counter to the words they uttered. This technique has proved more suited to films and television than to the stage, but the play fails because the characters and the themes are neither important nor interesting enough to justify its length and elaboration. The method is an attempt to adapt to the theatre the 'stream of consciousness' used by James Joyce and Virginia Woolf in their novels.

In a letter written in 1925 the dramatist described himself as 'a bit of a poet, who has laboured with the spoken word to evolve original rhythms of beauty where beauty apparently isn't . . . and to see the transfiguring nobility of tragedy in as near the Greek sense as one can grasp it, in seemingly the most ignoble, debased lives.' O'Neill sensed the permanence of certain tragic themes, so it was not surprising that in his trilogy, *Mourning Becomes Electra* (1931), he should transplant the legend of Electra to nineteenth-century New England immediately after the American Civil War. General Ezra Mannon (Agamemnon) returns from the War to his wife Christine (Clytemnestra), who has fallen in love with Adam Brant (Aegisthus), Ezra's nephew. Christine with Adam's help poisons her husband. Her daughter Lavinia (Electra), who herself is in love with Adam, knows of her mother's guilt, and persuades her brother Orin (Orestes) to murder Adam in revenge. Christine shoots herself. In their turn Lavinia and Orin are unable to escape from their own guilt, and finally Orin also commits suicide, leaving Lavinia to a life of remorse in the family mansion that has become a grim monument to the tragedy.

The tragedy is worked out in murder and suicide, but has its source in the incestuous feelings of Lavinia and her father, Orin and his mother, Lavinia and Orin. The Mannons are damned by their own powerful, perverted love and hatred for each other. Orin expresses this in a speech to Hazel Niles, whom he had hoped to marry:

> No! She can't have happiness! She's got to be punished! (*suddenly taking her hand—excitedly*) And listen Hazel! You mustn't love me any more. The only love I can know now is the love of guilt for guilt which breeds more guilt—

until you get so deep at the bottom of hell there is no lower you can sink and you rest there in peace! (*He laughs harshly and turns away from her.*)

O'Neill's dialogue does not stand up to the intensity of the feelings he is trying to convey. Much of it is afflicted by the clichés of the Hollywood script-writer, whilst other passages are flat. He is not a writer who can touch the imagination with a phrase or carry us away with the rhythmic force of a speech. Here is a passage in which Ezra Mannon is pleading with Christine:

MANNON: I want to find what that wall is that marriage put between us! You've got to help me smash it down! We have twenty good years still before us! I've been thinking of what we could do to get back to each other. I've a notion if we'd leave the children and go off on a voyage together—to the other side of the world—find some island where we could be alone a while. You'll find I have changed, Christine. I'm sick of death! I want life! Maybe you could love me now! (*in a note of final desperate pleading*) I've got to make you love me!

CHRISTINE (*pulls her hand away from him and springs to her feet wildly*): For God's sake, stop talking. I don't know what you're saying. Leave me alone! What must be, must be! You make me weak! (*Then abruptly*) It's getting late.

MANNON (*terribly wounded, withdrawn into his stiff soldier armour—takes out his watch mechanically*): Yes—six past eleven. Time to turn in. (*He ascends two steps, his face towards the door. He says bitterly*) You tell me to stop talking! By God, that's funny!

CHRISTINE (*collected now and calculating—takes hold of his arm, seductively*): I meant—what is the good of words? There is no wall between us. I love you.

MANNON (*grabs her by the shoulders and stares into her face*): Christine! I'd give my soul to believe that—but—I'm afraid!

Despite the clumsiness of the dialogue, the trilogy comes near to creating the effects at which O'Neill aimed and a brooding atmosphere hangs over the mansion. This measure of success is due to O'Neill's dogged honesty: here is something he wants to say about the human condition so strongly that the clumsiness itself becomes part of the honesty of expression.

In *The Iceman Cometh* (1946) O'Neill returns to the low life he had described in *Anna Christie*. The scene is a bar for human derelicts, one of whom says, 'The lie of a pipe-dream is what gives life to the whole misbegotten mad lot of us, drunk or sober.' Hickey, a salesman and an occasional visitor to the bar, sends the bums out into the world to face reality and to recognise that their pipe-dreams are all illusions. They fail, because though they pretend to feel guilty about their condition, they are in truth satisfied with their lives and their pretences. Hickey himself is finally revealed as a haunted man who is trying to persuade himself that he is independent. In a fit of madness he has killed his wife. *The Iceman Cometh*—the Iceman symbolises death—contains some of O'Neill's most convincing writing, based on direct knowledge of these scenes and characters. The introduction of too many bums, some of whom only repeat what the author has already said, leads to excessive length, a persistent weakness in O'Neill's plays.

His knowledge of the material was even more intimate in *Long Day's Journey into Night*, a re-creation of his own family. The play is interesting to read, for it tells us so much of the writer himself; on the stage the alternate spurts of resentment and affection may become tedious. The family is caught in a crisis. Mary Tyrone, mother of the two boys, has resumed taking drugs to the distress of her family; Edmund, the younger son, is told that his illness is tuberculosis. Although there is no resolution of their problems, the family's past history, their motives, their self-deceit, their feelings of guilt for their part in each other's troubles, are gradually brought out in an intricate pattern of revelation. The interest rarely slackens, and our understanding of the family steadily deepens. The final scene, in which Mary, now living in a drug-hazed past, brings out her wedding-gown is the most moving in all O'Neill's plays, all the more affecting because it is so gently done. She states the main theme of the play when she says: 'But I suppose life has made him like that, and he can't help it. None of us can help the things life has done to us. They're done before you realise it, and once they're done they make you do other things until at last everything comes between you and what you'd like to be, and you've lost your true self for ever.'

Like Edmund they are all conscious of their mistakes and they all hanker after an unreal world:

> The fog was where I wanted it to be. Halfway down the path you can't see this house. You'd never know it was here. Or any of the other places down the avenue. I couldn't see but a few feet ahead. I didn't meet a soul. Everything looked and sounded unreal. Nothing was what it was. That's what I wanted—to be alone with myself in another world where truth is untrue and life can hide from itself.

O'Neill stands out above his predecessors, contemporaries and successors in the American theatre. He had no room for pretence and false sentiment. He had little elegance of style, but he wrote powerfully about life as he saw it. He said something serious and of permanent validity about some aspects of human experience. His faults are easy to see in parts of his work—turgidity, repetition, an unrelievedly tragic view of life. His virtues are equally clear—honesty, strength, determination. It is perhaps a pity that he spent much of the middle part of his career in a search for novelty of method and idea, but his best work is impressive. O'Neill's view of life was consistently tragic, and most of his plays are on the subject of pain and suffering, some of it self-inflicted, some inflicted on loved ones. He was an ambitious writer who lacked only a sensitivity of style to place him among the truly great dramatists.

Sinclair Lewis

SINCLAIR LEWIS (1885–1951) was born in a small town in Minnesota about three hundred miles from Chicago and remote from other large cities in the U.S.A. at that time. He was educated at Yale University and then became a reporter. From reporting he graduated to writing short stories for popular magazines such as *The Saturday Evening Post*; from this it was a natural step for him to write novels. The first of his novels to attract attention was *Main Street* (1920) in which he criticised the narrow outlook on life of people living in provincial American cities. This was followed by *Babbitt* (1922) in which this criticism was developed; *Arrowsmith* (1925), the story of an idealistic young doctor who is corrupted by his experiences in practice; *Elmer Gantry*, an attack on commercialism, publicity-seeking and hypocrisy in American religious sects; and *Dodsworth* (1929), which describes a trip to Europe by a retired American motor-car manufacturer and his wife and the impressions made upon them by their experiences.

Dodsworth is the last of the novels we think of as typical of Sinclair Lewis in their unsympathetic attack on the dull, self-satisfied, restricted and often dishonest way of life of many prosperous Americans in the 1920s. Subsequently he wrote *It Can't Happen Here* (1935) in which he warned Americans that Nazi ideas might conquer their country because many of them neither recognised nor cared about the danger. His later novels like *Cass Timberlane* (1945) and *Kingsblood Royal* (1947) were well-told stories, but added nothing to his reputation as a critic of American society.

Sinclair Lewis came to maturity as a writer at the same time as the U.S.A. was coming to maturity as a nation. After the First World War the American people realised that they had great power and wealth and that their influence in world affairs would grow steadily. Sinclair Lewis saw that despite this wealth and power many Americans at that time knew little of the world outside their own cities and townships, and that their interests were often confined to their own businesses, their families, a restricted group of friends who shared their own limited tastes and belonged to the same clubs and organisations. This was the age before internal air-lines opened up the states of the Union to each other, before national radio and television networks brought Americans throughout the nation into touch with each other's ideas and lives. The narrowness and ignorance that he criticised no longer exists so widely or so crudely, but the picture of one section of American society in the 1920s which Lewis presents remains a striking one.

In his most famous novel, *Babbitt*, Sinclair Lewis added a word to the English language and a character as recognisable as Mr Micawber or Sherlock Holmes to the gallery of portraits in English literature. This novel describes a period of two years or so in the life of a middle-aged realtor (estate-agent and property-developer) in Zenith, a provincial American city with a population of some hundreds of thousands. In its size and situation Zenith is not unlike Minneapolis at that time.

George F. Babbitt is a successful business-man whose home, car, social life all give evidence of a comfortable prosperity. Sometimes the methods he uses in his business disturb his sense of honesty, but not for long. He is a leading figure in the Elks, the Chamber of Commerce, the Zenith Boosters' Club, a member of the Outing Golf and Country Club, the Chatham Road Presbyterian Church, and after some hesitation he is finally persuaded to join the Good Citizens' League. Babbitt is a great joiner—to be a member is to be accepted and at the clubs he makes the business contacts needed for his prosperity. Yet although he is conveyed on this roundabout of activities, and outwardly he seems to enjoy this ceaseless movement without change, he is often dissatisfied within himself. As a young man he had had visions of the future:

> When Babbitt had graduated from the State University, twenty-four years ago, he had intended to be a lawyer. He had been a ponderous debater in college; he felt that he was an orator; he saw himself becoming governor of the state.
>
> While he read law he worked as a real-estate salesman. He saved money, lived in a boarding-house, supped on poached egg on hash. . . . Babbitt's evenings were barren then, and he found comfort in Myra Thompson, a sleek and gentle girl who showed her capacity by agreeing with the ardent young Babbitt that of course he was going to be governor some day. . . . Of love there was no talk between them. He knew that if he was to study law he could not marry for years. . . . But Myra was a dependable companion. She was always ready to go skating, walking; always content to hear his discourses on the great things he was going to do, the distressed poor whom he would defend against the Unjust Rich, the speeches he would make at Banquets, the inexactitudes of popular thought which he would correct.

But the docile Myra led him into a marriage which cut short his law studies. Now in his middle-forties Babbitt resents the loss of his youth without the fulfilment of his hopes. He tries to break out of the narrow circle of real estate deals, the Boosters' Club and a humdrum domestic life. He expresses sympathy for workers on strike, refuses to despise all immigrants as ignorant louts, has a half-hearted affair with a widow, Mrs Tanis Judique, and joins the 'Bunch', a group of harmless, but noisy, young Bohemians. In the end the pressures that converge on him —his wife's illness, the loss of his friends, his unpopularity at the clubs, the falling-off of business—force him to return to the old meaningless round. He realises that there can be no escape for him now, and that he must find what consolation he can in his prosperity and social position. His son, Ted, elopes and gives up his University career, which he had found irksome, to become a mechanic. Babbitt, to the surprise of his family and friends, gives his approval, hoping that his son will find the freedom that he has missed:

> I've never done a single thing I wanted to in my whole life! I don't know's I've accomplished anything except just get along. I figure out I've made about a quarter of an inch out of a possible hundred rods. Well, maybe you'll carry on things further. I don't know. But I do get a kind of sneaking pleasure out of the fact that you knew what you wanted to do and did it. Well, those folks in there will try to bully you, and tame you down. Tell 'em to go to the devil! I'll back you. Take your factory job, if you want to. Don't be scared of the family. No, nor all of Zenith. Nor of yourself, the way I've been. Go ahead, old man! The world is yours!

Ted represents the next generation of Americans that will break loose from the stifling conventions of provincial life. Sinclair Lewis was not anti-American. The purpose of his work was not merely to condemn. He thought that at that time many Americans did not see the fences that hemmed them in, and that they would break down the fences once they knew there was a wider world beyond them. Babbitt and his friends saw only material values:

Of education:

> I've found out it's a mighty nice thing to be able to say you're a B.A. Some client that doesn't know what you are and thinks you're just a plug business man, he gets to shooting off his mouth about economics or literature or foreign trade conditions, and you just ease in something like 'When I was in college—course I got my B.A. in sociology and all that junk—'. Oh, it puts an awful crimp in their style!

Of art:

> In other countries, art and literature are left to a lot of shabby bums living in attics and feeding on booze and spaghetti, but in America the successful

writer or picture-painter is indistinguishable from any other decent business man; and I, for one, am only too glad that the man who has the rare skill to season his message with interesting reading matter and who shows both purpose and pep in handling his literary wares has a chance to drag down his fifty thousand bucks a year, to mingle with the biggest executives on terms of perfect equality, and to show as big a house and as swell a car as any Captain of Industry.

Of culture:

Culture has become as necessary an adornment and advertisement for a city today as pavements or bank-clearances. It's Culture, in theatres and art-galleries and so on, that brings thousands of visitors to New York every year and, to be frank, for all our splendid attainments we haven't yet got the Culture of a New York or Chicago or Boston—or at least we don't get the credit for it. The thing to do then, as a live bunch of go-getters, is to *capitalise Culture*: to go right out and grab it.

Pictures and books are fine for those that have the time to study 'em, but they don't shoot out on the road and holler 'This is what little old Zenith can put up in the way of Culture.' That's precisely what a Symphony Orchestra does do.

Sinclair Lewis saw Babbitt and his world with the eye of a reporter. In some ways Babbitt resembles H. G. Wells's Mr Polly: both are men approaching middle-age who realise that the romantic inclinations of their youth have been swamped by the cares of a business in which they have little interest. Wells touches up the portrait of Mr Polly with sentiment. He makes Mr Polly as likeable as he can, but Sinclair Lewis observes Babbitt coldly and reports upon him. Even when Mr Polly sets fire to a row of shops and deserts his wife, the shopkeepers make more from the insurance than they did from the shops and Miriam gets along better without her husband. Even if we see why Babbitt in those circumstances would behave in that way, we still feel he has behaved badly in his affair with Tanis Judique, and that he is a snob in his dealings with Eathorne and Overbrook. In the end Mr Polly escapes right out of his world to a backwater where he can daydream with agreeable companions, but time and reality do not exist. Babbitt remains in his world from which there is no escape. There is no sentiment for him; he lives in a world of hard, uncomfortable fact.

The great virtue of *Babbitt* is that it presents a detailed study of a man; we know his history, his education, his ambitions, his frustrations, his friends, his family, his work, his clubs, his office; we know what he wants, what he thinks, how he feels. He is set firmly in the foreground, but the background of the city and the times he lives in is clear and sharp. We see everything from his point of view—places, people, organisations. It is a one-sided picture of course. Not all prosperous business men were philistines, ignorant and careless about anything except money, and the underdogs are not always as deserving as Sinclair Lewis makes them appear. But the satirist and the reformer do not claim that they are completely accurate in the pictures of society they present. As a novelist, Sinclair Lewis preserved the reporter's gift of selecting the significant and interesting aspects of his story and hammering at these. His writing is neither subtle nor varied, but his vigour never flags. He paints a vivid portrait of a representative man of the 1920s whose name will always be Babbitt.

E. M. Forster

IN *A Room with a View* old Mr Emerson tells Lucy that 'there's nothing worse than a muddle in all the world'. Both in his life and in his novels EDWARD MORGAN FORSTER (born 1879) gives the impression of an immensely civilised and urbane man. He is too clear-sighted an observer of life not to see that life is full of muddles, and that most of these muddles are caused by defective personal relationships, people's inability to understand each other. Although their lives intersect, their views of what things in life are important are completely different. Margaret Schlegel sees this when she says to her sister Helen, in *Howards End:*

It's one of the most interesting things in the world. The truth is that there is a great outer life that you and I have never touched—a life in which telegrams and anger count. Personal relations, that we think supreme, are not supreme there. There love means marriage settlements, death, death duties. So far I'm clear. But here my difficulty. This outer life, though obviously horrid, often seems the real one—there's grit in it. It does breed character. Do personal relations lead to sloppiness in the end?

Because Forster puts personal relations first, the story is not the most significant element in his novels. The story is a framework in which these personal relations can be shown. In *Aspects of the Novel* Forster says, 'the novel tells a story . . . and I wish that it was not so, that it could be something different—melody, or perception of the truth, not this low atavistic form'.

Often the most obviously dramatic events in his novels are given little emphasis—the stabbing in *A Room with a View*, the killing of Lionel Bast in *Howards End*, Miss Quested's experiences in the cave in *A Passage to India.* This last incident is the pivot of the novel, and changes the lives of the main characters, but we never learn whether anything happened in the cave, let alone what it was.

In fact Forster seems at times to draw a distinction between drama and life, implying that drama is not real life, rather an interruption of life. Helen writes to Margaret:

Once you said that life is sometimes life and sometimes only a drama, and one must learn to distinguish tother from which, and up to now I have always put that down as 'Meg's clever nonsense'. But this morning, it really does seem not life but a play. . . .

And so it proved on this occasion, for Helen's romance with Paul faded as quickly as it had flared. Life to Forster was often dull and inconclusive, and one of the causes of muddle is to expect too much from it. Here are two passages which express this attitude, the first from *A Passage to India*, the second from *Howards End*:

Most of life is so dull that there is nothing to be said about it, and the books and talk that would describe it as interesting are obliged to exaggerate, in the hope of justifying their own existence. Inside its cocoon of work or social obligation, the human spirit slumbers for the most part, registering the distinction between pleasure and pain, but not nearly as alert as we pretend. There are periods in the most thrilling day during which nothing happens, and though we continue to exclaim: 'I do enjoy myself,' or, 'I am horrified,' we are insincere. 'As far as I feel anything, it is enjoyment, horror'—it's no more than that really, and a perfectly adjusted organism would be silent.

Looking back on the past six months, Margaret realized the chaotic nature of our daily life, and its difference from the orderly sequence that has been fabricated by historians. Actual life is full of false clues and sign-posts that lead nowhere. With infinite effort we nerve ourselves for a crisis that never comes.

For the last forty years of his life Forster as a novelist has shown himself to be a perfectly adjusted organism, for he has written critical essays, the libretto of an opera, a biography, and a chapter of autobiography, but no novels. In a long life he has written only five novels, *Where Angels Fear to Tread* (1905), *The Longest Journey* (1907), *A Room with a View* (1908), *Howards End* (1910), and *A Passage to India* (1925). His father, an architect, died soon after Forster's birth, and he was brought up by female relatives in a house in Hertfordshire, which he later wrote about as Howards End. He went to Tonbridge School, which he disliked; in *The Longest Journey* he condemns the lack of understanding and imagination shown at a public school, Sawston. At Cambridge, where he was happy, he came under the influence of the philosopher, G. E. Moore, who taught the importance of personal relations and of the contemplation of beauty in art. Others of his generation shared his admiration for Moore's ideas, and they became known as 'the Bloomsbury group'. In addition to Forster, the group included Virginia Woolf, Lytton Strachey, Lord Keynes, the economist and art-patron, and two art-critics, Roger Fry and Clive Bell.

Forster travelled in Greece, Germany, and Italy, using Italy as the setting for *Where Angels Fear to Tread* and *A Room with a View*. In 1912 he visited India with Lowes Dickinson, the writer on philosophy, whose biography he later wrote. He returned to India in 1921 as private secretary to the Maharajah of Dewas Senior, completing his finest novel, *A Passage to India*, after this second visit.

Three of his novels show him dealing with personal relations of increasing complexity. In *A Room with a View* the clash is between the conventional middle-class standards of behaviour and the tactless, warm-hearted Emersons. At the beginning Lucy Honeychurch, the heroine, and her older cousin, Charlotte Bartlett, are disappointed because in their pension in Florence they have not been given rooms with a view of the river as they had been promised. Hearing them, old Mr Emerson, without being introduced, says his room and his son's have a view of the river, something they do not value, and offers to change rooms with them. To Lucy the tactless way in which the offer is made at first outweighs its kindness. The son, George, later shocks Lucy, twice by kissing her, and a third time when she comes across him, her brother, and a clergyman friend, in the woods immediately after they have been swimming naked in a pond. Finally Lucy learns to accept and be grateful for George's willingness to give pleasure to others and to accept enjoyment for himself, but only after old Mr Emerson has warned her that she will never be happy unless she frankly recognises and acts upon her own natural affections.

George is contrasted with Cecil Vyse, a conventional, pompous, priggish young man with no capacity for enjoyment or for giving pleasure. Lucy breaks off her engagement to him when she realises that his coldness and artistic snobbery are intolerable. In many ways this novel resembles those of Jane Austen; the characters are drawn from a comfortable, leisured middle class; little happens, but the interest lies in the interplay between the subtly varied characters. Forster is particularly successful in drawing charming, unremarkable people, like Lucy's mother and brother.

In *Howards End* the clash is between the Schlegels, cultured and acting on impulse, and the Wilcoxes, thrusting and business-like. The theme of the novel is attitudes to other people: Henry Wilcox wants to use people, Helen Schlegel to change them, Charles Wilcox to dominate them, Tibby Schlegel to ignore them. After a struggle Margaret Schlegel learns to accept people as they are, to understand them, 'to connect', as she puts it. In the crisis the strong men of action, Henry and Charles Wilcox, are broken, and the pliable survive.

Howards End is the novel which makes it plainest why Forster deprecated the fact that a novel tells a story. The story contains melodramatic incidents like the death of Lionel and the recognition of Henry by his former mistress, now Lionel's wife; the plot depends on coincidence and convenient deaths. Forster's interest in the mechanics of the story is obviously slight, for the death of Ruth Wilcox, Henry's first wife, and Helen's brief affair with Lionel occur off-stage. The emphasis is on the consequences, not on the actions themselves. Forster is both reticent and stoical; death, even of such a charming woman as Ruth, rarely awakens deep regret.

Howards End expresses some of Forster's views on society in the Edwardian period. He obviously sympathises with Margaret's dissatisfaction with the position of women: Henry's attitude to his own conduct and to Helen's, his callousness towards Jackie, show that there were different moral standards for men and women. The novel also reflects the acute class-distinctions of the time: the gap between the Schlegels and Lionel cannot be bridged. Henry is right when he says, 'They aren't our sort, and one must face the fact.' The Schlegels are always conscious that their 'life of cultured but not ignoble ease' depends on the possession of a comfortable private income. Forster could see that this kind of life, typified by Howards End, the middle-class home, was coming to an end—'Life's going to be melted down, all over the world'. The prophecy came true, for the Hilton where the house was situated was in fact Stevenage.

In *A Passage to India* the failure to connect is between the Indians and the English rulers in India. With Major Callendar and Mrs Turton this failure springs from their utter self-centredness—they do not realise that Indians have an existence of their own beyond catering for the needs and whims of their rulers. But even where there is a genuine desire for understanding between Doctor Aziz and Fielding, the contact cannot be made. In between Forster exhibits a gradation of attitudes: Miss Quested, who wishes to see the real India, which she keeps separate in her mind from the Indians; Ronny Heaslop, still a little self-conscious about asserting British superiority in all things; the Nawab Bahadur, willing to give credit for stray acts of kindness, but finally exasperated by injustice; Mrs Moore, with an intuitive understanding of Doctor Aziz, but too weary to make it effective; Godbole, the Hindu mystic, who best understands what is happening, but thinks it is of no importance.

In this novel Forster came as near as he could to freeing himself of the story. The main interest lies in the reactions of the characters to an incident that never occurred. Doctor Aziz, a Muslim and assistant medical officer, is accused of assaulting Miss Quested, a young Englishwoman, in one of the caves at Marabar. He is condemned by the whole of the British community except the schoolmaster, Fielding, and Mrs Moore, mother of Miss Quested's fiancé. At the trial Miss Quested realises that she does not know that Doctor Aziz followed her into the caves, and he is acquitted, to the disgust of the British and the joy of the Indians. Miss Quested is rejected as a traitor by the British, and stays for some time with Fielding at the College. His sympathy for Miss Quested makes Doctor Aziz distrustful of him, and destroys the understanding that had grown up between the two men.

The book is notable for detachment and irony. The following extract gives something of its flavour:

People drove into the club with studious calm—the jog-trot of country gentlefolk between green hedgerows, for the natives must not suspect that they were agitated. They exchanged the usual drinks, but everything tasted different, and then they looked out at the palisade of cactuses stabbing the purple throat of the sky; they realised that they were thousands of miles from any scenery that they understood. The club was fuller than usual, and several parents had brought their children into the rooms reserved for adults, which gave the air of the Residency at Lucknow. One young mother—a brainless but most beautiful girl—sat on a low ottoman in the smoking-room with her baby in her arms; her husband was away in the district, and she dared not return to her bungalow in case the 'niggers attacked'. The wife of a small railway official, she was generally snubbed; but this evening, with her abundant figure and masses of corn-gold hair, she symbolised all that is worth fighting and dying for; more permanent a symbol, perhaps, than poor Adela. 'Don't worry, Mrs Blakiston, those drums are only Mohurram,' the men would tell her. 'Then they've started,' she moaned, clasping the infant and rather wishing he would not blow bubbles down his chin at such a moment as this. 'No, of course not, and anyhow, they're not coming to the club.' 'And they're not coming to the Burra Sahib's bungalow either, my dear, and that's where you and your baby'll sleep to-night,' answered Mrs Turton, towering by her side like Pallas Athene, and determining in the future not to be such a snob.

Virginia Woolf

E. M. Forster was one of a number of writers who found a meeting-point in the Bloomsbury home of Leonard Woolf and his wife, Virginia. VIRGINIA WOOLF (1882–1941) was a writer's daughter, a writer, and a writer's wife. Her father was Sir Leslie Stephen, a man of great intellectual and physical energy—critic, biographer, mountaineer, free-thinker, editor of the *Dictionary of National Biography*, a man devoted to regular thirty-mile walks. His literary criticism, which remains very readable, was notable for his attempt to apply standards of judgment to the criticism of novels. The Woolfs were related to the Darwins, the Symondses, and the Stracheys, other families with a tradition of writing. At home, where she was educated with her sister Vanessa, Virginia met these and other leading literary figures of the period.

With such a background her interests were almost inevitably intellectual and literary, so that not only her career as a writer, but also the kind of writer she did in fact become, might have been predicted. Her range of experience was restricted, but within that range she was extremely sensitive to impressions. This sensitivity shaped her views both of life and of the novel: in her essay on *Modern Fiction* she wrote:

> Examine for a moment an ordinary mind on an ordinary day. The mind receives a myriad impressions—trivial, fantastic, evanescent, or engraved with the sharpness of steel. From all sides they come, an incessant shower of innumerable atoms . . . if a writer were a free man and not a slave, if he could write what he chose, not what he must, if he could base his work upon his own feeling and not upon convention, there would be no plot, no comedy, no tragedy, no love interest or catastrophe in the accepted style. . . . Life is not a series of gig-lamps symmetrically arranged; life is a luminous halo, a semi-transparent envelope surrounding us from the beginning of consciousness to the end.

In a novel written according to this conception, the main interest does not lie in the story or in the characters. Instead the novelist records impressions, seeing life not as a clearly defined pattern of events, but as successive moments of experience, in which the same event may be quite different for different people. Characters are not constructed from slabs of qualities—kindness, extravagance, hypocrisy, for instance; the human personality is the product of all these moments of experience, much less consistent, much less clear-cut than it appears to be in the conventional novel. Virginia Woolf said and believed of the carefully devised plots and neat characterisation of these novels, 'Life is not like that.'

In her novels she used a technique called both 'interior monologue' and 'stream of consciousness'. In interior monologue the thoughts, impressions, emotions, memories, mental images, speculations are recorded as they occur in the mind of the character. Virginia Woolf applies this technique most thoroughly in *The Waves* (1931), which consists almost entirely of passages of interior monologue by the six characters, the course of whose lives from childhood to old age are traced by this means. Here is an example:

'Louis and Neville,' said Bernard, 'both sit silent. Both are absorbed. Both feel the presence of other people as a separating wall. But if I find myself in company with other people, words at once make smoke rings—see how phrases at once begin to wreathe off my lips. It seems that a match is set to a fire; something burns. An elderly and apparently prosperous man, a traveller, now gets in. And I at once wish to approach him; I instinctively dislike the sense of his presence, cold, unassimilated, among us. I do not believe in separation. We are not single. Also I wish to add to my collection of valuable observations upon the true nature of human life. My book will certainly run to many volumes, embracing every known variety of man and woman. I fill my mind with whatever happens to be the contents of a room or a railway carriage as one fills a fountain-pen in an inkpot. I have a steady unquenchable thirst. Now I feel by imperceptible signs, which I cannot yet interpret but will later, that his defiance is about to thaw. His solitude shows signs of cracking. He has passed a remark about a country house. A smoke ring issues from my lips (about crops) and circles him, bringing him into contact. The human voice has a disarming quality—(we are not single, we are one). As we exchange these few but amiable remarks about country houses, I furbish him up and make him concrete. He is indulgent as a husband but not faithful; a small builder who employs a few men. In local society he is important; is already a councillor, and perhaps in time will be mayor. He wears a large ornament, like a double tooth torn up by the roots, made of coral, hanging at his watch-chain. Walter J. Trumble is the sort of name that would fit him. He has been in America, on a business trip with his wife, and a double room in a smallish hotel cost him a whole month's wages. His front tooth is stopped with gold.'

From this passage the reader learns something about Bernard and about Trumble, a little about Louis and Neville. The little incident is easily visualised.

Bernard, Louis, Neville, Jinny, Rhoda, Susan live as children in the same house, their distinct personalities perceptible even then. Later their lives separate, although pairs of them have contacts with each other, and the whole group meets twice. From their monologues on these occasions and their reflections when alone, Virginia Woolf builds up a picture of their lives, their personalities, and their relationships. *The Waves* has no plot in the normal sense of the word; it does not end with a marriage, or a death, or the resolution of a problem. Much of the detail is deliberately vague: Susan is in love with Bernard, Rhoda has a love affair with Louis and leaves him, but we know little that is exact about the times, the places, the course of their relations. What we get are impressions of six people, their lives, their emotions, their hopes, their doubts.

There is one other person of importance in the book, Percival, an influence rather than a character. He appears only indirectly in the minds of the six, most of whom admire him as a man of decision and physical action, rather than one who contemplates life as they tend to do. After the six have given a farewell party in his honour, Percival goes off to India where he is killed in a riding accident. The reflection of Percival never gives the impression of a real person, and it illustrates the narrow range of experience and character on which Virginia Woolf could draw. Her women characters are more convincing than the men, and the introspective more convincing than the active, partly of course because the technique of interior monologue lends itself more readily to recording thought and feeling than to narrative. In *Mrs Dalloway*, Peter Walsh, another restless man, returns from India; one suspects that Virginia Woolf did not feel comfortable with decisive and energetic men at close quarters.

Nor was her prose suited to plain narrative: indeed many of its elements—metaphor, simile, words chosen for suggestion, echoing of sounds and images—are close to poetry:

'How fair, how strange,' said Bernard, 'glittering, many-pointed and many-domed London lies before me under mist. Guarded by gasometers, by factory chimneys, she lies sleeping as we approach. She folds the ant-heap to her breast. All cries, all clamour, are softly enveloped in silence. Not Rome herself looks more majestic. But we are aimed at her. Already her maternal somnolence is uneasy. Ridges fledged with houses rise from the mist. Factories, cathedrals, glass domes, institutions and theatres erect themselves. The early train from the north is hurled at her like a missile. We draw a curtain as we pass. Blank expectant faces stare at us as we rattle and flash through stations. Men clutch their newspapers a little tighter, as our wind sweeps them, envisaging death. But we roar on. We are about to explode in the flanks of the city like a shell in the side of some ponderous, maternal, majestic animal. She hums and murmurs; she awaits us.'

Although *The Waves* most clearly illustrates some of Virginia Woolf's ideas about the novel, it is not the most suitable book to begin with. The most immediately enjoyable is probably *Orlando* (1928), a fantastic historical story of a character who represents a family, by repute the Sackville-Wests, through three hundred and fifty years. Orlando goes on from generation to generation, changes sex and century, but is always youthful and high-spirited, ready for the next adventure. The novel is full of vigour, humour, and imagination, the episodes and descriptions much clearer than in her other novels. The novel closest to the conventional form is *Mrs Dalloway*. This is particularly interesting because in her other work Virginia Woolf is continually referring to one of its main themes, the need to protect from intrusion an inner core of the personality:

> And there is a dignity in people; a solitude; even between husband and wife a gulf; and that one must respect, thought Clarissa, watching him open the door; for one would not part with it oneself, or take it, against his will, from one's husband, without losing one's independence, one's self-respect—something, after all, priceless.

To the Lighthouse is probably the most successful of her works, and Mrs Ramsay the most appealing of her characters.

In addition, Virginia Woolf wrote many critical essays, some of the best being collected in *The Common Reader*.

She was greatly depressed by the outbreak of the Second World War, and was found drowned in 1941. At the inquest a verdict of suicide was returned.

Lytton Strachey

LYTTON STRACHEY (1880–1932), who had a family connection with Virginia Woolf, wrote a number of biographies: *Eminent Victorians* (1918), *Queen Victoria* (1921), *Elizabeth and Essex* (1928). In the introduction to the first of these he explained his aims and motives as a biographer:

To preserve, for instance, a becoming brevity—a brevity which excludes everything that is redundant and nothing that is significant—that, surely, is the first duty of the biographer. The second, no less surely, is to maintain his own freedom of spirit. It is not his business to be complimentary; it is his business to lay bare the facts of the case, as he understands them. That is what I have aimed at in this book—to lay bare the facts of some cases, as I understand them, dispassionately, impartially, and without ulterior intentions.

He criticised earlier writers of biography in English:

With us, the most delicate and humane of all the branches of the art of writing has been relegated to the journeymen of letters; we do not reflect that it is perhaps as difficult to write a good life as to live one. Those two fat volumes, with which it is our custom to commemorate the dead—who does not know them, with their ill-digested masses of material, their slipshod style, their tone of tedious panegyric, their lamentable lack of selection, of detachment, of design?

'Human beings', he said, 'are too important to be treated as mere symptoms of the past.' He affirmed that ignorance is the first requisite of the historian—that is, ignorance of a mass of trivial fact that will only blur the sharp vision of the artist. He described his own method:

If he is wise, . . . he will attack his subject in unexpected places; he will fall upon the flank, or the rear; he will shoot a sudden, revealing searchlight into obscure recesses, hitherto undivined. He will row out over that great ocean of material, and lower down into it, here and there, a little bucket, which will bring up to the light of day some characteristic specimen, from those far depths, to be examined with a careful curiosity.

The characteristic specimens in this book are General Gordon, Florence Nightingale, Cardinal Manning and Dr Arnold of Rugby

School, none of them in the first rank of importance in this age, but each typical of some aspect of its genius. The first two paragraphs of the book show the method at work:

> During the year 1883 a solitary English gentleman was to be seen, wandering, with a thick book under his arm, in the neighbourhood of Jerusalem. His unassuming figure, short and slight, with its half-gliding, half-tripping motion, gave him a boyish aspect, which contrasted, oddly, but not unpleasantly, with the touch of gray on his hair and whiskers. There was the same contrast—enigmatic and attractive—between the sunburnt brick-red complexion—the hue of the seasoned traveller—and the large blue eyes, with their look of almost childish sincerity. To the friendly inquirer, he would explain, in a low, soft, and very distinct voice, that he was engaged in elucidating four questions—the site of the crucifixion, the line of division between the tribes of Benjamin and Judah, the identification of Gibeon, and the position of the Garden of Eden. He was also, he would add, most anxious to discover the spot where the Ark first touched ground, after the subsidence of the Flood: he believed, indeed, that he had solved that problem, as a reference to some passages in the book which he was carrying would show.
>
> This singular person was General Gordon, and his book was the Holy Bible.

This is not immediately recognisable as a portrait of General Gordon, eminent as soldier, administrator, engineer, the martyr of Khartoum, about whom legends had proliferated. It is rather the picture of a religious eccentric. But then, it is not the business of the biographer to be complimentary, but to 'lay bare the facts of the case, as he understands them . . . dispassionately, impartially and without ulterior intentions.' This Strachey does with a sense of style and form, clinical observation, and considerable wit. His work has changed the writing of biography in this century. He has been called a 'debunker', a deflator, as indeed he is. But this was the result, rather than the purpose of his writing: he set out to make the writing of biography an art instead of a blunt instrument. As both his observation and his pen were sharp, his subjects suffered some clean cuts.

'The facts of the case, as he understands them.' Like most people Strachey's understanding was incomplete. Not all the people he wrote about were as dispassionate as he was, nor were their calculations as exact as his, but they tend to turn out as reflections of his own temperament to some extent. He had a deficient understanding of the part that abstract ideas, passions, ideals, played in the actions of some men. He rescued biography from pious admiration, however, and showed that it could be written with elegance. He questioned accepted ideas, and showed that beneath the smooth public surface of these men and women there was often a curious, unsuspected kind of life which could be converted into amusing reading.

His two full-length biographies are, perhaps, better balanced, but his distinctive qualities as a biographer are most clearly seen in *Eminent Victorians.*

Aldous Huxley

THE reader cannot help thinking that Lytton Strachey takes a malicious pleasure in describing the oddities and absurdities of human behaviour. This trait is shared by ALDOUS HUXLEY (1894–1963). Like Strachey Huxley also belonged to an extremely intelligent family, for his grandfather was T. H. Huxley, the eminent Victorian biologist, his father a biographer and editor, and his brother Julian only less distinguished as a biologist than his grandfather. All of them had in addition highly developed powers of self-expression. Taking for granted such a concentration of intellect, perhaps both Strachey and Huxley were rather intolerant of human weaknesses.

It was originally intended that Aldous Huxley should also be a biologist, but a defect in his eyesight made this impossible. Instead he turned to literature. He retained something of the attitude of the biologist, however, and in his early novels, *Crome Yellow* (1921), *Antic Hay* (1923) and *Point Counter Point* (1928), he exhibited under the microscope the crawling, decadent life of a section of English society in the years immediately following the First World War. It is a picture of aimless young people trying to live a life of pleasure, but finding little satisfaction in it. Everything about them is false—their intellectual and artistic pretensions, their relations with each other, their knowledge of themselves. Showing neither mercy nor sympathy for them, Huxley dissects their lives and their behaviour without compunction. The satire is as cold and biting as a north-east wind in February; individual scenes are admirable—Lord Edward Tantamount drawn away from his biological experiments by the sound of Bach at his wife's party, Humphrey Gumbril's first encounter with Rosie; minor characters like Mr Boldero are amusing, though others, Philip Quarles's father for instance, are tiresome; and Aldous Huxley can give a witty turn to his sentence. Emotionally, the books are sterile: little Philip's death in *Point Counter Point*, Humphrey's affection for Emily, these are just as cold as the satire. The characters are fond of lengthy comments on art or architecture or biological control which have little to do with the story or the situation. Whilst these would have made suitable material for articles in periodicals, in the novels they are out of place, for the characters tend to voice Huxley's own opinions in his own accents. Huxley merely changes hats when he mounts a fresh hobby-horse.

The theme of *Brave New World* (1932) was better suited to his talents. In this novel Huxley describes a scientific Utopia in which the human will and human individuality are subordinated to the conditions in which men are compelled to live; they are bred and indoctrinated to accept without question the work and the place in society which have been decided for them by the scientists who control the world. Man's problems have disappeared, because man is not allowed to realise that problems can exist for him. 'And that,' put in the Director sententiously, 'that is the secret of happiness and virtue—liking what you've *got* to do. All conditioning aims at that: making people like their unescapable social destiny.'

Brave New World should be read and compared with George Orwell's *1984*: one deals with a world in which man is scientifically controlled; in the other he is politically controlled.

Huxley also wrote essays, travel-books, short stories (*The Gioconda Smile* among them), film-scripts, a book about his success in improving his eyesight, and another about the effects of the drug mescalin on his powers of perception. He was one of the earlier English writers to settle in America, in his case California, so reversing the traffic across the Atlantic in which Henry James and T. S. Eliot had changed their countries.

Evelyn Waugh

In the same year as *Point Counter Point* there appeared a much better-humoured, a much more amusing, a much less laboured, and a much more scathing exposure of the idle young people of the twenties— *Decline and Fall* by Evelyn Waugh (1903–1966). This was followed two years later by another raking satire on the Bright Young Things, *Vile Bodies*. In these two novels Waugh's targets, all squarely hit, included private schools, film-makers, progressive prison-governors, American hot-gospellers, newspaper gossip-writers and feverish parties. Waugh has a comic inventiveness that keeps the stories spinning along with a succession of ludicrous incidents which have an absurd logic of their own. He also starts in these early books a splendid collection of eccentric characters with Dr Fagan, the sanctimonious impostor; Captain Grimes who has equal talent for getting into and for getting himself out of trouble; Colonel Blount of Doubting Hall; and Margot Beste-Chetwynde, the brightest though not the youngest of all Bright Young Things. Waugh handles dialogue deftly; in this passage Paul Pennyfeather is being interviewed by Sir Wilfred Lucas-Dockery, the prison-governor:

Paul was led in.

'I understand you wish to continue cellular labour instead of availing yourself of the privilege of working in association. Why is that?'

'I find it so much more interesting, sir,' said Paul.

'It's a most irregular suggestion,' said the Chief Warder. 'Privileges can only be forfeited by a breach of the regulations witnessed and attested by two officers. Standing Orders are most emphatic on the subject.'

'I wonder whether you have narcissistic tendencies?' said the Governor. 'The Home Office has not as yet come to any decision about my application for a staff psycho-analyst.'

'Put him in the observation cell,' said the Chief Warder. 'That brings out any insanity. I've known several cases of men you could hardly have told were mad —just eccentric, you know—who've been put on observation, and after a few days they've been raving lunatics. Colonel MacAdder was a great believer in the observation cells.'

'Did you lead a very lonely life before conviction? Perhaps you were a shepherd or a lighthouse-keeper, or something of the kind?'

'No, sir.'

'Most curious. Well, I will consider your case and give you my answer later.'

Waugh used his own experience as the basis of certain episodes in these novels. Like Paul Pennyfeather he did not complete his degree course at Oxford and then spent a short period as an unsuccessful schoolmaster. His time as a reporter on the *Daily Express* was even shorter and more unsuccessful. Indeed in 1928 at the age of twenty-five Waugh had tried a number of things including the study of art and the learning of cabinet-making, yet had accomplished little despite his obvious talent. He then became engaged to the daughter of Lord Burghclere, but his fiancée's father was not impressed by his prospects as a cabinet-maker. At this stage Waugh wrote a life of Rossetti and quickly followed this with his two early novels. It seems remarkable that he did not become a writer from the beginning, for his father had been a publisher, literary critic and biographer and his brother, Alec, had at the age of nineteen published *The Loom of Youth*, a story of public-school life that attracted some attention and notoriety.

Evelyn Waugh's first marriage lasted only a year. In 1930 he was received into the Roman Catholic Church; he was henceforward a Catholic, a royalist and a classicist. During the 1930s he travelled widely in Abyssinia, East and South Africa, Fez, the West Indies and Mexico. He used his experiences as material for newspaper articles, travel books and novels. He visited Abyssinia to report the Italian-Abyssinian War for the *Daily Mail*, and two of his novels of the thirties, *Black Mischief* and *Scoop*, are set in countries which resemble that country in some respects. In *Black Mischief* Waugh introduces Basil Seal, a self-centred cad of great charm who appears also in two later novels. This is one of the few novels in which the heroine is eaten. In *Scoop* Waugh again satirises a newspaper magnate, Lord Copper, owner of *The Daily Beast*. He confuses two cousins, William Boot, a country-lover who writes articles on natural history, and John Boot, a successful novelist and experienced traveller. William is sent to Ishmaelia to report a war for *The Daily Beast* with instructions to 'continue cabling victories until further notice'. Basil Seal re-appears in *Put Out More Flags* up to his old tricks in a new historical setting, the period of the 'phoney' war, 1939–40. He was getting a little old for these escapades, however, and the outbreak of the war in earnest brought to an end for ever the kind of world in which Basil and Ambrose Silk and Peter Pastmaster could survive unchanged.

Waugh's later work has been greatly influenced by his war service. Although he was almost thirty-six at the outbreak of war, he regarded himself as a fighting soldier. He gained a commission in the Royal Marines in 1939 and later served in a commando unit in the Middle East, in the Royal Horse Guards and in the British Military Mission to Yugoslavia. During the few months before the invasion of Europe he was sent on indefinite leave because he was regarded as too old for the strenuous campaign that lay ahead. He used this period before his departure for Yugoslavia to write *Brideshead Revisited*, subtitled *The Sacred and Profane Memories of Captain Charles Ryder*. This novel is a study of the members of a Catholic family, several of whom lapse from their faith, but who, in the end, discover that they cannot abandon their religion. On that level *Brideshead Revisited* demonstrates that, despite temptation and sin, man has a fundamental need for faith. This truth is illustrated in a story told with the wit, the love of the absurd and extravagant, the merciless observation of human weakness that marked Waugh's earlier satires. Here the emphasis is perhaps more on character, less on comic incident, and Ryder himself in his comments on the other characters and their behaviour is more obviously echoing the author's own beliefs than anyone in the books he had written in the 1930s. Some readers have found the mixture of piety and comedy uncomfortable; others think the comedy has a deeper tone and see nothing incongruous between the two elements in the story. Waugh's early books were often heartless in such incidents as the accident to Lord Tangent, Prendergast's death and Prudence's horrid fate, but here there are both pathos and wit. On the one hand we have Ryder's malicious father, deliberately misunderstanding events in order to embarrass his son, amusing as any of Waugh's elderly eccentrics; on the other, we have Lady Marchmain, kindest and most sincere member of her family, but fated to lose her brothers and to estrange her husband and children. This is at the least an immensely accomplished and entertaining novel; whether it is anything more depends on the reader's taste. This extract shows that in *Brideshead Revisited* even the absurdities are rather graver than they used to be:

Bridey was a slow and copious eater. Julia and I watched him between the candles. Presently he said: 'If I was Rex'—his mind seemed full of such suppositions: 'If I was Archbishop of Westminster,' 'If I was head of the Great Western Railway,' 'If I was an actress,' as though it were a mere trick of fate that he was none of these things, and he might awake any morning to find the matter adjusted—'if I was Rex I should want to live in my constituency.'

'Rex says it saved four days a week not to.'

'I'm sorry he's not here. I have a little announcement to make.'

'Bridey, don't be so mysterious. Out with it.' He made the grimace which seemed to mean 'not before the servants.'

Later when port was on the table and we three were alone Julia said: 'I'm not going till I hear the announcement.'

'Well,' said Bridey, sitting back in his chair and gazing fixedly at his glass. 'You have only to wait until Monday to see it in black and white in the newspapers. I am engaged to be married. I hope you are pleased.'

'Bridey. How . . . how very exciting! Who to?'

'Oh, no one you know.'

'Is she pretty?'

'I don't think you would exactly call her pretty; "comely" is the word I think of in her connexion. She is a big woman.'

'Fat?'

'No, big. She is called Mrs. Muspratt; her Christian name is Beryl. I have known her for a long time, but until last year she had a husband; now she is a widow. Why do you laugh?'

'I'm sorry. It isn't the least funny. It's just so unexpected. Is she . . . is she about your own age?'

'Just about, I believe. She has three children, the eldest boy has just gone to Ampleforth. She is not at all well off.'

'But, Bridey, where did you find her?'

'Her late husband, Admiral Muspratt, collected match-boxes,' he said with complete gravity.

Julia trembled on the verge of laughter, recovered her self-possession and asked: 'You're not marrying her for her match-boxes?'

'No, no; the whole collection was left to the Falmouth Town Library. I have a great affection for her. In spite of all her difficulties she is a very cheerful woman, very fond of acting. She is connected with the Catholic Players' Guild.'

'Does papa know?'

'I had a letter from him this morning giving me his approval. He has been urging me to marry for some time.'

In 1947 Waugh went to Hollywood to discuss the filming of *Brideshead Revisited*. Although he could not agree with the film company about the screen adaptation of the novel, his visit was not wasted, for whilst he was there he became fascinated with the elaborate death-rites observed by the bereaved Californians and encouraged by the undertakers. The result of this was *The Loved One*, a macabre farce, set in 'Whispering Glades', a profitable temple consecrated to the human corpse. The climax occurs when Aimée Thanatogenos commits suicide in the workroom of Mr Joyboy, the chief embalmer, who is faced with the problem of disposing of an unwanted body. His pride and delight has been in the treatment of bodies, but the circumstances make Aimée's body particularly embarrassing to him. *The Loved One* is a return to the heartless farce, as this situation shows.

In 1950 Waugh wrote *Helena*, a fictional biography of Saint Helena who discovered the true cross on which Jesus died. The portrait of the saint is a human one with little vanities and weaknesses.

Waugh next wrote a war trilogy consisting of *Men at Arms* (1952), *Officers and Gentlemen* (1955) and *Unconditional Surrender* (1961). The central figure, Guy Crouchback, has much in common with the author:

he is a Catholic who enlists at the beginning of the war although he is approaching forty. He spends long periods training in England, but serves in West Africa and Crete and is sent on the Military Mission to Yugoslavia. At one time he is placed on the list of unemployed officers. Of the three books the first, *Men at Arms*, is much the best, principally for the glorious character of Apthorpe, who is everything that Guy is not. The bogus Apthorpe is promoted, whilst Guy, who volunteered from pure patriotism and serves humbly yet devotedly, is passed over. The trilogy is a record of Guy's growing disillusionment, of his discovery that the Army and the country even in war are full of self-seeking, false and hollow men who thrust men like Guy out of their way to the top. The two later books are rather sour in tone, but as long as Apthorpe is alive, he brings a rich humour to events, and his campaign against Ritchie-Hook for control of his Thunder-box is very funny.

The Ordeal of Gilbert Pinfold is a fictional treatment of an interlude in Waugh's life when he suffered from hallucinations, principally voices that were maligning him.

Waugh was an aristocrat who clung to tradition and deplored the shallowness, the gimcrack pleasures, the decay of standards which he saw in modern life. He attacked what he disliked with a cutting wit; his beliefs, his opinions, his criticisms, isolated him from his age, and it is not therefore surprising that he should have felt that modern life is a conspiracy against everything he was attached to, perhaps even against himself.

Robert Frost

IN 1912 some of the Georgian poets welcomed a visitor from America who stayed in England for three years. He was ROBERT FROST (1874–1963), perhaps the poet held in the highest respect by his own generation, the marks of esteem culminating in an invitation to read one of his own poems at the inauguration of President Kennedy. Although Frost remained friendly with the English writers he met and was praised by them for 'the calm eagerness of emotion' that characterised his poetry, his roots remained firmly planted in the soil of New England where he farmed for many years.

His work is deceptively simple. In familiar, often colloquial, language he describes a commonplace experience as in 'The Road Not Taken':

> Two roads diverged in a yellow wood,
> And sorry I could not travel both
> And be one traveler, long I stood
> And looked down one as far as I could
> To where it bent in the undergrowth;
>
> Then took the other, as just as fair,
> And having perhaps the better claim,
> Because it was grassy and wanted wear;
> Though as for that the passing there
> Had worn them really about the same,
>
> And both that morning equally lay
> In leaves no step had trodden black.
> Oh, I kept the first for another day!
> Yet knowing how way leads on to way,
> I doubted if I should ever come back.
>
> I shall be telling this with a sigh
> Somewhere ages and ages hence:
> Two roads diverged in a wood, and I—
> I took the one less traveled by,
> And that has made all the difference.

Simple as it is this poem communicates the uncertainty and perplexity of man, not only about the rightness of the choice made, but also about the difference it has made to his life. The poem is as profound as the reader makes it; it raises many questions and allows of many interpretations. Obviously the two paths in the wood symbolise a turning-point in a man's life. But you could argue that this is a sad poem about the failure to take an opportunity; or an even sadder one about the inevitability of rejecting one possibility when you accept another. It may be about a man's loss of freedom of action as he grows older and more involved in the world's affairs, or even about the loss of innocence. Is Frost referring to his own decision to become a poet and wondering what his life might otherwise have been? The only interesting questions are those to which there is no clear-cut answer and Frost opens the doors to speculation. There is not an emphatic word in the four verses, but they make their impression on the reader or listener.

Frost knows the countryside in a way that only someone who has lived and worked there for many years can know it. He feels a bond with it:

> The land was ours before we were the land's.
> She was our land more than a hundred years
> Before we were her people. . . .

He observes the rural scene closely. In 'Birches' he describes in detail what he has seen and heard:

> Often you must have seen them
> Loaded with ice a sunny winter morning
> After a rain. They click upon themselves
> As the breeze rises, and turn many-colored
> As the stir cracks and crazes their enamel.
> Soon the sun's warmth makes them shed crystal shells
> Shattering and avalanching in the snow-crust—
> Such heaps of broken glass to sweep away
> You'd think the inner dome of heaven had fallen.

Other poems which illustrate Frost's ability to combine simplicity of utterance with profundity of implication are 'Stopping by Woods on a Snowy Evening' and 'Mending Wall'. In the latter Frost tells how he and his neighbour each year patrol the boundary between their land repairing any breaks in the wall. Frost cannot see what purpose the wall serves:

> Before I built a wall I'd ask to know
> What I was walling in or walling out,
> And to whom I was like to give offence.

His neighbour only replies, 'Good fences make good neighbours.' These two points of view exemplify two different outlooks on life, and Frost does not claim that his own is right and his neighbour's wrong. He seldom makes judgments of that kind, preferring to present a situation that gives rise to reflection.

Most of his poems are short, but 'The Death of the Hired Man' is rather longer. An old labourer returns to a farm where he has often worked and which he has several times left at awkward times to earn more money. The farmer and his wife argue whether they are under an obligation to take him in:

> 'Warren,' she said, 'he has come home to die:
> You needn't be afraid he'll leave you this time.'
>   'Home,' he mocked gently.
>   'Yes, what else but home?
> It all depends on what you mean by home.
> Of course he's nothing to us, any more
> Than was the hound that came a stranger to us
> Out of the woods, worn out upon the trail.'
>
> 'Home is the place where, when you have to go there,
> They have to take you in.'
>
>   'I should have called it
> Something you somehow haven't to deserve.'

When the farmer goes to see the old man he finds him dead. The poem with its background of a farmer's life, its simple story, and its quietness, reminds one of Wordsworth's 'Michael', and the two poets have some things in common. Frost is, however, not openly didactic as Wordsworth so often is; the lesson is there, but the reader makes of it what he chooses. In many ways Frost has a dignified, rather old-fashioned air that sets him apart from the other poets of his generation. He does not insist, nor strive for novelty, but makes his effects with a notable economy of means.

Robert Graves

ROBERT GRAVES (born 1895) wrote poetry during the First World War and fifty years later is still writing poetry with no sign of exhaustion. He appeared in Siegfried Sassoon's *Memoirs of an Infantry Officer* as David Cromlech, whilst he himself wrote his own impressions of the Army and the war in *Goodbye to All That*, a lively work in which he freely expresses his likes and, more often, his dislikes. During the 1930s he wrote two historical novels about the Roman emperor, Claudius, called *I, Claudius* and *Claudius the God*. In these he explored the devious mind and motives of an emperor who often had to rely on his wits to survive the intrigues of the Roman court. He builds a complex and fascinating character, part idealist and part opportunist, wholly credible in the vicious circle in which he strove to live.

When these novels were written Graves's poetry was out of fashion, though his work has always been respected by the critics. His poems have always been private communications, lucid and cool even when they spring from deep passion. They are not declamatory or didactic; he does not analyse society's ills or prescribe political cures; they are not full of obscure allusions or images violently yoked together. Often he is giving precise expression to his own feelings, his reactions to his experiences. These have stirred him, but he applies his intellect to them so that he can make clear to himself what was the nature of the experience and what effect it has had upon him. The reader is admitted to observe, but Graves does not point any moral or urge any action. It is enough for him to find out the truth about himself. The poems are all short, and simple in language and form, for Graves is trying to distil his experience, not adulterate it.

In his Foreword to the *Collected Poems* (1965) Graves says, 'My main theme was always the practical impossibility, transcended only by a belief in miracle, of absolute love continuing between man and woman.' This is certainly true of his later poetry, but there was a period after the war when his peace of mind was disturbed by morbid fears and nightmares. Although he has cut out some of these poems from his collected works, 'The Pier Glass' and 'The Castle' remain of these dark visions:

> . . . to run the head against these blind walls,
> Enter the dungeon, torment the eyes

With apparitions chained two and two,
And go frantic with fear
To die and wake up sweating by moonlight
In the same courtyard, sleepless as before.

Graves is also fond of grim jokes in songs like 'Lift-Boy', in which the attendant receives a warning:

But along came Old Eagle, like Moses or David;
He stopped at the fourth floor and preached me Damnation:
'Not a soul shall be savèd, not one shall be savèd.
The whole First Creation shall forfeit salvation:
From knife-boy to lift-boy, from ragged to regal,
Not one shall be savèd, not you, not Old Eagle,
No soul on earth escapeth, even if all repent—'
So I cut the cords of the lift and down we went,
With nothing in our pockets.

Few of Graves's poems take natural description as their subjects, but 'Rocky Acres' is an exception. Usually he writes love lyrics, often with a doubt about the permanence of love. Such are 'The Foreboding' and 'The Visitation', which ends thus:

And though a single word scatters all doubts
I quake for wonder at your choice of me:
Why, why and why?

In 'The Wreath' he wonders how someone who loved him so could reject him, promising like Shakespeare to make immortal by his verse her faithlessness:

You shall be punished with a deathless crown
For your dark head, resist it how you may.

No matter how close has been their union, Graves knows that she keeps a part of her being secret from all men, as in these lines from 'The Secret Land':

Every woman of true royalty owns
A secret land more real to her
Than this pale outer world.

and these from 'Golden Anchor':

I have been honest in love, as is my nature;
She secret, as is hers.

Although he sometimes exults in his love ('Recognition' and 'Name Day') he never counts on its permanence. His feelings are summarised in 'The Three-Faced':

Who calls her two-faced? Faces, she has three:
The first inscrutable, for the outer world;
The second, shrouded in self-contemplation;
The third, her face of love,
Once for an endless moment turned on me.

There is consistency both in the choice of subject and in the quality of the verse. There are things to admire in all his poems—reticence, proportion, terseness, lucidity—and scarcely a word that jars. Graves has written as many good poems as any English poet of the century, but he has written few that are memorable. They give off light rather than heat. He has tamed the beast ('Down, wanton, down!'), but robbed it of some vitality.

J. B. Priestley

IN a letter to James Agate, the dramatic critic, J. B. PRIESTLEY (born 1894) wrote, 'There are some writers who can bide their time and then turn out something like a masterpiece every five years. I am not one of them. I am too restless, too impatient, too prolific of ideas. I am one of the hit-or-miss school of artists.'

These two kinds of writer have always existed: in our own century Priestley and Chesterton on the one hand, E. M. Forster on the other. At the beginning of the nineteenth century there was the same kind of contrast in output between Sir Walter Scott and Jane Austen. If, as Priestley himself says, there are some misses amongst the many books and plays he has written, this fact does not destroy the merits of the undoubted achievements amongst the others.

Early in his career he had a resounding success with *The Good Companions*. If he had been satisfied to repeat his success with more genial, expansive novels of the same kind, he could have lived very comfortably on the capital of goodwill that this book earned for him with the reading public. His next novel, *Angel Pavement*, was, however, completely different in mood, setting, and manner of development. Some writers find a formula that suits their talents—crime-stories, historical novels, drawing-room comedy, or kitchen-sink drama—and are able to turn out two or three variations on this theme year after year. Priestley's fertility has not been of this nature: he has written novels, plays, essays, literary criticism, travel books, biography, short stories, even a libretto for an opera. Yet, even to mention the different genres still fails to indicate fully his versatility. His plays include broad comedies like *Laburnum Grove* and *When We are Married*; sensitive domestic studies like *Eden End* and *The Linden Tree*; a modern morality play in *Johnson over Jordan*; an exploration of character using an experimental technique in *Music at Night*; three plays in which Priestley expounded theories of time and individual experience; a political extravaganza, *Bees on the Boatdeck*, and an expression of his social ideals in *They Came to a City*.

Many of his later novels have been topical in their themes—wartime conditions suggested *Daylight on Saturday* and *Blackout in Gretley*, demobilisation *Three Men in New Suits*, the Festival of Britain *Festival at Farbridge*. Priestley has not only been 'prolific of ideas' as he claimed. He has always been able to clothe them with characters and plot.

Among this abundant output selection is necessary, for it is not possible even to mention everything he has written. And so it is necessary to limit the choice: from his novels *The Good Companions*, *Angel Pavement* and *Bright Day*; from his plays *Eden End*, *Time and the Conways*, *Johnson over Jordan* and *The Linden Tree;* from his other works *English Journey*, *Midnight on the Desert*, and *Delight*. This leaves out *Faraway*, a fine romantic novel which will appeal to a young, imaginative reader, *An Inspector Calls*, a play which attacks vigorously complacency and hypocrisy and leaves a question at the end, and that monumental guide to the development of modern civilisation, thought, and literature—*Literature and Western Man*.

The Good Companions is a generous novel: generous in length, inventive in incident and character, genial in outlook. It is a novel in the English tradition, tracing its descent from Defoe through Fielding, Smollett and Dickens, discarding coarseness and acquiring refinement at each stage. In the first part of the story Priestley describes how three people escape from the narrow existences they are used to: Jess Oakroyd, a carpenter from Bruddersford in Yorkshire, loses his job and tires of his nagging wife; Miss Trant, a spinster approaching middle age, is at last freed of the responsibility for looking after her father by his death; Inigo Jollifant, a young music-teacher in a private school, rebels against the petty tyranny of the headmaster's wife and walks out of the school. They make their way across England to meet by chance at the Station Refreshment Rooms at Rawsley in the Midlands. Here they find six forlorn members of a concert-party, called the Dinky Doos, who have been deserted by their manager.

The second part tells how Miss Trant decides to put her savings into the party to reform it as the Good Companions. Inigo Jollifant joins them as pianist, Jess Oakroyd as carpenter and odd-job man. They travel around the country and, despite setbacks, they enjoy both success and adventure. In the third part the Good Companions break up, most of them finding fulfilment for their ambitions or personal happiness.

The English reader has always liked long, warm-hearted novels of this kind, but length and ardour are not enough in themselves. Priestley gives us an idea, that in hard times loyalty and friendliness will pull people through their troubles. Then there is a procession of clearly drawn, immediately recognisable characters; some like Jess Oakroyd run through the book, their likenesses well filled out, but new characters like Mrs Tarvin and Mr Timpany enliven their own episodes in the book, then disappear. Priestley has, too, a strong sense of the nature of different places so that the journey from small town to small town never becomes monotonous. It is a novel without a climax, but something is always happening; the ability to keep a story moving is more important and rarer than some novelists think. Finally, Priestley's style is clear and vigorous; there is scarcely a memorable sentence in the book, but there is hardly an obscure one either.

Angel Pavement is not an expansive book like *The Good Companions*. Instead of telling how a group of people break out from their former lives, it describes how one man, Mr Golspie, breaks into the closed world of a London firm of timber suppliers, Twigg and Dersingham. It is not a warm, cheerful book, nor a story of a group bound together by comradeship. Here most of the characters are lonely individuals, worried about their employment and uncertain in their personal relationships. It is a novel about a large, impersonal city, full of people but empty of affection, in which the animation of the cinema and the tea-shop is false and superficial. There are again striking characters like Turgis and Smeeth, and the sense of place is seen in the descriptions of the concert at Queen's Hall and of the glittering but tawdry restaurant that Turgis visits. Although not a tragedy, *Angel Pavement* is often disturbing for it analyses the sickness of twentieth-century life. It is a much more profound book than *The Good Companions* and likely to survive as a picture of commercial life in London between the wars.

In *Bright Day*, Priestley's own favourite amongst his novels, Gregory Dawson takes stock of his life. He is a writer in his forties prosperously engaged on churning out film-scripts which he knows to be unworthy of him. A meeting with an old acquaintance takes him back to his youth in Bruddersford, and, in particular, to his memories of the Alington family. Priestley excels in the depiction of family life in, for instance, *Eden End*, *Time and the Conways* and *The Linden Tree*, but there is no more delightful family group than the Alingtons in his work. Obviously Gregory Dawson has more in common with Priestley himself than smoking a pipe, though the character is not simply a self-portrait. Certainly the reader who wishes to understand Priestley should read *Bright Day* from which he will learn much about his outlook, about his views on success and failure, and about a man's experiences, ambitions, disillusionment and consolations.

Of Priestley's other prose works *Delight* is a collection of short essays which can be dipped into with pleasure whenever the reader has even five minutes to spare; *English Journey* gives Priestley's impression of people and places as he travelled through the country in 1934 during the depression; *Midnight on the Desert* is a chapter of autobiography, reflective rather than narrative, worth comparing with *Bright Day*. The author spends a night thinking, remembering, describing his life in the past and in the present, thinking occasionally about his future.

Eden End (1934) is a play about a Yorkshire doctor's family to which a prodigal daughter who ran away years before to become an actress returns, hoping to find peace, only to discover that she has disturbed the lives of her father, sister and brother. The characters and the life of the family are so intimately drawn that even Priestley himself wondered how he came to write the play, 'because everything in it is imagined—I have never known any people like the Kirby family—and I know nothing in my own life that would suggest to me this particular theme of the pathetic prodigal daughter'. It is surprising, too, how often in his plays and novels Priestley returns to Yorkshire for his settings, and how authentic they seem, when he has not lived there for almost fifty years. Perhaps he himself feels an exile, attached to Yorkshire but unable to return there. He describes the conception and writing of the play in this way: 'I brooded for a long time over the people of this play and their lives, and then wrote it quickly and easily: and to my mind this is the way that plays ought to be written. The long brooding brings depth and richness; and the quick writing compels the whole mind, and not merely the front half of it, to work at the job.'

Time and the Conways (1937), another family play, is Priestley's own favourite amongst his time-plays. Act I shows the Conway family in 1919 happily celebrating a birthday; Act II shows them nearly twenty years later with all their bright hopes and plans disappointed; Act III goes back to the family party, but this time the gaiety and the ambitions are empty and pathetic after the revelations of Acts II and III have been transposed. The second act becomes an ironic commentary on Act III, Kay's prophetic vision giving point to what would otherwise have been a humdrum story.

Johnson over Jordan is very different in technique from these plays. Robert Johnson, an ordinary City clerk, has just died and is caught between this life and the next. The play is a phantasmagoria in which scenes from his life, friends from his past, buried parts of his personality, are flashed before him in a kind of dream which he both watches and takes part in. The play moves freely backwards and forwards in time; some of the characters are depicted realistically, others like the vices and virtues in the old morality plays; the beginning of each act is naturalistic, much of the later parts symbolic. Johnson is a modern Everyman. Reaction to the play has been sharply divided, a sign that it has something to say. Some have found the central character insufficient to maintain interest, others have found his re-created life profoundly moving. In reading, the effect of the play is fragmentary, but in production the fragments build up into a pattern that portrays the life, the aspirations, and the failures of an ordinary man.

In *The Linden Tree* Priestley returns to the family play. The central character, Professor Robert Linden, is threatened with imposed retirement from his post in a provincial university. When three of his four children return to visit him he feels out of sympathy with the cold, hard attitude of the younger generation. Something of his own gentleness and idealism survives in his youngest daughter, Dinah, and the relationship between the two is the most affecting feature of the play. In the end, the Professor, like the intellectual equivalent of a Hemingway hero, determines to stay on at the University to campaign for the standards he believes in, though he realises that his ideas have been pushed aside and that he cannot succeed in his struggle. In outline the play sounds drab and melancholy, but the quiet, unquenchable faith of Professor Linden illuminates it.

In addition to writing his novels, essays and plays, Priestley has actively supported many political and social ideas, most of them left-wing. His mind has always been active and vigorous, and the words to express them have come readily to him. He always has something to say and nearly always says it effectively.

Somerset Maugham

THE best guide to the life and work of WILLIAM SOMERSET MAUGHAM (1874–1965) is his own book *The Summing Up*. Whilst he denies that this is an autobiography, it tells the reader enough about his life to understand how his career developed, and it also explains the ideas that have guided him as a writer. He also takes an extraordinarily detached view of his own gifts and defects, so that the book is illuminating both about his own work and about authorship in general. It merits a place beside Trollope's autobiography.

Maugham was born in Paris, but after the death of his parents while he was still a boy, he was brought up in Kent by an uncle who was a clergyman. He attended King's School, Canterbury, where he ordered that his ashes should be buried after death, though he claimed to have been very unhappy at school. He was mocked by both staff and pupils because he stammered badly. Frank Swinnerton said: 'He never forgot this humiliation or the stammer. They were the cause of his brevity in both speech and writing.'

After leaving school Maugham studied medicine at Saint Thomas's Hospital in London and qualified as a doctor. Later he wrote, 'I do not know a better training for a writer than to spend some years in the medical profession'. He did not practise as a doctor and chose writing as a career, at first with little success. His first novel, *Liza of Lambeth* (1897), described the life in London slums he had seen as a medical student, and its realism shocked many readers.

During the period from 1907 to 1933 Maugham's plays were very popular, and at one time four were running simultaneously in London. They were mostly witty, cynical pieces which now seem like rather faded memories of Oscar Wilde's plays. Maugham summed them up shrewdly: 'I had then very high spirits, a facility for amusing dialogue, an eye for a comic situation, and a flippant gaiety.' The best of this batch is probably *The Circle* (1921), for the satirical comments on the society of his day have now lost their point.

Maugham took his novels and short stories more seriously. He regarded *Of Human Bondage* (1915) as his best work, a book which he wrote to free himself from the pains and unhappy recollections of his childhood and youth. 'It is not an autobiography, but an autobiographical novel; fact and fiction are inextricably mingled; the emotions are my own, but not all the incidents are related as they happened, and some of them are transferred to my hero not from my own life, but from that of persons with whom I was intimate.'

The story tells of Philip Carey's loneliness as a boy brought up by his uncle, of his sensitiveness, particularly about his club foot, of his time as an art-student in a bohemian group in Paris, and, mainly, of his unhappy love for a shallow, vulgar and selfish waitress in London, Mildred. Philip becomes a medical student and obtains a post as ship's doctor. The novel is notable for its frank, unsentimental detail of life in a poor part of London, and for the characters of Philip Carey, Mildred, and Fanny Price, a dedicated but untalented artist.

During the First World War Maugham served as a British secret agent in Switzerland and Russia, and he later used these experiences in his Ashenden stories. Ashenden had much in common with Maugham: 'Ashenden admired goodness, but was not outraged by wickedness.' Afterwards Maugham travelled widely, particularly in the East and in America. On his journeys he kept a notebook in which he jotted down scenes, characters, conversations which he had noticed, and which later served as materials for his short stories. Maugham has described his purpose as a writer of short stories:

> I wanted to write stories that proceeded, tightly knit, in an unbroken line from the exposition to the conclusion. I saw the short story as a narrative of a single event, material or spiritual, to which by the elimination of everything that was not essential to its elucidation a dramatic unity could be given. I had no fear of what is technically known as 'the point'. It seemed to me that it was reprehensible only if it was not logical, and I thought that the discredit that had been attached to it was due only to the fact that it had been too often tacked on, merely for effect, without legitimate reason. In short, I preferred to end my short stories with a full-stop rather than with a straggle of dots.

In short stories such as *Rain*, *The Letter*, *Jane*, *Mr Harrington's Washing*, and *The Round Dozen* Maugham used this method most effectively, and he is a dull reader who is not interested and amused. Maugham's talent for brevity, his quick eye for character and situation, were admirably suited to the short story.

Maugham's later novels include *The Moon and Sixpence*, based on the life-story of the French artist, Gauguin. In this version Charles Strickland, a respectable and successful middle-aged stockbroker, abandons his wife, his family, and his career, so that he can live and develop his interest in painting in Tahiti. Here he lives with a native woman and, after destroying his paintings, dies of leprosy.

Cakes and Ale (1930) tells the life-story of Albert Driffield, a man of humble family who, partly by longevity, becomes a celebrated novelist.

Driffield himself, despite Maugham's denials, is supposed to have been modelled on Thomas Hardy; certainly, Alroy Kear, a malicious portrait of a writer with more talent for publicising himself than for literature, is based on Hugh Walpole. Driffield's first wife, Rosie, a former barmaid, who generously gives and receives pleasure from the men she meets, illustrates one of Maugham's views of human character: 'I am not my brother's keeper. I cannot bring myself to judge my fellows; I am content to observe them. My observation has led me to believe that, all in all, there is not so much difference between the good and the bad as the moralists would have us believe.' The first few pages of this novel are an admirable example of a skilful novelist's ability to engage the interest of his readers.

Maugham was a craftsman, not a great artist. He had neither the distinction of style nor the creative imagination that mark the work of the finest writers. He was, however, outstandingly successful and popular. For these reasons his merits have perhaps been underestimated. 'Poetic flights and the great imaginative sweep were beyond my powers,' he admitted. 'On the other hand I had an acute power of observation, and it seemed to me that I could see a great many things that other people missed. I could put down in clear terms what I saw. . . . On taking thought it seemed to me that I must aim at lucidity, simplicity, and euphony. I have put these three qualities in the order of the importance I assigned to them.'

Maugham regarded himself as a story-teller, a title in which he took some pride. 'I have had some sort of story to tell and it has interested me to tell it. To me it has been a sufficient object in itself. It has been my misfortune that for some time now a story has been despised by the sophisticated.' In particular he disliked and mistrusted the novelist in whose work propaganda was the chief aim and the story incidental and clumsily told. With some scorn he spoke of 'a large mass of ignorant people who want knowledge that can be acquired with little labour. They have thought that they were learning something when they read novels in which the characters delivered their views on the burning topics of the day. A bit of love-making thrown in here and there made the information they were given sufficiently palatable.'

In achieving lucidity and simplicity, Maugham failed to touch life at enough points to be a great novelist, and his gifts were best suited to the short story. His career showed how far professional skill can take a writer, but indicated that a novelist who is content to observe human behaviour without the desire to say anything about its significance sets limits on his achievement.

F. Scott Fitzgerald

F. SCOTT FITZGERALD (1896–1940) wrote three novels, and left a fourth incomplete, in which men had achieved outstanding success which they could, through their talents, reasonably hope to consummate. In the event, each of them falls under the influence of a woman in an attachment that leads to his downfall. This was the theme of Fitzgerald's own life, too; at Princeton, in his marriage, and as a young writer, a triumphant success seemed there for the taking, but each time it slipped through his hands.

Fitzgerald was born in St Paul, a town in the mid-western state of Minnesota. On his father's side the family enjoyed an established social position, and there was wealth in his mother's family. Despite his father's failure in a business career, Fitzgerald was educated at a well-known private Catholic school and at Princeton. He tried hard to impress his contemporaries both as an athlete and as a writer, making himself rather unpopular by his thrustfulness. His efforts to win recognition as a literary figure at Princeton were on the point of fulfilment when the neglect of his academic work led to low gradings and debarment from activities not connected with his studies. After an absence of several months caused by illness, Fitzgerald returned to Princeton for only a short time before he joined the U.S. Army in 1916. He spent the rest of the war in training-camps in America instead of seeing service abroad as he had hoped. Whilst he was stationed in Alabama he met Zelda Sayre, a beautiful and popular girl, in much the same circumstances as Jay Gatsby met Daisy in *The Great Gatsby*. With the end of the war the brilliant and handsome young officer became a young man with no money and meagre prospects, so Zelda broke off their engagement. After an unsuccessful spell with an advertising agency in New York, Fitzgerald returned to St Paul to rewrite a novel for publication, hoping that its success would win back Zelda for him.

In 1920 the novel was published as *This Side of Paradise;* it was favourably reviewed and sold remarkably well for a first novel. Fitzgerald was regarded as the first novelist of the post-war generation, and he was able to sell his short stories to the leading American magazines. The same year he married Zelda, his position and prospects having been transformed in the space of a few months.

This Side of Paradise tells of the sentimental education of a self-conscious young aesthete who is a student at Princeton. He progresses by way of petting parties, drunken escapades, poetic affirmations of his passion for a succession of girls, seduction by Eleanor, ro self-knowledge and a vague, visionary faith in socialism. Today the book seems an obviously juvenile attempt at fictionalised autobiography in which the central figure, Amory Blaine, takes himself and his ideas very much more seriously than they deserve. Although it shocked some people at the time it now seems harmless enough.

Fitzgerald immediately began a second novel, originally to be called *The Flight of the Rocket*, but published in 1922 under the title of *The Beautiful and Damned*, which he described in a letter thus: 'My new novel . . . concerns the life of one Anthony Patch between his 25th and 33rd years (1913–21). He is one of those many with the tastes and weaknesses of an artist but with no actual creative inspiration. How he and his beautiful young wife are wrecked on the shoals of dissipation is told in the story.'

Both Anthony and his wife, Gloria, expect more from their marriage than they are able to put into it, they grow disillusioned and seek refuge in drink, parties, and absurd ambitions, until both their personalities disintegrate. Anthony expects to inherit the fortune of his millionaire uncle, Adam Patch, nicknamed 'Cross' Patch, who disinherits him after finding him at a particularly wild party. His character gives a vigour to this novel that the first had lacked. There is an ironic twist at the end, when Anthony, drained of hope and vitality by his experiences, learns that he has won a law-suit which gives him possession of his uncle's fortune at a time when he can no longer enjoy its fruits.

So far Fitzgerald had seemed a young writer of vast promise whose quick observation, keen ear for dialogue, and lively narrative style were often obscured by his emotional involvement in his characters and themes. These books were self-centred, and Fitzgerald was regarding some of his own characteristics with an indulgent and self-pitying eye. With *The Great Gatsby* (1925) he leaps forward. Hitherto, the best passages in his novels had been islands in a swamp, but now he set his feet confidently on firm land.

Jay Gatsby, born Jimmy Gatz, is a self-made young man from the Middle West with an immense fortune derived from racketeering. Some years before, when he had been poor and obscure, he had fallen in love with Daisy, a beautiful girl from a prosperous family. Although in the meantime Daisy has married Tom Buchanan, an enormously wealthy young man, Gatsby is obsessed by his memories of their love affair. Daisy, though charming and affectionate, is shallow and selfish. In the end, whilst driving Gatsby's car, she knocks down and kills Myrtle Wilson, Tom's mistress. When the distracted husband calls on Tom to enquire about Myrtle's death, Tom sends him to Gatsby whom Wilson kills in revenge for his wife's death. Although Tom and Daisy have been responsible for Gatsby's death, they are too selfish and callous to show any compunction.

They were careless people, Tom and Daisy—they smashed up things and creatures and then retreated back into their money or their vast carelessness, or whatever it was that kept them together, and let other people clean up the mess they had made. . . .

The story develops in a succession of dramatic flashes that give the effect of a film-script. The use of the flashback, rather than a chronological sequence of events, strengthens this impression. In his earlier novels the principal character had been a projection of the novelist himself, and his problems had been partly Fitzgerald's own. Here he uses a narrator, Nick Carraway, who has much in common with himself, but attention is focussed on Gatsby, a man whom he can observe with detachment. Carraway sees, understands and pities Gatsby, but he does not identify himself with his strange friend. There is an intricate pattern of personal relationships between Tom and Daisy, Daisy and Gatsby, Myrtle and Tom, Nick and Jordan Baker, each reflecting on the others. From them all emerges a highly-coloured picture of a section of American society in the 1920s.

There are many things to admire in this novel—the pathos of Gatsby's funeral, the effective contrasting of three parties at Tom's house, Gatsby's neo-palatial residence and Myrtle's apartment, the comic automobile accident after Gatsby's party, the moment of realisation when Tom thinks he is about to lose both his wife and his mistress at the same time, the symbolism of the valley of ashes where Myrtle is killed with the lifeless eyes of Doctor Eckleburg dominating the scene from a hoarding. The style is light and clear, the observation of detail sharp, the ear for dialogue unerring, so that, despite the tragic climax which has been shadowed from the first, the effect is wryly comic, rather than grim.

By the mid-twenties Fitzgerald and Zelda were living a restless life, wandering extravagantly from place to place, from country to country, to France and Switzerland as well as the eastern states. Both had a feverish love of excitement, of gaiety, of wild parties under which Zelda's mind broke down and Fitzgerald found it difficult to concentrate on writing. He made several attempts to write another novel, but did not complete anything except short stories until the publication of *Tender is the Night* in 1934. Here Fitzgerald returns to the treatment in the form of a novel of the problem of his own life. Dick Diver, a young and talented American psychiatrist, takes an interest in the treatment of Nicole, a schizophrenic girl receiving treatment in a Swiss clinic. Nicole becomes dependent on Dick so that he marries her from mixed feelings of sympathy and fascination. He neglects his career so that he can give his time to Nicole until eventually he in his turn is dependent on her wealth for his way of life. He loses his self-respect, takes to drink, and sinks into failure and poverty whilst Nicole becomes the mistress of Tommy Barban whose strength, callousness and aggressiveness excite her. In the end, Nicole has drawn all Dick's strength of mind and character from him so that their roles are reversed. This was Fitzgerald's own favourite novel and there are excellent things in it, such as the period picture of the Riviera before it became a crowded summer-holiday resort. There is also a striking gallery of characters, more varied than in any of his other novels. It has never succeeded like *The Great Gatsby*, however, perhaps because the main theme of Dick's decay is often allowed to slip into the background. There are two versions of the novel, much the better being Fitzgerald's late revision which begins, not on the Riviera, but in the Swiss clinic where Nicole is a patient.

Fitzgerald, already disturbed by Zelda's mental deterioration, was further discouraged by the lukewarm reception of this novel. He spent some time in Hollywood as a script-writer, before he died in 1940 from a heart-attack brought on by his own dissipation and the stresses to which he was subjected. He left behind an unfinished novel, *The Last Tycoon*. In this Monroe Stahr, a film-producer with great energy, creative ability, integrity and leadership is ruined by a combination of his own pride and the hostility of a rival producer and a union leader. His life is complicated by two women, Kathleen, whom he loves but who marries another man, and Cecilia, the narrator, to whom he turns for consolation after Kathleen's marriage. The part that he completed and the draft of the rest shows this novel to be more ambitious and powerful than anything Fitzgerald had so far written, with several skilfully connected themes that he was particularly suited to develop. Once again, he was cheated when success was within his reach.

Frustrated ambition ran through his life and his novels. His temperament demanded not mere success, but an overwhelming triumph and universal acclaim. He wrote three essays, published in *The Crack-Up*, which showed how he failed in the moment when fulfilment was at hand.

Two forces warred within his personality, and the destructive force finally won, so that this man of abounding talent left behind him a number of short stories of varying merit, some revealing letters and autobiographical essays, and only three completed novels, two of them immature, one a masterpiece. Possibly he was given too much when he was too young.

Ernest Hemingway

THE novels of Evelyn Waugh often seem to be projections of his own life and personality. With ERNEST HEMINGWAY (1899–1962) the relationship between his life and his work is more complex: incidents and scenes from his own life are reproduced in his novels, and the leading characters have much in common with their creator; on the other hand, the code of conduct which runs through his work he also applied to himself, so that his life appears like a draft for one of his novels.

Hemingway has a consistent view of man and life. His principal characters are tough men whose appetite for danger leads them into situations where injury, wounds and death are almost inevitable. They are also sentimental men who form strong attachments to women or children, and these attachments make them equally vulnerable to emotional wounds. They pitch themselves into struggles that they cannot hope to win, but they show that, although a man must lose, he can lose with dignity and honour. On the surface Hemingway's novels seem perhaps to encourage immorality, for they deal with sexual promiscuity, ruthless killing, hard drinking, desertion from the Army, and smuggling. In fact, Hemingway had a strict moral code. Loyalty and courage are the great virtues, though they take unusual forms—a man is loyal to a woman he is not married to, and he may show great courage in deserting from the Army. The code is worked out emotionally, not intellectually; if what the hero does feels right to him, then it is right, even though it is opposed to the moral standards accepted in society. Following his emotions leads a man into strange and dangerous places, but he must not flinch from danger. Finally, death may be the only way in which he can show his loyalty.

Hemingway was born near Chicago, the son of a doctor who was a keen fisherman and hunter, and naturally initiated his son into these sports. At school Hemingway's eye was damaged whilst he was boxing, the first of many injuries he was to suffer. When he left school, instead of going to college, he obtained a post as reporter on the Kansas City *Star*. By giving a false age, he was able to join an American ambulance unit serving on the North Italian front where he was severely injured in the knee in July 1918. His experiences there provide the basis for *A Farewell to Arms*. After the war he returned to America where he worked as a newspaper man in the U.S.A. and Canada. In 1921 he was sent as a foreign correspondent for the Toronto *Star* to Paris, where he supported himself by journalism until the appearance of his novel, *The Sun Also Rises*, published in Britain as *Fiesta* (1926). The hero, Jake Barnes, sexually impotent through a wound received in the war, has a hopeless love affair with Lady Brett Ashley in Paris and Spain. Brett in particular and her circle represent the 'lost generation' which, reaching maturity during the war, has suffered the loss in the war of loved ones, disillusion, and the destruction of its ideals. Here we see the Hemingway theme of the mutilated man tormented by his own feelings.

His second novel, *A Farewell to Arms* (1929), established Hemingway's reputation. Frederic Henry, an American ambulance driver serving with the Italian Army, falls in love with a British nurse, Catherine Barkley, whilst he is recuperating from a wound in the knee. When he returns to the front, he is caught up in the Italian defeat and the disorderly retreat from Caporetto. He only just escapes execution by the Italian battle police as a suspected German spy, and decides to desert. He rejoins Catherine, who is now pregnant, dodges arrest, and escapes by rowing-boat to Switzerland with her, where he is interned. At this point their dangers appear to be over, but Catherine dies in giving birth to a still-born son. Even when a man is congratulating himself on his survival, fate keeps in wait a last bitter twist.

A Farewell to Arms showed war to be a messy business, not a glorious adventure. Men are killed without reason and without justice. This conception, commonplace enough now, was still a striking one in 1929. Hemingway made clear what soldiers thought and felt when they were wounded, when they were trying to escape from the enemy, when they suspected their comrades of treachery. Often a writer's style acts as a buffer between his feelings and the reader's grasp of them, but Hemingway had the good reporter's eye for telling detail and his power of plain statement. He strips away padding; in scenes of action the story moves quickly; the dialogue is terse, staccato, with the rhythms of speech. There is no attempt to heighten the dramatic effect by literary devices —once the story has gained momentum the characters move from crisis to crisis with violence always present or impending. The drama is in the events and does not need pointing:

> I watched the shore come close, then swing away, then come closer again. We were floating more slowly. The shore was very close now. I could see twigs on the willow bush. The timber swung slowly so that the bank was behind me and I knew we were in an eddy. We went slowly around. As I saw the bank again, very close now, I tried holding with one arm and kicking and swimming the timber toward the bank with the other, but I did not bring it any closer.

I was afraid we would move out of the eddy and, holding with one hand, I drew up my feet so they were against the side of the timber and shoved hard toward the bank. I could see the brush, but even with my momentum and swimming as hard as I could, the current was taking me away. I thought then I would drown because of my boots, but I thrashed and fought through the water, and when I looked up the bank was coming toward me, and I kept thrashing and swimming in a heavy-footed panic until I reached it. I hung to the willow branch and did not have strength to pull myself up but I knew I would not drown now. It had never occurred to me on the timber that I might drown. I felt hollow and sick in my stomach and chest from the effort, and I held to the branches and waited. When the sick feeling was gone I pulled in to the willow bushes and rested again, my arms around some brush, holding tight with my hands to the branches. Then I crawled out, pushed on through the willows and on to the bank. It was half-daylight and I saw no one. I lay flat on the bank and heard the river and the rain.

Here the reader can see clearly what happened and knows how Frederic Henry felt.

Hemingway has been criticised because his characterisation is sharp, rather than deep. In fact he is describing men's behaviour at a crisis point in which their past history and former personal relations have little relevance. Their reactions at the time to events are interesting and credible. His men are, however, much more convincing than his women, and in this novel Catherine is little more than an adolescent's erotic day-dream. Hemingway was so masculine in outlook that he seemed to see women as appurtenances to men.

His next two books were about bullfighting, *Death in the Afternoon* (1932), and big-game hunting, *The Green Hills of Africa* (1935). Neither is a novel; both are about the ritual killing of animals. Killing and dying were important parts of Hemingway's creed, and some of his books seem almost to create a liturgy about slaughter. His next novel was *To Have and Have Not* (1937) about a boat-owner called Harry Morgan who, in the depression, turns to smuggling to support his family. He is shot whilst he is helping a gang of bank-robbers to escape, and his final words are the moral to the story — 'One man alone ain't got — no chance.'

Hemingway's travels in Africa produced also two of his best short stories, *The Short Happy Life of Francis Macomber*, in which Macomber is shot dead by his wife just as he has freed himself from her domination, and *The Snows of Kilimanjaro*. When the Spanish Civil War broke out, Hemingway, whose sympathies were with the left-wing Republicans, went there as a war correspondent. He wrote a play called *The Fifth Column* in which a dissolute American journalist in Spain acts as a modern

Scarlet Pimpernel in helping the Republicans, but this was never successful on the stage. Perhaps it might have been remembered more clearly if it had not been eclipsed by Hemingway's finest novel, *For Whom the Bell Tolls* (1940). In this, Robert Jordan, an American college lecturer, has gone to Spain on a year's leave, which he is spending in helping the Republicans, especially by dynamiting trains and bridges. He now joins a group of guerrillas in the hills in order to blow up a bridge of some tactical importance. He falls in love with Maria, a Spanish girl, and spends three days with her whilst he is waiting to complete his mission. Pablo, the guerrilla leader, steals his detonators, but Jordan succeeds in blowing up the bridge. Whilst escaping he breaks his leg in a fall from his horse and he is left there to kill a Fascist officer and to be killed himself.

For Whom the Bell Tolls is a long novel, but Hemingway maintains the tension through the interplay of the several themes—the plan to blow up the bridge, the love story of Jordan and Maria, the jealousies between the Communist groups, the rivalry between Jordan and Pablo. Here the characterisation is fuller than in *A Farewell to Arms*. At times Hemingway uses a stream-of-consciousness technique in which the characters recall their past lives and throw light on their present attitudes and situations. There is also a wider range of characters, among them Pilar, Pablo's formidable wife, General Golz, the Russian, and Anselmo, Jordan's faithful guide. Maria's simplicity is natural enough in a girl with her background and history, and she serves, like Carmen, as a focus for passion and jealousy. The weakest part of the novel is perhaps her dialogue with Jordan, but otherwise Hemingway's writing is taut and vivid. This is the novel by which Hemingway is most likely to be remembered.

Across the River and into the Trees (1950) was a self-indulgent book in which Hemingway used the story of Colonel Richard Cantwell as an opportunity to express his views on a variety of subjects, notably the Hürtgen Forest offensive in the latter stages of the Second World War. Here Hemingway had accompanied American forces as a war correspondent and he had been appalled at the high rate of casualties sustained in a hopeless attack. Earlier in the war he had had a plan for luring U-boats to the surface by acting as a decoy and then destroying them. Fortunately for Hemingway he was unable to persuade the Navy to operate his scheme. Subsequently he flew with the RAF over many parts of Europe, took part in the invasion of Europe, and is supposed to have reached Paris many miles in front of the liberating forces. He interpreted his rôle of war correspondent very freely.

In 1954 Hemingway was awarded the Nobel Prize for Literature, the selection no doubt having been influenced by the publication of *The Old Man and the Sea* (1952). Santiago, an old Cuban fisherman, goes far out to sea after a long spell of bad luck in the hope of catching a large fish. There, after a long battle, he catches a marlin so huge that he cannot bring it on board but has to tie it to the boat and drag it home. On the way the marlin is attacked by sharks which, despite Santiago's heroic efforts to beat them off, eat the marlin and leave Santiago only with the skeleton of the fish. It is a short novel in which every word seems right. The story is full of fine things—the old man's relations with the young boy who both idolises and protects him; his respectful talks to the marlin after he has hooked it; his musings about the past.

It is also a story about death and courage. It shows that a brave creature can be killed, but not disgraced, and that a brave man can be brought to the limits of his endurance and enhance his pride and self-regard. The book can also be regarded as an allegory just as can *The Tempest.* Santiago the fisherman can be regarded as Hemingway the novelist making one last gesture, his spirit rising above past failures and the fatigue of age. Hemingway was not of course an old man, but he had had an eventful, trying life, punctuated by accidents, wounds and injuries. He had been obsessed by the idea of death and in the end he surrendered to it when, in 1962, he shot himself. His life and work can be summed up in one sentence he himself wrote: 'The world breaks everyone and afterwards many are strong at the broken places.'

William Faulkner

WILLIAM FAULKNER (1897–1962) drew a map of Yoknapatawpha County with the town of Jefferson in the middle and added the legend, 'William Faulkner, Sole Owner and Proprietor'. He lived most of his life and died in the town of Oxford in Lafayette County in Mississippi, on which Jefferson and Yoknapatawpha are based. As indissolubly as Hardy with Wessex and Trollope with Barsetshire is Faulkner linked with Yoknapatawpha, in which fifteen of his novels and most of his stories are set.

As with Hardy each novel is part of a grand design, a body of work which expresses a view of life the author has recognised and accepted from living in the area and from knowing the inhabitants and their families' roots in past generations. Yoknapatawpha is not merely the background of Faulkner's novels; it is the subject of them. The place and the people cannot be separated; if they had been born and brought up elsewhere with a different ancestry and heritage, Bayard Sartoris, Gavin Stevens, V. K. Ratliff, would be changed unrecognisably.

Faulkner has a strong sense of family as well as a strong sense of place. This feeling probably derives from his admiration for his great-grandfather, Colonel William Cuthbert Falkner (the novelist himself added the 'u' to the family name). The Colonel was twice tried for and acquitted of murder; he was a colonel in the Civil War, a railroad pioneer, a popular author, and finally the victim of a murderous attack by a former partner whom he had defeated in an election for the state legislature. This romantic figure appears in several of Faulkner's novels, as Colonel John Sartoris, as Thomas Sutpen in *Absalom, Absalom!* and as Lucius Quintus Carothers McCaslin in *Go Down, Moses*. In all his manifestations he is brave, impulsive, ruthless, and sexually assertive with both white and coloured women.

Faulkner knows that these men were responsible for much harshness and injustice, but they also built up their plantations, ruled their families and their slaves, applied their own code of living unhindered by legal processes, family claims, or moral scruples. As a result they achieved something in their lives. That way of life was destroyed by the Civil War, but though the props were knocked from under the old system nothing was put in their place. So Faulkner's novels often deal with decay and disintegration, with once honourable families running to seed, with negroes deprived of the protection of their white masters and oppressed, with share-croppers trying to scratch a living from the impoverished soil.

Faulkner's views are expressed by Gavin Stevens, an intelligent and humanitarian lawyer defending a negro on a charge of murdering a white man, in *Intruder in the Dust*:

> I'm defending Lucas Beauchamp. I'm defending Sambo from the North and East and West—the outlanders who will fling him decades back not merely into injustice but into grief and agony and violence too by forcing on us laws based on the idea that man's injustice to man can be abolished overnight by police. Sambo will suffer it of course; there are not enough of him yet to do anything else. And he will endure it, absorb it and survive because he is Sambo and has that capacity.

He believes that an alien way of life has been forced on the South and it is resented. The injustice to Sambo, who represents the negro oppressed by the white man, can only be cured by the lapse of time and the growing-up of a new way of life that will be accepted. Events since Faulkner's death have changed the basis of this argument.

Lucas Beauchamp is saved by Chick Mallison, a white boy, one part of whom admires the negro and cannot believe him to be guilty of murder, and the other part demands that the negro must accept his place—'We got to make him be a nigger first. He's got to admit he's a nigger. Then maybe we will accept him as he seems to intend to be accepted.' In the end Chick resolves the conflict within himself and thereby becomes a man.

Similar crises in the lives of young men and boys provide the themes of several other novels. In *The Sound and the Fury* Quentin Compson cannot face the fact of his sister's corruption and promiscuity and he kills himself. In *The Bear*, a short story that forms part of *Go Down, Moses*, Ike McCaslin goes with a hunting-party into the woods where he takes part in the killing of an old bear of mythical strength and cunning. This experience marks the beginning of his manhood too. In the woods Ike leaves behind the artificiality of civilised life and comes to recognise and admire the noble qualities of man, whether white or coloured, and of beast. Faulkner regarded his own periodic hunting expeditions as necessary for the renewal of his own vitality and expresses this belief in *The Bear*, the best of his short stories.

In the latter part of his career Faulkner wrote the Snopes trilogy: *The Hamlet* (1940), *The Town* (1957), and *The Mansion* (1959). In these stories Flem Snopes, son of a struggling share-cropper, devotes himself to the making of money and the gathering of power that goes with it, until, first, he dominates the hamlet of Frenchman's Bend, later the town of Jefferson. In the process he displaces Will Varer, who has hitherto dominated the life of Frenchman's Bend; marries his voluptuous daughter, Eula; supplants Major DeSpain as president of the Bank; becomes the wealthiest and most powerful man in the town. He does all this by giving other people the opportunity to make fools of themselves and taking advantage of their folly. He has no charm, limited intelligence, but great shrewdness; he is also single-minded in pursuit of money and power. Eula finally reveals that he is sexually impotent, so confirming the cause of the emotional sterility which has been evident throughout his career.

Flem represents the forces that have filled the vacuum in the life of the South caused by the destruction of its former way of life in the Civil War. His sterility, lack of feeling, obsession with material possessions, symbolise the new ruling principles. A man need not be clever, or attractive, or forceful, or heroic in stature to become master of a people who have lost their direction. In the end Flem is killed by his cousin, Mink Snopes, in revenge: when Mink was charged with murder, Flem made no attempt to help him, and later when Mink tried at the instigation of Flem to escape, he was caught and the sentence doubled. Although, on the face of things, Mink was the most miserable of men as a farmer, as a husband, as a convict, he preserves within himself something of the spirit of the old South—its passion, its vindictiveness, its loyalty, its ruthlessness, its code of conduct. He is therefore able to destroy Flem, a task which more powerful and more intelligent men had tried and been worsted. The contrast between the two men is most clearly brought out when Flem is talking to Mink about the murder of Jack Houston:

'You mean you ain't got any money? You mean to stand there and tell me he never had nothing in his pocket? Because I don't believe it. By God, I know better. I saw inside his purse that same morning. He never carried a cent less than fifty. . . .' The voice ceased, died. Then it spoke in a dawning incredulous amazement and no louder than a whisper: 'Do you mean to tell me you never even looked? *never even looked*?'

The Hamlet shows also another side of Faulkner—his love of a tall story, of humorous exaggeration. This characteristic is shared by a number of American writers, notably those who wrote about rural life in the vernacular, such as Mark Twain, Bret Harte and Artemus Ward. The horse-auction at the beginning of Book Four of *The Hamlet* is a particularly good example of Faulkner's powers of humorous narrative. It is a comedy of character as well as incident, with the personalities of Henry Armstid, Bookwright, the Texan, Eck Snopes, Mrs Armstid,

Ratliff and Mrs Littlejohn nicely contrasted with each other. Anyone who can read *Huckleberry Finn* can read this episode with enjoyment.

Faulkner's narrative methods were not often so clear, so it is perhaps as well to make the point that his novels are not obscure in places because he was unable to write clearly, any more than Picasso's forms are distorted because he cannot draw. There is plenty of evidence to the contrary. In *The Sound and the Fury* (1929), however, the story of the degradation of the Compson family is told through the minds of four narrators—Benjy, an imbecile; Quentin, his mind distracted on the day of his suicide; Jason, their callous and self-centred brother; and Dilsey, the family's negro housekeeper. Benjy confuses the past and present, jumping backwards and forwards in time as one experience reminds him of another; he also exists solely on the plane of physical feeling, sights, sounds, the taste of food, smells (Caddy, the sister he idolises, smells like trees) the feeling of going to bed or the burning sensation of the stove. He cannot think about his experiences. At first reading, his account is a mere jumble, for the pattern of events can be grasped only after reading the other three sections and then returning to Benjy's story. Quentin too is confused between past and present, obsessed by his sister's depravity and his own imminent death. Incidents in his account are beautifully clear—the negro at the crossing and Bland rowing on the river, for instance. But, for the most part, this novel demands an effort on the reader's part to understand it. Faulkner is not primarily telling a story: he is showing how these events affected the minds and wills of the four narrators. The technique he uses is the stream of consciousness, the flow of impressions within the mind, not an objective narrative.

As I Lay Dying (1930) also consists of a series of interior monologues, fifty-nine in number, distributed between at least fourteen characters, and all short. These monologues describe and comment on the death of Addie Bundren and the nightmare journey with the body to bury it at Jefferson. The death and the journey coincide with and intensify crises in the lives of Addie's husband and five children. Here the technique brings out vividly the motives for human behaviour, the emotional relationships between the characters, and the patterns of their lives.

A simpler variant of the same method is seen in *The Town*, where the story is told by three narrators, Ratliff, Gavin Stevens, and Charles Mallison. The reader is not intended to accept any of these accounts as the true one; they are expressions of events as they seemed to the individual. Faulkner would not have accepted the concept of final truth about human behaviour.

A similar contradiction exists in Faulkner's style. He often wrote simply and directly, especially in purely narrative passages. In description, however, he has a fondness for elaboration, for piling up detail, for a profusion of adjectives, which leads him into writing long, formless sentences. These can usually be disentangled, but sometimes they are confused both in grammar and in meaning. Here is an example from *The Hamlet:*

> When he passed beyond the house he saw it—the narrow high frame like an epicene gallows, two big absolutely static young women beside it, who even in that first glance postulated that immobile dreamy solidarity of statuary (this only emphasised by the fact that they both seemed to be talking at once and to some listener—or perhaps just circumambience—at a considerable distance and neither listening to the other at all) even though one of them had hold of the well-rope, her arms extended at full reach, her body bent for the down pull like a figure in a charade, a carved piece symbolising some terrific physical effort which had died with its inception, though a moment later the pulley began again its rusty plaint but stopped again almost immediately, as did the voices also when the second one saw him, the first one paused now in the obverse of the first attitude, her arms stretched downward on the rope and the two broad expressionless faces turning slowly in unison as he rode past.

It is odd that a writer who is sensitive to the idioms and rhythms of speech should sometimes be so insensitive in his own writing. Such phrases as 'solidarity of statuary' and 'the first one paused now in the obverse of the first attitude' are downright ugly.

Faulkner makes lavish use of the grotesque in some of his novels. Every family seems to have its idiot boy, and rape, incest and fratricide flourish. In a book like *Sanctuary* the means used to make good his thesis about human corruption seem excessive.

Faulkner had much in common with his great-grandfather. Like him, he was small in stature, quick-tempered, impulsive, determined to win attention. One embodied in his life, the other in his writings, the spirit of the place where they lived. Colonel Falkner owned land and a railroad in Lafayette County, but he was not, for all his fire and spirit, 'Sole Owner and Proprietor' as was, and still is, William Faulkner of the County of Yoknapatawpha.

Graham Greene

GRAHAM GREENE was born in 1904, a year later than Evelyn Waugh. Both men were brought up in the Church of England, went to Oxford, became journalists, were converted to Roman Catholicism, have written novels, and introduced their religious beliefs into their work. Despite all this their works are quite dissimilar. Waugh is a comic novelist, who writes with a sense of style in like manner. He is also an orthodox Catholic. Greene has written a number of unhappy novels about seedy characters, and his Catholicism is peculiar to himself. The principal characters seem to be intent on testing God's faith in man, rather than on expressing man's faith in God.

Greene has divided his work into 'entertainments' and novels. The entertainments he wrote mainly in the first part of his career whilst he was establishing himself as a writer. In them a man with no settled place in society is engaged in some illegal and dangerous enterprise which arouses the opposition of a wealthy and powerful capitalist. In the course of his adventures he meets a woman who feels both pity and love for him. After he has betrayed her, he himself is destroyed by the capitalist, accepting his death as inevitable and just. These principal characters are neither heroes nor villains. Life has outmanoeuvred them: they are friendless, live in depressing surroundings, and usually suffer from indigestion. Their spasms of idealism and loyalty cannot last against the pressure of their past deprivation and their present danger. The stories follow a formula, but Greene dangles these men and women expertly, there is a brisk succession of incidents, and the style is taut and nervous. They are accomplished entertainments after all in a fashion that has become increasingly popular since Greene stopped writing them in the forties. Now the seedy spy or counter-spy who is hunted down is the commonest figure in our suspense fiction.

To *Brighton Rock*, published in 1938, much of the atmosphere of the earlier stories clings, as the first sentence shows: 'Hale knew, before he had been in Brighton three hours, that they meant to murder him.' Hale is in fact murdered by Pinkie, a seventeen-year-old gangster, who is the central character of the story. In Pinkie, Greene created a vicious teenage delinquent who kills without anger. Although such youths have become a part of post-war criminal history, Greene's was an imaginative creation before the type became familiar in real life. Pinkie knows that he will be caught; he also knows as a Catholic that his soul is hopelessly damned by his crimes, but he cannot stop himself. He tricks Rose, a waitress who can connect him with the murder of Hale, into marrying him, though he is incapable of affection, and sex both nauseates and fascinates him. Although some of the crucial incidents in the story, such as Pinkie's meeting with Rose, are contrived, Greene does penetrate the personality of Pinkie, especially in exposing his inability to feel any warm emotion for another human being. The religious element in the story is less convincing to most people: for all Pinkie's sins, and despite his damnation, he was a Catholic. And at the end the priest tells Rose, 'A Catholic is more capable of evil than anyone. I think perhaps—because we believe in Him—we are more in touch with the devil than other people.' It is a strange distinction that only a Catholic can damn himself as utterly as Pinkie did.

In 1939 Greene visited Mexico to gather information about the persecution of the Catholic Church in some of the provinces there. He wrote a travel book, *The Lawless Roads*, about his experiences on this journey, and subsequently used them in his next novel, *The Power and the Glory* (1940). Like most of Greene's fiction this is a pursuit story. In this case the quarry is a priest, the last priest left in the province after the others have been driven out or killed or forced to abandon their faith. He is neither good nor brave nor attractive—he is a 'whiskey-priest', father of an illegitimate daughter, weak-willed and often afraid. We never get to know his name, nor that of his pursuer, the lieutenant who is ruthlessly determined to extirpate religion from the province. Twice the lieutenant has the priest in his power, but fails to recognise him. We know that the third time will come and that there will be no escape this time. The priest has known this from the beginning, when, in order to attend a sick woman, he misses the boat that would have taken him to safety. 'I shall miss it then. I am meant to miss it.' Later he is able to leave the province and to act as a parish priest again in security. He is lured back, however, by a half-caste he knows will betray him, in order to hear the dying confession of an American criminal. When he arrives, the criminal does not confess and the lieutenant is waiting for him.

The theme of the novel is Greene's constant query—damnation or salvation? The priest dies in a state of sin, for Don José, who has been terrified into renouncing his priesthood, refuses to hear his confession. He knows that he is weak and sinful and denies that he is a martyr: 'Oh no. Martyrs are not like me. They don't think all the time—if I had drunk more brandy I shouldn't be so afraid.'

The pictorial element in *The Power and the Glory* is much stronger than in Greene's other novels, the dialogue much sparser. One of his weaknesses has been a fumbling for the idiom which will convince the reader of a character's background and personality. Perhaps we find it impossible to place his characters in society because they do not talk like anyone we should recognise. The sense of place in this novel is marked in passages like this:

At sunset on the second day they came out on to a wide plateau covered with short grass: an odd grove of crosses stood up blackly against the sky, leaning at different angles—some as high as twenty feet, some not much more than eight. They were like trees that had been left to seed. The priest stopped and stared at them: they were the first Christian symbols he had seen for more than five years publicly exposed—if you could call this empty plateau in the mountains a public space. No priest could have been concerned in the strange rough group; it was the work of Indians and had nothing in common with the tidy vestments of the Mass and the elaborately worked out symbols of the liturgy. It was like a short cut to the dark and magical heart of the faith—to the night when the graves opened and the dead walked.

During the war Greene worked in a Government department in Sierra Leone, the setting of *The Heart of the Matter* (1948). This tells how Scobie, the Deputy Commissioner, destroys himself by his sentimental pity for others—for a Portuguese captain; for his wife; for Helen, his mistress. Although he cannot bear to hurt people, he puts himself into a position where he must hurt either his wife or Helen. As he cannot extricate himself from his dilemma, he commits suicide. Greene has admitted in an article in *The Sunday Times* (16.1.66) that the book has been misunderstood; he says: 'All these discussions about whether Scobie stood a chance of salvation after his suicide—not what I meant at all. I meant Scobie as an object lesson, if I "meant" him to be anything at all, showing how awful pity is—I mean pity as opposed to compassion—and how it is really the expression of a kind of pride. But everybody seemed to take the book as the story of a good man driven to self-destruction by his dreadful wife. Well, as I say, it must be my fault.'

And in part it is Greene's own fault. In the last scene, after Scobie's death, his wife and Father Rank discuss his fate and God's mercy, the priest implying that salvation for him remained a hope. Louise is made so demanding, Scobie so anxious to please her, that the balance of the book as Greene intended it is disturbed.

Scobie asked little of life: his office was as bare as he could make it; he did not seek Helen's love or his wife's return; he was not hurt when passed over for promotion. He was content to be dull and a failure; other people forced what they regarded as the prizes of life upon him, and he could not cope with them. Scobie is a proof of something Greene had written in an earlier book: 'You can't cure success. Success is a mutilation of the natural man.'

Querry in *A Burnt-Out Case* is another man who has been mutilated by success. He arrives at a leper village in the Belgian Congo, burnt out by his success as an architect and as a womaniser in Europe. His moral condition is paralleled by the physical condition of his servant, Deo Gratias, whose body leprosy has ravaged and mutilated before leaving him, a burnt-out case. 'I want nothing,' Querry says. 'I suffer from nothing. I no longer know what suffering is.' Deo Gratias awakens his interest in others again and he helps in the work of the colony, particularly in a building project. He is told, 'Sometimes I think that the search for suffering and the remembrance of suffering are the only means we have to put ourselves in touch with the whole human condition. With suffering we become part of the Christian myth.' Like other Greene characters Querry does suffer and die for the mistakes of others. He is shot by Rycker, the husband of a young woman for whom he had felt sorry. Like Scobie his own pity is the cause of his destruction. Instead of the success that was thrust upon the unwilling Scobie, Querry has virtues foisted on him by other people—Father Thomas thinks he is a good Catholic at heart, Parkinson the popular journalist thinks he has gone to the Congo to sacrifice himself for the good of others, Marie thinks she is in love with him. The absurdity of the illusions that have led to his death strike Querry at the end: '"Absurd," Querry said, "this is absurd or else . . ." but what alternative, philosophical or psychological, he had in mind they never knew.' It was absurd that he, a burnt-out case, unable to feel suffering or sympathy, should have been killed by a jealous husband of the girl he had pitied; or else, there had been a plan in his life which he realised only at the moment of death. Querry was a lapsed Catholic and the novel ends with the same question as Greene's other novels. For all his sins and for all his denials had Querry found salvation at the end?

Greene has been writing novels about the adulteries of lapsed Catholics in hot climates for over twenty years, and through them posing questions about the nature of good and evil. In his latest novel *The Comedians* he asks whether harmless neutralism is better than active commitment to an evil cause. As Dr Magiot puts it: 'Catholics and Communists have committed great crimes, but at least they have not stood aside like an established society, and been indifferent. I would rather have blood on my hands than water like Pilate.' The question is different in *The Comedians*, but the elements in the novel can be traced in his earlier work.

George Orwell

WAUGH was a believer in aristocracy, the principle that some people are superior to others and better fitted therefore to rule and to influence others. His life in the main followed the pattern of an English gentleman's: public school, Oxford, country landowner. GEORGE ORWELL (1903–50), on the other hand, led an uncomfortable life in which he never found his niche in society. He was born Eric Hugh Blair in Bengal where his father was a minor official in the Indian Customs and Excise service. The name he chose to write his books under was more solid and more English in sound; unconventional as his life and beliefs were, one side of him seems to have longed to conform to traditional English virtues, such as taking up the white man's burden, and English pursuits like hunting and fishing. From his days at preparatory school, however, he was often an outsider; there, he was accepted on reduced fees and was poorer than the rest of the boys. He was taken into the school because it was hoped he would do it credit by winning a scholarship to a public school. In fact, he won two and chose to go to Eton where, despite his ability, he did little work and failed to distinguish himself. Instead of going to Oxford or Cambridge, Orwell served from 1922 to 1927 in Burma in the Indian Imperial Police. Later he wrote two fine essays, *Shooting an Elephant* and *A Hanging*, about incidents in his career there. These are marked by a power of extraordinarily clear, concrete description which serves as a basis for his penetrating comments on the events. In 1934 he published a novel, *Burmese Days*, in which are mingled a revulsion against the kind of life led by the English in Burma and a fascination with some aspects of it such as hunting trips.

When Orwell came home on leave, he determined not to return to this kind of life. Instead, he went to Paris with little money or prospect of earning a living, and lived for nearly two years in acute poverty. When he returned to England after borrowing his fare, he had to live there in doss-houses for a time until he found work. Out of these experiences he wrote *Down and Out in Paris and London* (1933), a rather scrappy book but with vivid sketches of the life he had led. Back in England he wrote two more novels, *A Clergyman's Daughter* and *Keep the Aspidistra Flying*, both about characters cut off from their normal lives and failing to adapt themselves to their unfamiliar circumstances. Gordon Comstock, the hero of *Keep the Aspidistra Flying*, gives up a comfortable job so that he can write, but is glad eventually to get married and lead a dull, secure, suburban life. These two aspirations co-existed in Orwell himself.

Orwell's pictures of poverty in *Down and Out in Paris and London* encouraged Victor Gollancz, the publisher, to commission a book from him on the life of the poor in industrial England. This appeared in 1937 as *The Road to Wigan Pier*, a book which shows more sympathy for the unemployed miner than understanding of his outlook. By the time it was published Orwell had gone to Spain to write about the Spanish Civil War. Orwell often thought that it was not enough merely to observe and write about an experience, but that it was necessary to share the experience. As a result he joined the Republican Army and was soon wounded and disillusioned. Although he believed that the left-wing had justice on its side, he soon realised that much of the propaganda it put out was false, and that different factions on the left, especially the Communists, spent more energy on persecuting each other than on fighting their real enemies. Hemingway described these intrigues also in *For Whom the Bell Tolls*. Orwell's disgust came out later in both *Animal Farm* and *1984*. He wrote *Homage to Catalonia* (1938), an honest piece of reporting of the Spanish War, which both sides rejected because it was honest.

During the Second World War Orwell, unfit for the Army through his wound in the throat, worked for the B.B.C. in its overseas services. He also wrote his finest book, *Animal Farm*, published in 1945, which he described as a fairy story. In fact, it is an animal fable which points two morals, one universal, the other topical. It exposes the corruptibility of man, showing how the reformer abuses power when he seizes it from the tyrant, and how in a revolutionary situation the most ruthless man will oust his colleagues as rivals, and exploit the workers by cruelty and lies. The parallel with Russia was so obvious and unwelcome at a time when Russia was an ally that Orwell had considerable difficulty in getting the book published. When it did appear, it was an immediate success, the first of Orwell's books to sell in any number, though he had enjoyed a literary reputation for some years.

In an essay about Swift, Orwell said, '*Gulliver's Travels*, in particular, is a book which it seems impossible for me to grow tired of.' *Animal Farm* has many of the virtues of Gulliver: the appeal of the simple narrative, the sharply-defined descriptions, the implicit comment on the folly and villainy of mankind, the effect of complete naturalness once the opening situation has been accepted. In one respect *Animal Farm* is finer than *Gulliver* — the characterisation is more varied, with Boxer, the loyal, hard-working cart-horse, Squealer, the dictator's yes-man, Benjamin, the donkey, intent on survival, and Mollie, the vain white mare.

The fable was particularly suited to Orwell's talents. Human relationships were the weak point of several of his novels, but the animals, each representing one quality, corresponded to his stern, moral view of life. *Animal Farm* enabled him to present politics and economics in terms of morality with great effect. He was so clear-sighted and wrote such lucid prose that he was able to create a detailed and convincing picture of a strange world. It is a book that can be enjoyed on different levels: as a child's story, as a morality, as a political satire. It has one other uncommon virtue—brevity. In ninety pages it says all that a powerful mind has to say on an important aspect of life.

With his overpowering sense of duty, Orwell drove himself hard, making no allowances for physical weakness and the effect of wartime conditions. He undermined his health and from 1947 on he was a sick man suffering from tuberculosis. He went on writing, and in 1949 published *1984*, a horrific vision of a possible future. In this book Orwell projected into the future the austerity, shoddiness and sheer ugliness of wartime Britain and the tyranny, ruthlessness and dishonesty of the Communist state which had come to power in so many countries in Eastern Europe. We are heading for a state, Orwell says, in which the individual will be ground to dust by the machinery of the one-party state, when man will be unable to distinguish between truth and lies, when the ordinary human emotions will have been crushed out of existence. Winston Smith, an official in the Ministry of Truth, whose work is to falsify history in the interests of the Party, meets a clerk, Julia, and each is attracted to the other. They re-create an individual life for a short time and plan to revolt against the Party. Inevitably they are discovered, are tortured, betray each other, and die. Winston Smith and Julia are the weakest part of the novel, for they lack faith and vitality. The machinery of the one-party state is, however, very impressive: Newspeak which twists the meaning of words to the Party's purposes so that 'peace' means 'war'; the Two Minutes Hate; Big Brother; the telescreens watching over each room. The criticism that there is nothing new in this apparatus of tyranny seems misconceived, for Orwell was saying that this is the way we are going now, that we were already headed for the destination of 1984 by following the direction in which 1948 was pointing. It is a depressing book; Orwell said, 'It wouldn't have been so gloomy if I hadn't been so ill.' But it is also a powerful book, well worth reading alongside Aldous Huxley's *Brave New World*.

Orwell died in 1950 at the age of forty-six from a haemorrhage at a time when, after years of struggle, he had established himself as a writer of distinction. He sacrificed himself to his own sense of duty. He left behind in *Animal Farm* a masterpiece of its kind, several interesting novels, some honest autobiographical works, and a number of intelligent and vigorously-written essays. He was not meant to live to a comfortable old age.

C. Day Lewis, Louis MacNeice, Stephen Spender, W. H. Auden

DURING the first half of the 1930s people in England lived in the shadow of the great depression with its accompaniment of industrial decay, unemployment and poverty. Rearmament took the edge off unemployment in the second half of the decade, but emphasised the growing threat of Fascism and the imminence of war. Many intellectuals, deeply disturbed by the troubles of their times, saw in Marxist Communism the solution to these problems. Amongst them was a group of poets who came together at Oxford just before 1930. They included C. DAY LEWIS (born 1904), LOUIS MACNEICE (1907–1963), STEPHEN SPENDER (born 1909); and they looked to WYSTAN HUGH AUDEN (born 1907) as their leader. They all accepted MacNeice's statement that 'a poet should be able-bodied, fond of talking, a reader of the newspapers, capable of pity and laughter, informed in economics, appreciative of women, involved in personal relationships, actively interested in politics, susceptible to physical impressions.'

Certainly they were interested in the world as they knew it, its sights, its people, its crises. The subjects of poetry were not only the picturesque and impressive aspects of life, noble or tragic deeds, inspiring characters. Auden describes a scene of industrial squalor:

> Get there if you can and see the land you once were proud to own,
> Though the roads have almost vanished and the expresses never run:
> Smokeless chimneys, damaged bridges, rotting wharves and choked canals,
> Tramlines buckled, lying on their sides across the rails;
> Power-stations locked, deserted, since they drew the boiler fires,
> Pylons falling or subsiding, trailing dead high-tension wires.

Spender also has a poem about pylons,

> Those pillars,
> Bare like nude, giant girls that have no secret.
> Like whips of anger
> With lightning's danger
> There runs the quick perspective of the future.

It was a real world in which poverty existed with unemployment, as in Day Lewis's 'Carol':

Oh hush thee, my baby,
Thy cradle's in pawn:
No blankets to cover thee
Cold and forlorn.
The stars in the bright sky
Look down and are dumb
At the heir of the ages
Asleep in a slum.

The hooters are blowing,
No heed let him take;
When baby is hungry
'Tis best not to wake.
Thy mother is crying,
Thy dad's on the dole:
Two shillings a week is
The price of a soul.

This child's elder brothers and sisters appear in 'An Elementary School Classroom' by Stephen Spender:

Far far from gusty waves, these children's faces
Like rootless weeds the torn hair round their paleness;
The tall girl with her weighed-down head; the paper-
seeming boy with rat's eyes; the stunted unlucky heir
Of twisted bones, reciting a father's gnarled disease,
His lesson from his desk. At back of the dim class
One unnoted, mild and young: his eyes live in a dream
Of squirrel's game, in tree room, other than this.

The right of the wretched and the poor to a more satisfying life was affirmed by Louis MacNeice:

It is so hard to imagine
A world where the many would have their chance without
A fall in the standard of intellectual living
And nothing left that the highbrow cared about.
Which fears must be suppressed. There is no reason for thinking
That, if you give a chance to people to think or live,
The arts of thought or life will suffer and become rougher
And not return more than you could ever give.

The difficulty lay in a lack of communication between the intellectuals and those whom they wanted to help. The poets were writing about something they had observed from the outside, not experienced themselves. Auden is aware of this in 'A Communist to Others':

We cannot put on airs with you
The fears that hurt you hurt us too
        Only we say
That like all nightmares these are fake
If you would help us we could make
Our eyes to open, and awake
        Shall find night day.

On you our interests are set
Your sorrow we shall not forget
        While we consider
Those who in every country town
For centuries have done you brown,
But you shall see them tumble down
        Both horse and rider.

To this generation the testing-ground for their beliefs seemed to be Spain where the Civil War brought about a confrontation between the left-wing and Fascism. In this situation the concerns of yesterday appeared trivial, and the shape of the future was to be determined by the outcome of the Spanish war:

Yesterday the installation of dynamos and turbines,
The construction of railways in the colonial desert;
        Yesterday the classic lecture
On the origin of mankind. But today the struggle.

Yesterday the belief in the absolute value of Greece,
The fall of the curtain upon the death of a hero;
        Yesterday the prayer to the sunset
And the adoration of madmen. But today the struggle.

. . . .

Tomorrow the rediscovery of romantic love,
The photographing of ravens; all the fun under
        Liberty's masterful shadow;
Tomorrow the hour of the pageant-master and the musician,

The beautiful roar of the chorus under the dome;
Tomorrow the exchanging of tips on the breeding of terriers,
        The eager election of chairmen
By the sudden forest of hands. But today the struggle.

The struggle, Auden concludes, will not be settled by fate, but by human will: there would be no reversal of the result because it was the wrong result:

> The stars are dead. The animals will not look.
> We are left alone with our day, and the time is short, and
>   History to the defeated
> May say alas but cannot help or pardon.

Amongst the other fine poems that Spain produced, two of the finest are 'A Letter from Aragon' by John Cornford and 'Ultima Ratio Regum' by Stephen Spender, both to be found in *Poetry of the Thirties* edited by Robin Skelton.

In the end Spain proved not to be the life-and-death conflict that the poets, the politicians and the idealists thought it would be, but a skirmish on a badly-chosen battlefield. In 'September 1, 1939' Auden has lost faith in political solutions to man's problems and states that love for one's fellow-man is the hope of the world:

> All I have is a voice
> To undo the folded lie,
> The romantic lie in the brain
> Of the sensual man-in-the-street
> And the lie of Authority
> Whose buildings grope the sky:
> There is no such thing as the State
> And no one exists alone;
> Hunger allows no choice
> To the citizen or the police;
> We must love one another or die.

Since 1939 Auden has lived most of his time in New York, though with regular visits to England and Austria. Although he reversed the direction of Eliot's voyage across the Atlantic, he also has been converted to Anglicanism, and has written three long poems about his spiritual journey. His later poems have been more sober than those written in the 1930s for which he remains best-known.

Much of Auden's best verse is not concerned with politics. In fact it is possible to argue that his pre-occupation with politics, his obsessive topicality in the thirties, led him to use his talents wastefully. He has written grave and touching love-lyrics such as:

> Lay your sleeping head, my love,
> Human on my faithless arm. . . .

The best of his satires are directed against the whole trend of modern life; such works as 'Song for the New Year' and 'The Unknown Citizen' are not comments on individual events. These show both his technical virtuosity and his intellectual high spirits:

> I shall come, I shall punish, the Devil be dead,
> I shall have caviare thick on my bread
> I shall build myself a cathedral for home,
> With a vacuum cleaner in every room.
>
> I shall ride on the front in a platinum car,
> My features shall shine, my name shall be star:
> Day long and night long the bells I shall peal
> And down the long street I shall turn the cart wheel.

The same qualities are seen also in *The Ascent of F6* (1936), a verse-play he wrote in collaboration with his friend, Christopher Isherwood. The mixture of narrative, symbolism, political ideas, Freudian psychology and social satire is too rich for most digestions, but the brief sketches of human types are often effective. Auden also has a gift for narrative verse, as in the well-known ballad beginning thus:

> O what is that sound which so thrills the ear
>   Down in the valley drumming, drumming?
> Only the scarlet soldiers, dear,
>   The soldiers coming.

Auden's talent is so obviously abundant and varied that his acceptance as their natural leader by his contemporaries causes no surprise. He is an intensely interesting personality, and in his best work he seems to be observing his own mind and emotions with an intimate knowledge and at the same time a detachment that is at least tinged with irony. He thinks of other people—except Isherwood—in the mass and conceives politics in abstract terms. His true subject is himself and it seems regrettable that at times he has cast round for less interesting ones.

C. Day Lewis expressed most vividly in 'The Conflict' the precarious situation of the poet whose instinct was to shed all care and sing, but whose reason told him that he must act in support of his ideals:

> Singing I was at peace,
> Above the clouds, outside the ring;
> For sorrow finds a swift release in song
> And pride its poise.

Yet living here,
As one between two massing powers I live
Whom neutrality cannot save
Nor occupation cheer.

None such shall be left alive:
The innocent wing is soon shot down
And private wars fade in the blood-red dawn
Where two worlds strive.

Like Auden, Lewis wrote lyrical as well as topical and satirical verse. *From Feathers to Iron* is a sequence of poems tracing his own development through his experience of love, marriage and parenthood. He describes the joy he feels when he knows his wife is to have a baby; Nature joins in proclaiming the good news:

Today the almond tree turns pink,
The first flush of the spring;
Winds loll and gossip through the town
Her secret whispering.

Now too the bird must try his voice
Upon the morning air;
Down drowsy avenues he cries
A novel great affair.

He has this gift of taking images from Nature to give palpable form to his ideas. He has also a sensitiveness to the English scene, particularly to the shapes and colours of the sky:

You that love England, who have an ear for her music,
The slow movement of clouds in benediction,
Clear arias of light thrilling over her uplands,
Over the chords of summer sustained peacefully;
Ceaseless the leaves' counterpoint in a west wind lively,
Blossom and river rippling loveliest allegro,
And the storms of wood strings brass at year's finale:
Listen. Can you not hear the entrance of a new theme?

Here the metaphor linking scenery with music is sustained in gracefully flowing verse. Although in his earlier work, notably *The Magnetic Mountain* (1933)—the mountain symbolised man's quest for truth—he came under the influence of Auden in style and ideas, his natural bent was probably to this kind of cool and elegant lyric.

Lewis is descended from Oliver Goldsmith and has a little of his ancestor's literary versatility, for in addition to poetry he has written a number of detective stories under the name of Nicholas Blake. The economics of authorship are such that these have probably brought him far more money than his poetry.

On the death of John Masefield in 1967 Lewis was appointed Poet Laureate.

Stephen Spender's socialism was based not on abstract ideas of justice and equality, but on his own emotional reactions; pity, admiration, hope. He is the most rhetorical of this group of poets, invoking the reader to share his feelings, directing him by questions to respond in the same way. In a poem which begins, 'I think continually of those who were truly great', he writes:

> Near the snow, near the sun, in the highest fields
> See how these names are fêted by the waving grass
> And by the streamers of white cloud
> And whispers of wind in the listening sky.
> The names of those who in their lives fought for life,
> Who wore at their hearts the fire's centre.
> Born of the sun they travelled a short while toward the sun
> And left the vivid air signed with their honour.

There is a vigour here of both language and imagination different from anything in Auden or Lewis.

After the war the sufferings of the Jews in the Nazi extermination camps roused him to write 'Memento':

> Remember the blackness of that flesh
> Tarring the bones with a thin varnish
> Belsen Theresenstadt Buchenwald where
> Faces were a clenched despair
> Knocking at the bird-song-fretted air.
>
> Their eyes sunk jellied in their holes
> Were held up to the sun like begging bowls
> Their hands like rakes with finger-nails of rust
> Scratched for a little kindness from the dust.
> To many, in its beak, no dove brought answer.

More than his comrades, Spender wrote from emotional conviction.

In 'The Pylons', 'The Express', 'The Landscape near an Aerodrome', Spender drew on the products of an industrial civilisation for his material.

Louis MacNeice had the perceptive eye of a reporter observing man in his habitat. He describes 'Sunday Morning' in a suburb:

> Down the road someone is practising scales,
> The notes like little fishes vanish with a wink of tails,
> Man's heart expands to tinker with his car
> For this is Sunday morning, Fate's great bazaar. . . .

He talks about the many kinds of readers who use 'The British Museum Reading Room':

> Cranks, hacks, poverty-stricken scholars,
> In pince-nez, period hats or romantic beards
>   And cherishing their hobby or their doom,
> Some are too much alive and some are asleep
> Hanging like bats in a world of inverted values,
> Folded up in themselves in a world which is safe and silent:
>   This is the British Museum Reading Room.

These pictures are bright and clear with details that catch the attention. The verse is fluid, the style lucid, often witty. MacNeice saw plainly enough the emptiness of the materialistic world in which he lived, but he was never convinced of the Utopia which socialism promised to bring. He was a classical scholar and had the restraint and the scepticism of an eighteenth-century writer. The latter part of his career was spent largely in writing for radio, for which he wrote some effective poetic drama.

Although these four poets are remembered together as Communist poets of the 1930s, they all turned away from their common faith. Auden became a Christian, the others wrote poetry less often afterwards and usually on non-political themes. No one can know whether they would have been greater poets during their most productive period if their minds and hearts had been engaged by other ideas and feelings.

Dylan Thomas

AUDEN and his circle dominated the English poetic scene in the 1930s. The poetry regarded as characteristic of their work, though not necessarily the truest to their individual gifts, expresses their views on topical events and subjects in a conversational style. It was the conversation of intimates who understood each other's allusions and who shared the same social, political and intellectual background. Their work was not wholly cerebral, for conditions like widespread poverty and events such as the Spanish Civil War stirred deep feelings, though their enthusiasms and hatreds were often for concepts rather than for individuals.

A reaction was bound to come. DYLAN THOMAS (1914–1953) used poetry to release emotion in a flood of images. He defined his own poetry in these words: 'A poem by itself needs a host of images. I make one image . . . let it breed another, let that image contradict the first, make, of the third image out of the other two together, a fourth contradictory image, and let them all, within my imposed formal limits, conflict.' A poet who calls up a host of images, some contradictory and conflicting, takes the risk that his readers will not be able to follow the leaps of his own imagination, and that they will be baffled by what sometimes looks to them like wilful obscurity. If a host is to be effective, it needs marshalling. In these verses there is a central idea worked out through compatible images:

> The force that through the green fuse drives the flower
> Drives my green age; that blasts the roots of trees
> Is my destroyer.
> And I am dumb to tell the crooked rose
> My youth is bent by the same wintry fever.
>
> The force that drives the water through the rocks
> Drives my red blood; that dries the mouthing streams
> Turns mine to wax.
> And I am dumb to mouth unto my veins
> How at the mountain spring the same mouth sucks.
>
> The hand that whirls the water in the pool
> Stirs the quicksand; that ropes the blowing wind
> Hauls my shroud sail.
> And I am dumb to tell the hanging man
> How of my clay is made the hangman's line.

There are twin principles of life and death at work in Nature and in the poet himself—life and death come from the same source. Notice also how precisely Thomas observes the 'imposed formal limits' of his stanza. Although he was often prodigal of words, especially adjectives, and tropes, his management of metre and verse-form was careful and accomplished. This poem makes its impact, but it is difficult without an interpreter to make anything coherent of these lines:

> She makes for me a nettle's innocence
> And a silk pigeon's guilt in her proud absence,
> In the molested rocks the shell of virgins,
> The frank, closed pearl, the sea-girl's lineaments.
> Glint in the staved and siren-printed caverns,
> Is maiden in the shameful oak, omens
> Whalebed and bulldance, the gold bush of lions
> Proud as a sucked stone and huge as sandgrains.

The consciousness of death we saw in the first of these poems haunted Thomas. His most eloquent poems are about death: 'Do not go gentle into that Good Night', a protest against death; 'And Death Shall Have No Dominion' and 'A Refusal to Mourn the Death, by Fire, of a Child in London', both denials of the supremacy of death; 'After the Funeral', a tribute to a dead Welsh woman, Ann Jones, in which he says that the force of the personality he remembers is so strong that she almost calls back to life 'a stuffed fox and a stale fern' in the room where the funeral party has gathered:

> These cloud-sopped, marble hands, this monumental
> Argument of the hewn voice, gesture and psalm
> Storm me for ever over her grave until
> The stuffed lung of the fox twitch and cry Love
> And the strutting fern lay seeds on the black sill.

Even in 'Fern Hill', a poem celebrating the delight of childhood, full of light and colour, gay in movement and mood, death casts its shadow across the last three verses.

Thomas's poetry is also full of sexual symbols, as in 'Light Breaks Where No Sun Shines' and in the 'Ten Sonnets', which are an interpretation of Christ's life in Freudian terms. Those likely to be offended by it will understand only snatches of the sequence.

In addition to his poetry Thomas wrote some lively and amusing prose works, most of them autobiographical in a fantastic manner. *Portrait of the Artist as a Young Dog* (1940) is perhaps the most interesting. Thomas's own comment on one of his prose books is in some measure true of them all: 'a mixture of Oliver Twist, Little Dorrit, Kafka, Beachcomber, and good old three-adjectives-a-penny, belly-churning Thomas, the Rimbaud of Cwmdonkin Drive.' He reached his widest audience with the radio production of *Under Milk Wood, A Play for Voices.* This is a picture of a small Welsh town peopled by touchingly articulate eccentrics through one day of its existence. Once heard, it remains a permanent part of one's memory with characters such as Captain Cat, Polly Garter, Ogmore Pritchard, and Gossamer Beynon as distinctive as those in a Dickens novel. Polly Garter's songs have a wistful, childlike quality too as a bonus. This is surely the finest work yet written for radio.

In every generation there seems to be one writer who captures the attention of the public for reasons that have little to do with his work. In 1914 it was Rupert Brooke; in the latter part of his life and in the years that followed his early death Dylan Thomas was such a writer. Extravagant claims have been made for the poetry of a picturesque figure, and others in reaction against this adulation have reduced him to a dwarf. His work is very uneven; often he drove words and images too hard and his poetry became so dense in texture that it blocked the passage of feeling and meaning to the reader. Where he let the light in, however, in a handful of poems, he wrote superbly and in a manner that is uniquely his. If these poems were lost, we should have nothing with which we could replace them. There are not many poets of whom one can say that.

PART THREE: 1945 Onwards

Arthur Miller

ONE of the first playwrights to attract attention after the end of the Second World War was an American, ARTHUR MILLER (born 1915). His first successful play, *All My Sons* (1947), arose out of the war. The title is taken from a speech by the main character of the play, Joe Keller, owner of an engineering factory, who has sent out defective engine-parts for use in American bombers during the war. At the time he was able to shift responsibility on to his partner who has been jailed, but after the war his guilt is brought home to him by his own family, particularly by his dead son, Larry. Also a pilot, he had realised his father's guilt and had deliberately crashed his plane as a mark of his contrition and despair at the deaths of twenty-one of his fellow airmen. Keller at first defended his action:

> Who worked for nothin' in that war? When they work for nothin', I'll work for nothin'. Did they ship a gun or a truck outa Detroit before they got their price? Is that clean? It's dollars and cents, nickels and dimes; war and peace, it's nickels and dimes, what's clean?

Finally he realises that his duty is not merely to himself and his family:

> Sure, he was my son. But I think to him they were all my sons. And I guess they were, I guess they were.

Keller shoots himself.

Most of Miller's plays are American tragedies which involve a criticism of the standards of American society. Here the attack is upon the businessman, the capitalist, who puts his profits before the lives of others.

Miller's next play, *Death of a Salesman*, was more ambitious, both in theme and technique. The central figure, Willy Loman, a sixty-three year old commercial traveller, also kills himself. His life has been devoted to selling, never questioning the necessity to produce and sell. Now he is old and unsuccessful, there is no place for him in the firm he has worked for or even in the society he has lived in. He realises he has spent his life serving a system which is worthless and has no care for the individual. The play is a condemnation of American business, and it was commonly regarded as the tragedy of a typical American. It was less successful in Britain, largely because Willy's assumptions are not shared by most British people: his faith in a system, his loyalty to and affection for his firm are not emotions that British people feel. The tragedy therefore loses much of its poignancy.

In *Death of a Salesman* the action jumps backward and forward in time, here and there in place, reflecting the breaking-down of order in Willy Loman's mind. This device has been called 'expressionism', but the term is used loosely to indicate an abandonment of realism, the use of the resources of the stage not to reflect real life but to emphasise a theme or intensify an emotion.

One of the main themes of the play is Willy's relationship with his two irresponsible, unsuccessful sons, the same situation that exists in O'Neill's *Long Day's Journey into Night*. A comparison of the two plays is wholly in favour of O'Neill, partly because he makes the situation more credible, mainly because the dialogue is so much better written.

In the early 1950s Senator Joseph McCarthy rocked America by his accusations of widespread Communism in the State Department and Civil Service and by his persecution of anyone against whom he could work up a charge of left-wing or even radical sympathies. Amongst those he attempted to bring under his examination was Arthur Miller. It was clear both from his associations and from his plays that Miller thought that the American way of life demanded reform, often denied justice to the individual, and that he favoured radical and left-wing ideas. As a protest against the witch-hunting of McCarthyism he wrote *The Crucible*: 'I saw accepted the notion that conscience was no longer a private matter, but one of state administration. I saw men handing conscience to other men and thanking other men for the opportunity of doing so.'

Miller found a parallel between the activities of McCarthy and the Salem witch-trials by religious fanatics in New England in 1692. There is no outright mention of McCarthy but the likeness is unmistakable and damning. Hysteria, intolerance, malice, ignorance, gullibility are displayed in a merciless light. As a topical play *The Crucible* had a great and deserved success; whether it will maintain its position is doubtful, for there is a repetitiveness which at the time was effective, but now weakens its impact.

Of Miller's later plays *A View from the Bridge* is the best. It is about a New York dock-worker, Eddie Carbone, who is infatuated by his wife's niece. Eddie and his wife have smuggled in two illegal Italian immigrants who stay with them. Catherine, the niece, falls in love with Rodolpho, whom Eddie regards as effeminate because he is blond, sings tenor and laughs a great deal. When he sees that he will be unable to keep Catherine and Rodolpho apart, Eddie betrays the two Italians to the immigration authorities. Eddie provokes a fight with Rodolpho's companion, Marco, in which he is stabbed to death by his own knife. Miller himself has described the theme of the play as 'a passion which, despite its contradicting the self-interest of the individual it inhabits, despite every kind of warning, despite even its destruction of the moral beliefs of the individual, proceeds to magnify its power over him until it destroys him.' This is a solidly constructed play with clear, simple characterisation, lively dialogue and a strong story. In it Miller uses the device of an 'engaged narrator', a lawyer called Alfieri, to whom Eddie goes for help. He introduces the action; his advice to Eddie is sensible comment on the action; at the end he points the moral of the tragedy. The device neither adds to nor subtracts from the effect of the play to a significant extent.

Miller has not succeeded in writing the great American tragedy that appears to have been his ambition, but he has written workmanlike plays on important themes. Perhaps it is the imaginative power of Eugene O'Neill that he has lacked.

Tennessee Williams

It is only by coincidences of age, nationality and profession that Arthur Miller and Thomas Lanier Williams are connected. Williams, always known as Tennessee Williams, was born in 1914, and he is an American playwright. Apart from these facts the two have very little in common. At the centre of Miller's plays is an idea which is worked out through his characters: Williams's plays are about festering emotions. He has nothing to say about political freedom, economic systems, the moral rightness or wrongness of the actions he sets down, or about persecution of men for their beliefs, but he has a great deal to show us about the reactions of neurotic and unbalanced people in times of emotional crisis. Miller's plays are constructed according to a design, but the development of Williams's is intuitive; he introduces snatches of poetry or music, a storm, off-stage noises, a symbolic object or creature, a new character or group of characters to create the mood he is seeking to establish. His work is suggestive, impressionistic. The two plays of these authors that have something in common are perhaps their least typical—Miller's *A View from the Bridge* and Williams's *The Rose Tattoo.*

In Williams's first play, *The Glass Menagerie*, the central character, Laura Wingfield, is a partial cripple whose shyness and lack of confidence isolate her from the world. Deprived of contact with people, she consoles herself by caring for her collection of glass animals, particularly the unicorn, and by playing old gramophone records. Whilst Laura is passive, her mother, Amanda, a more active character, also lives in an unreal world, that of her own youth, when as a Southern belle she was sought after by a stream of 'gentlemen callers'. Finally she is able to persuade her son, Tom, to bring to dinner a young man, Jim O'Connor, whom both he and Laura had known at high school. Jim, a nice, ordinary, young man begins to thaw Laura's diffidence by his interest and kindness, trying to build up her self-confidence. Whilst they are dancing, he knocks the unicorn off the table and breaks off the horn, so making it like the other animals on the shelf. After kissing Laura, who had admired him in school, Jim tells her that he is in love with, and engaged to, another girl, and cannot call on Laura again.

This play is a delicate and moving study of personality, of the irruption of a normal man into a world of fantasy. Laura, Tom, and Amanda are all victims of their own illusions, yet in each of them the illusion takes a different form. There is no violent action in the play, the climax being the kiss that Jim gives to Laura and his confession that he is engaged already. It is an altogether subtler play than Williams's next, *A Streetcar Named Desire*.

This is set in New Orleans, where two streetcars named Desire and Cemetery run on the same track. These two motives, sexual allurement and self-destruction, co-exist in the principal character, Blanche DuBois, who has come to live with her sister, Stella, and her husband, Stanley. Stanley's friend, Mitch, is attracted by Blanche, but Stanley warns him off marrying her because he thinks her neurotic and insincere. Blanche provokes Stanley into raping her, and is finally taken off to a mental home appealing for help to 'the kindness of strangers'. Her world of illusion is brutally shattered. Williams has often been accused of exaggerating cruelty, violence and savagery in his plays, especially since they are often given realistic settings that contrast with the emotional distortions. His answer is that these primitive impulses lie only just below the surface of civilised life.

In *The Rose Tattoo* Serafina, a widow in a Sicilian community, mourning for the death of her husband, keeps his ashes in a marble urn in the house, another example of symbolism. A passionate woman, she has led a life of restraint until she meets a younger truck-driver who, like her husband, has a rose tattoo on his chest. Williams introduces broad comedy into this play through the slow-witted young Sicilian men and their women. Again, however, the pretences of a woman without a man, in this case Serafina's illusions about her husband's fidelity, are suddenly dispersed by an intruder.

The 'cat' in *Cat on a Hot Tin Roof* (1955) is Maggie, the wife of an alcoholic former football-star, Brick Pollitt. One theme of the play is the forcing of Brick and his father, 'Big Daddy', to face their problems and admit the truth about themselves: Brick that he is an alcoholic with homosexual inclinations, 'Big Daddy' that he is dying of cancer. Maggie, who has quarrelled with her husband, brings him and his father together by saying falsely that she is expecting a baby, news that would make 'Big Daddy' pleased with his son. This again is a play of violent quarrels with the steamy heat of the Mississippi delta setting suited to the over-heated emotions of the Pollitt family.

The Night of the Iguana is set in a decaying Mexican hotel. The iguana is a lizard that has been caught and tied up by the workers at the hotel. Its fate symbolises the bondage of the characters: Maxine, the owner of the hotel, to her lust; the Reverend Shannon to his spiritual and moral weakness; Hannah, 'a spinster pushing forty', to her deprivation of love; Nonno, her grandfather, struggling to finish his last poem before he dies, to his feebleness and imminent death. Here Williams's fondness for creating moods through unexpected events and irrelevant characters is particularly noticeable with the result that the play is a loosely connected sequence of episodes, often momentarily effective but often on the verge of disintegration.

Williams seems to keep saying the same things about human nature, and as time has gone on to say them with increased violence until at times he is almost parodying himself. The same types of character reappear—the assertive male, degenerate men, self-deluding women, frigid spinsters afraid to feel emotion. Because it handles this theme more credibly and more delicately than his later plays, *The Glass Menagerie* is the most appealing of his works. It also gives scope to his poetic handling of dialogue that contrasts with the crudity of the action in other plays. *A Streetcar named Desire* and *Cat on a Hot Tin Roof* on the other hand have the dramatic force which Williams sought in order to shock his audience into accepting his view of the brutishness of modern, urban man. To shock is not, however, to convince.

Christopher Fry

A FEW years after the end of the Second World War a revival of poetic drama on the English stage looked possible. In 1949 a play by CHRISTOPHER FRY (born 1907), *The Lady's not for Burning*, was produced with striking success, and was followed the next year by Eliot's *The Cocktail Party*. These plays were not stately and static, but were written in a free, flexible verse, and Fry's play was full of brilliant verbal conceits. A brilliant cast led by John Gielgud was partly responsible for its success, together with a natural inclination after the war for something remote from the prosaic austerity of contemporary life. Fry's subsequent plays, *Venus Observed* and *The Dark is Light Enough*, were rather less successful, for once audiences looked beyond the verbal coruscations there was not a great deal in the plot, the characterisation or the themes to hold their interest.

John Osborne

MANY of the plays presented in the 1930s and 1940s were comedies set in the drawing-rooms or lounge-halls of middle-class families. They were constructed to a pattern calculated to amuse their audiences, but they did not touch the realities of modern life at any point. It was inevitable that when this kind of play became exhausted it would be succeeded by something utterly different. The decisive moment of change came in 1956 with the production of *Look Back in Anger* at the Royal Court Theatre. Its author, JOHN OSBORNE (born 1929), had acted in several plays at this theatre before his own was accepted. In it Osborne was protesting against the values that the middle-class smugly and unquestioningly accepted. The hero, Jimmy Porter, was the first angry young man, and the play the first of the 'kitchen-sink' dramas to make a powerful impact on a wide public. Jimmy worked in a sweet-shop which gave little scope for his intellect or energy; he lived in a poky flat in the Midlands; he was married to a long-suffering wife, Alison, on whom he poured all the resentment he felt against the society in which he led a frustrated life. He left Alison to carry on an affair with her friend, Helena, which failed because Helena was incapable of suffering as Alison did. When Alison returned, grief-stricken at the loss of her baby, she and Jimmy were re-united.

Jimmy often seems ill-tempered rather than angry, but at least his resentment is aroused by conditions that exist in real life, and some of his problems were shared by many young married couples of that generation. The prospects of happiness in his re-union with Alison look doubtful, for the causes of his dissatisfaction persist. Yet the play deserved the attention it attracted for several reasons: its setting was recognisable and its theme relevant to its age. It also helped to attract to the theatre a new public which had no interest in the artificial comedy of the last generation. This public was prepared to accept novelty in the theatre, and it encouraged a number of young playwrights and producers in their exploration of new themes and techniques. Anything unconventional, including many unfamiliar and unusual plays from the continent, was welcomed with the result that interest in the theatre became much livelier. Some of the novelties and imports were merely eccentric or shocking, but others did widen the range of public taste. *Waiting for Godot* and the Ionesco plays could hardly have been successfully produced if Osborne had not prepared public taste first. The audiences at the National Theatre are the successors of those at the Royal Court Theatre.

Osborne followed *Look Back in Anger* with *The Entertainer* (1957), a portrait of a seedy music-hall artist, Archie Rice. Perhaps, like Mrs Grundy, Jimmy Porter and Archie Rice will be remembered as character types when the plays are almost forgotten. A more ambitious project was *Luther* (1961) in which Osborne explored the mind and conscience of another rebel. The subject was a natural one for him, because Luther also questioned the whole basis of the society in which he had to live. Osborne has always been a protester, his target the 'Establishment', the people who exercise influence and power without having to prove their claim to their positions. Luther can see the falsity and the corruption of the Roman Catholic church as it then existed; whilst he is attacking its rottenness, he is confident that he is right. Doubt seeps in again when he has to find something to replace it. Cajetan, the Papal legate, is right when he says to Luther:

I've read some of your sermons on faith. Do you know all they say to me?
LUTHER: No.
CAJETAN: They say: I am a man struggling for certainty, struggling insanely like a man in a fit, an animal trapped to the bone with doubt.

Later, he admits to his former mentor, Staupitz:

LUTHER: I listened for God's voice, but all I could hear was my own.
STAUPITZ: *Were* you sure?
(*Pause*)
LUTHER: No.

Luther is the struggle of a man with his own conscience, the record of his attempt to work out his individual relationship with God. In the end he doubts his own success and is grateful for the comfortable relationship he has established with his wife, Katherine. His chronic constipation symbolises the blockage in his own mind and faith. It is an interesting play with a conflict that is mainly internal. Only the scene with Cajetan has the conventional dramatic impact of character opposed to character. It has a similar theme to Shaw's *Saint Joan*, the struggle of the individual conscience against the established power of the Church, but the episodic form of Osborne's play is clumsier than Shaw's. Joan's character, though not her conscience, is much more complex than Luther's. Shaw's play is richer in texture, the prose much finer, yet there is an intensity in *Luther* that grips an audience: 'Here I stand; God help me; I can do no more. Amen.'

Harold Pinter and Arnold Wesker

HAROLD PINTER (born 1930) and ARNOLD WESKER (born 1932) were also actors before they became playwrights, so following the example of Shakespeare. Pinter's first plays were written for television, and his stage-plays too, with small casts, paucity of action and revelation of attitudes through dialogue, would adapt easily to the small screen in the lounge. *The Birthday Party* tells how a young artist of modest talent, despite his resistance to conformity, is carried off to a conventional life. *The Dumb Waiter* is about a simple-minded assassin who is murdered by his partner in the crime. Pinter's experience as an actor has taught him what will hold the attention of an audience. His great gift is in the reproduction of apparently commonplace talk, naturalistic, repetitive, often circular, in which the characters seem to be warily testing out each other's reactions, and their own, to what they say. Although the words used are the simplest, the dialogue full of pauses, hesitations, gropings after meaning, in Pinter's hands the effect is of poetry, strongly rhythmical, characters answering each other, repeating each other's phrases, almost like a chant. This quality is seen particularly in *The Caretaker* (1960):

DAVIES: Who was that feller?
ASTON: He's my brother.
DAVIES: Is he? He's a bit of a joker, en' he?
ASTON: Uh.
DAVIES: Yes . . . he's a real joker.
ASTON: He's got a sense of humour.
DAVIES: Yes, I noticed.
(*Pause*)
He's a real joker, that lad, you can see that.
(*Pause*)
ASTON: Yes, he tends . . . he tends to see the funny side of things.
DAVIES: Well, he's got a sense of humour, en' he?
ASTON: Yes.
DAVIES: Yes, you could tell that.
(*Pause*)
I could tell the first time I saw him he had his own way of looking at things.

This kind of dialogue has much in common with the patter of music-hall comedians who had this gift of arousing expectancy through the trivial. This can be seen even more plainly in the following passage:

(*Silence*)
(*A drip sounds in the bucket. They all look up.*)
(*Silence*)
DAVIES: You still got that leak.
ASTON: Yes.
(*Pause*)
It's coming from the roof.
MICK: From the roof, eh?
ASTON: Yes.
(*Pause*)
I'll have to tar it over.
MICK: You're going to tar it over.
ASTON: Yes.
MICK: What?
ASTON: The cracks.
(*Pause*)
MICK: Think that'll do it?
ASTON: It'll do it, for the time being.
MICK: Uh.
(*Pause*)
DAVIES (*abruptly*): What do you—?
(*They both look at him.*)
What do you do . . . when that bucket's full?
(*Pause*)
ASTON: Empty it.

This could hardly be simpler, but played by actors with an acute sense of timing it cannot fail.

Although the dialogue and characters in Pinter's plays are superficially comic, he always leaves behind the feeling that the jokes conceal something mysterious and sinister. He leaves unexplained the precise nature of the mystery and much else. *The Caretaker* has no plot: an old tramp is taken to a junk-filled room and allowed to stay there for a time by two brothers who say they own and maintain the rooms on that floor of the building. He tries to play off one brother against the other, but finally they make him leave—that is all. We never know whether anything that the three characters say is true; they are all on the point of doing something—building a shed, decorating the room, going to Sidcup to get papers that will prove something, but we know they will never do these things. Their attitudes to each other keep changing through mistrust and suspicion quite irrationally. All kinds of questions are left unanswered at the end, but this is what Pinter intends. We hear snatches of conversation like this, we see odd people performing peculiar actions for no ascertainable reason. Humanity is absurd, Pinter seems to say, but there is something sad and even menacing in the absurdity.

Arnold Wesker's trilogy, consisting of *Chicken Soup with Barley*, *Roots*, and *I'm Talking about Jerusalem*, was also produced in 1960 at the Royal Court Theatre. If it were geometrically possible, one might say that Wesker's reputation rests four-square on this trilogy, for his subsequent plays, *The Kitchen*, *Chips with Everything*, and *The Four Seasons* have not met with the same enthusiastic reception. In the trilogy Wesker traced the history of the Kahns, a family of Jewish socialists from the East End of London, during the period 1936, the time of the Spanish Civil War, to 1956, the date of the Hungarian uprising against the Communist government. It is a history of disillusion, for in the 1930s they were confident that the Socialist era would soon dawn and dispel the misery and injustice of working-class life. At the beginning we see the Kahns and their friends enjoying their part in counter-demonstrations against London Fascists and Dave Simmonds eagerly going off to fight for socialism against General Franco in Spain. In Act II of *Chicken Soup with Barley* Dave and his wife Ada Kahn have already lost their faith: Ada says, 'Oh, yes! the service killed any illusions Dave may have once had about the splendid and heroic working class.' By this time, 1946, it is Ronnie Kahn who is fired by idealism:

> But it is, it is the beginning. Plans for town and country planning. New cities and schools and hospitals. Nationalisation! National health! Think of it, the whole country is going to be organised to co-operate instead of tear at each other's throat. That's what I said to them in a public speech at school, and all the boys cheered and whistled and stamped their feet—and blew raspberries.

Sarah Kahn, their mother, once full of energy and enthusiasm, has been worn down by caring for her weak and paralysed husband, Harry. The family is scattered and the brutal putting-down of the Hungarian rising has shattered Ronnie's faith in Communism. In the last scene Sarah states the theme of the play:

> We got through, didn't we? We got scars but we got through. You hear me, Ronnie? (*She clasps him and moans.*) You've got to care, you've got to care or you'll die.

Ronnie's instability is already seen at the end of this play. Although he does not appear in the second play, *Roots*, his ideas dominate it. This too is a play about a family, the Bryants, a complete contrast to the Kahns. Beatie Bryant, working as a waitress in London, has come under the influence of Ronnie Kahn, now a chef, who has introduced her to art and music, political consciousness and love. She returns to her family in Norfolk where they live a narrow, squalid and ignorant life. Beatie tries in vain to spread the ideas she has learnt from Ronnie amongst her family. When Ronnie is to be introduced to the family at a grand tea-party, he fails to appear but sends a letter to say that neither his relationship with Beatie nor his ideas about social reform will work. In the moment of her humiliation before her family Beatie finds that she really believes in all that Ronnie has told her, and that she has found her independence:

God in heaven, Ronnie! It does work, it's happening to me. I can feel it's happened. I'm beginning, on my own two feet—I'm beginning. . . .

The last of the plays takes us back to the Kahns, particularly Ada and her husband Dave Simmonds. The first two plays have been about a London family and a Norfolk family in their own environments; in this the Londoners have come to Norfolk where Dave hopes to earn an honest and dignified living as a craftsman making furniture, and to live as a member of a rural community. He fails to become a member of the community because he steals some old linoleum which his employer would gladly have given him if he had asked for it. As Ada tells him, 'Your ideals have got some pretty big leaks in places haven't they?' He fails as an independent craftsman because people cannot contract out of the kind of society in which they live. Dave sums it up:

Face it—as an essential member of society I don't really count. I'm not saying I'm useless, but machinery and modern techniques have come about to make me the odd man out. Here I've been, comrade citizen, presenting my offerings and the world's rejected them. . . . Maybe Sarah's right, maybe you can't build on your own.

Ronnie also realises the truth about himself:

Isn't that curious? I say all the right things, I think all the right things, but somewhere, some bloody where I fail as a human being.

At the end Ronnie, Dave, and Ada pack up and go back to London with Sarah. Ronnie's belief in an educated working-class and in socialism, Dave's hopes of a life as a craftsman, have vanished, but the family remains. They have come through, bearing the scars of their failures and disappointments, but their unity is the stronger for the tests it has undergone. The indomitable Sarah retains her beliefs and radiates her own warmth to the others. They have all come to realise that people matter more than ideas, that brotherhood is an emotion that has its most intense meaning within the family. All this is personified in Sarah, who might have been a sentimentalised Yiddisher momma, but is instead a Jewish mother with the courage to face and vanquish hardships. As she had said, 'You've got to care', and if you do care, not so much for humanity in general or for a theory, as for the people in your own life, everything else can be made tolerable. Beatie, on the other hand, coming from a family in which there was no affection, found her emotional satisfaction in her own growing awareness of life and emancipation.

John Arden

ALTHOUGH he has not yet written a play that has come as near accomplishing what he set out to do as Pinter did in *The Caretaker* and Wesker in *Chicken Soup with Barley*, the most interesting and promising of this generation of playwrights is probably JOHN ARDEN (born 1930). An early play, *Live like Pigs*, tells of the home-life of a family that has never acquired the moral and hygienic standards current in our society. Although they lead a revolting existence, Arden shows considerable sympathy for them as deprived people. The title is well chosen.

Arden's best-known play is *Serjeant Musgrave's Dance*. This was a commercial failure when it was first produced at the Royal Court Theatre in 1959, but in the recollection of those who saw it the play gathered significance. On its subsequent revival in 1965 it had a mixed reception : everyone found it stimulating to mind and emotions, but pointed to flaws in its construction and style. At least a play that has caused so much argument must have something in it that is worth discussion.

The disagreement about the play arises partly from its theme. Four soldiers who have deserted from the Army during a colonial war arrive at a mining town in the North of England during a pit-strike in the middle of last century. It is the middle of winter and freezing hard. Apparently they have come to find recruits for the Army, but in truth they have brought with them the body of a comrade who had been killed in the colonial war, and who had originally come from the town they are now visiting. Their leader, Serjeant Musgrave, is a fanatic determined to exact revenge for the death of Billy Hicks. After one of the party has been accidentally—and rather casually—killed in a scrimmage over a barmaid, the Serjeant, a violent pacifist, holds the town and its leading, hypocritical citizens up at gun-point until the dragoons arrive to arrest him and his followers.

The references to a colonial war, the killing of a British soldier after curfew-time and the reprisals taken for the murder had an obvious relevance to events in Cyprus at the time. To some extent, the welcome given to the play by the individual depended on whether he agreed with Arden's views on this subject. One of the difficulties of criticising contemporary works is the separation of one's political conscience from one's literary tastes. To some extent these topical references obscure the real theme of the play—that you cannot protest against killing by starting a massacre.

The play has a fervid climax when the body of Billy Hicks is strung up in the town square. Whilst this has great dramatic impact, the build-up to the scene is less effective. For a long time it is not clear to an audience what the theme of the play is: we do not know what Musgrave and his men are intent upon, nor does Arden arouse much suspense in the earlier scenes. Again, the play lacks conflict; except for a few feeble lay-figures like the Mayor, the parson and the Town Constable, everyone is against war and killing. Musgrave, a man of smouldering power, needs more opposition than he gets to show his fanaticism.

Again, inconsistencies in the language trouble the audience. One soldier says, 'He wor my mucker . . . he wor killed dead . . . what had I to care for a colonial war?' We do not believe that the same person could speak in two such different idioms. Arden introduces ballads into the realistic dialogue of the colliers with some discomfort to the ear. This question of a consistent style that the audience can accept from the characters is also an impediment in a later play, *Armstrong's Last Goodnight*. These are perhaps niggling criticisms against a playwright with the ability to project ideas on to the stage, but one feels that so far Arden has not succeeded in writing the wholly satisfying play he is capable of. He finds themes and he has a sensitivity to different kinds of speech, dialect, ballads, archaic language. He has an impressive kit of parts for writing a very good play, but he has not yet assembled it.

Samuel Beckett

SAMUEL BECKETT (born 1906) belongs to an older generation than these playwrights, but he is one of those writers who are recognised only when after years of composition they produce a work that takes the public fancy. This happened with Beckett in 1956 when *Waiting for Godot* was produced in London. Like all his later work this was originally written in French as *En attendant Godot* and then translated into English by the author. He has indeed lived in France since 1932, part of the time as secretary to a fellow-exile from Ireland, James Joyce. One early admirer of Beckett's work was Dylan Thomas whose book, *Adventures in the Skin Trade* with a hero called Samuel Bennet, was reputedly based on Beckett's first novel, *Murphy*. At that time Thomas was one of few admirers.

Beckett's work was against the stream of fashion of the 1930s when most writers concerned themselves with social and political themes. His interest has always been in the individual, particularly the derelict who has been stripped of possessions, ambition and sense of decorum. For this reason he picks characters who have no social milieu: tramps like Vladimir and Estragon in *Waiting for Godot*, or creatures like Nell and Nagg of *Endgame*, Krapp in *Krapp's Last Tape* and Malone in *Malone Dies*; these people preserve garbled memories of the past, but have no interest in the present or hope for the future. Here is an example from *Waiting for Godot*:

VLADIMIR: All the same, you can't tell me that this bears any resemblance to . . . (*he hesitates*) . . . to the Macon country, for example. You can't deny there's a big difference.

ESTRAGON: The Macon country! Who's talking to you about the Macon country?

VLADIMIR: But you were there yourself, in the Macon country.

ESTRAGON: No, I was never in the Macon country. I've puked my puke of a life away here, I tell you! Here! In the Cackon country!

VLADIMIR: But we were there together, I could swear to it. Picking grapes for a man called . . . (*he snaps his fingers*) . . . can't think of the name of the man, at a place called . . . (*snaps his fingers*) . . . can't think of the name of the place, do you not remember?

This can be interpreted as Vladimir, the artist, trying to make contact with his public, with Estragon as the puzzled representative of that public. Vladimir's own confidence is affected by Estragon's failure to accept what he tells him. Much of Beckett's work is concerned with the difficulty of communication.

Beckett feels that this disorientation applies to him as it does to the characters in his plays and stories, as can be seen in these lines from *Quatre Poèmes*, No. 3. The first verse shows him to be aware of and touched by the strangeness of the world, the second convinced of his own utter loneliness and of the meaningless nature of his existence:

> what would I do without this world faceless incurious
> where to be lasts but an instant where every instant
> spills in the void the ignorance of having been
> without this wave where in the end
> body and shadow together are engulfed
> what would I do without this silence where the murmurs die
> the pantings the frenzies towards succour towards love
> without this sky that soars
> above its ballast dust
>
> what would I do what I did yesterday and the day before
> peering out of my deadlight looking for another
> wandering like me eddying far from all the living
> in a convulsive space
> among the voices voiceless
> that throng my hiddenness

An Irish exile takes away with him something of exile: Yeats took its history and myths, Joyce a sense of its moral climate, Beckett a mixture of humour, desperation and nostalgia that is peculiarly Irish.

Beckett is not an easy author to read, for his matter is condensed and so many meanings are implicit in almost any passage of his work that he demands both great concentration and sensitivity from his readers. Perhaps the best works with which to begin are *Waiting for Godot* and his first novel, *Murphy*.

Waiting for Godot has almost no action; on two successive days Vladimir and Estragon, both of them tramps, wait beneath a tree in a barren landscape for someone called Godot from whom they expect help without knowing what:

VLADIMIR: I'm curious to hear what he has to offer. Then we'll take it or leave it.
ESTRAGON: What exactly did we ask him to do for us?
VLADIMIR: Were you not there?
ESTRAGON: I can't have been listening.

VLADIMIR: Oh . . . nothing very definite.
ESTRAGON: A kind of prayer.
VLADIMIR: Precisely.
ESTRAGON: A vague supplication.
VLADIMIR: Exactly.
ESTRAGON: And what did he reply?
VLADIMIR: That he'd see.
ESTRAGON: That he couldn't promise anything.
VLADIMIR: That he'd have to think it over.

On each of the two days a messenger is sent, apparently from Godot, to tell the two derelicts that although Godot cannot come that day, he will certainly be there next day. Whilst they are waiting, Pozzo and Lucky pass by. On the first day Pozzo, a practical man and possibly a landowner, is driving Lucky, a wretched, barely human creature, to market to sell him. The relationship between these two deprives them both of human characteristics. The same painful kind of association exists between the two tramps: dependent upon each other, they make each other miserable for most of the time. When Pozzo and Lucky again pass the tree on the second day, Pozzo has gone blind and Lucky has been struck dumb. Pozzo cannot say when this happened:

VLADIMIR: Dumb! Since when?
POZZO (*suddenly furious*): Have you not done tormenting me with your accursed time? It's abominable. When! When! One day, is that not enough for you, one day like any other day, one day he went dumb, one day I went blind, one day we'll go deaf, one day we were born, one day we'll die, the same day, the same second, is that not enough for you? (*Calmer*) They give birth astride of a grave, the light gleams an instant, then it's night once more. On!

The play explores human relationships and exposes the pathetic attempts which people make to fill the emptiness of their lives, their aspirations, the irrational hope that some external agent will rescue them from their condition. With its stark language and ludicrous little mimes it is often more like a charade than a play. At the end of each act the light gleams for an instant before night falls, this perhaps best expressing Beckett's comment on human existence.

His first novel, *Murphy*, is a convenient introduction to his work, for this has identifiable settings in Dublin and Islington for its action. The Islington episodes are believed to be descriptive of the author's own experiences in London as a youth. There are two connected plots: one is concerned with Murphy's former teacher, a man from Cork named Neary who could stop his heart more or less whenever he liked and keep it stopped, within reasonable limits, for as long as he liked. This rare faculty, acquired after years of application somewhere north of the Nerbudda, he exercised frugally, reserving it for situations irksome beyond endurance, as when he wanted a drink and could not get one, or fell among Gaels and could not escape, or felt the pangs of hopeless sexual inclination.

His particular inclination is towards a lady named Miss Counihan, who has, however, already given her affections to Murphy. He has gone off to London, intending as she believes to return and reclaim her once he has made good. Neary and his assistant, Wylie, set off to London in pursuit of Murphy, hoping to prove this rival unworthy of the lady. As he is, indeed, for not only is Murphy unemployed, but he is living with another woman. The core of the novel is the character of Murphy and his tortuous relationship with Celia: 'The part of him that he hated craved for Celia, the part that he loved shrivelled up at the thought of her.'

Celia is anxious for him to get a job as a male nurse in a mental asylum, and this of course separates them. Murphy vainly attempts to convert the asylum into his spiritual home, until he is forced to admit to himself that his own mind is inferior to that of some of the inmates. He has just decided to return to Celia when he is accidentally—or at least apparently accidentally—burnt to death in his room at the asylum.

'Death by burns,' said the coroner, 'perhaps I am expected to add, is a wholly unscientific condition. Burns always shocks, I beg your pardon, my dear Angus, always shock, sometimes more, sometimes less, according to their strength, their locus and the shockability of the burner. The same is true of scalds.'

'Sepsis does not arise,' said Dr. Killiecrankie.

'My physiology is rather rusty,' said the coroner, 'but no doubt it was not required.'

'We arrived too late for sepsis to arise,' said Dr. Killiecrankie. 'The shock was ample.'

'Then suppose we say severe shock following burns,' said the coroner, 'to be absolutely clear.'

The upside-down logic of this extract shows the mixture of humour and disbelief in the significance of human activity that is characteristic of Beckett.

In the meantime Neary had decided that it was not Miss Counihan that he desired, but the friendship of Murphy, whilst Miss Counihan, tired of waiting for the unfaithful Murphy, has opted for the assistant,

Wylie, who is equally attracted by her comfortable fortune. There is little certainty to hang on to here.

Is *Murphy* then a comic novel, or a tragic, or a pathetic? The answer is not really important. The events and their implications are often tragic, but they are masked by the ironic manner of the telling.

The reputations of those writers already discussed may reasonably be regarded as established. Some of them will continue to write, but it will be surprising if they produce work distinctively new in kind or quality. This is of course an unsafe assumption, for Shaw was almost seventy when *Saint Joan* was produced, and most of Hardy's poetry appeared when he was well over sixty. Vitality appears to diminish earlier in writers, especially poets, than in musicians, and it is difficult to think of any writer who has paralleled Verdi in producing two masterpieces profounder than his earlier work when in his seventies.

William Golding

ON the other hand WILLIAM GOLDING, born in 1911, is not a predictable author. Since he published his first novel, *Lord of the Flies*, in 1954, he has written *The Inheritors* (1955), *Pincher Martin* (1956), *Free Fall* (1959), and *The Spire* (1964). Each of these has been a highly original achievement with no suggestion that he is willing to repeat himself. *Lord of the Flies* is about a party of schoolboys isolated on a coral island after an aeroplane crash during an atomic war some time in the near future. Their attempts to organise their own society bring out the cruelties, jealousies, fears and hatred characteristic of primitive tribes and also of civilised communities where they appear in a more complex form. In *The Inheritors* Neanderthal man describes how he is destroyed by the new people, homo sapiens. The most impressive feature is Golding's ability to enter into the consciousness of Neanderthal man, his dependence on the senses, especially of smell, his curiosity about the new people, his innocence until, like Adam and Eve, he learns the difference between good and evil. Most historical novels point out the difference in the objects that form the background of life in a past age. Golding stresses the completely different way in which Neanderthal man apprehends his world.

In *Pincher Martin* a naval lieutenant is blown off the bridge of a destroyer by a torpedo. The novel tells of his struggle for survival, how he reached a barren rock, and his precarious, hopeless efforts to live until he is rescued.

> The end to be desired is rescue. For that, the bare minimum necessary is survival. I must keep this body going. I must give it drink and food and shelter. When I do that it does not matter if the job is well done or not so long as it is done at all. So long as the thread of life is unbroken it will connect a future with the past for all this ghastly interlude.

Through Pincher's thoughts and memories Golding builds up a picture of a man whose life has been a record of selfishness and greed. His name is apt, for he seizes everything that comes within his grasp and uses everyone for his own purposes. When he is confronted on his barren rock by the vision of a man dressed like a sailor, who asks him what he believes in, Pincher tells him, 'The thread of my life. . . . At all costs.' In the last chapter where Pincher's body is found, there is a twist in the story which turns it all upside down and completely changes its significance. It would be a great pity to deprive the reader of this experience.

Free Fall is again a new departure for Golding. It is largely a 'stream of consciousness' in which Sammy Mountjoy looks back on his life in an effort to find out at what point he had lost his freedom of choice and of action. *Free Fall* is a difficult novel to understand: events are not narrated in chronological order and their sequence has to be pieced together. That is not uncommon, however, in twentieth-century novels. The real difficulty lies in knowing what exactly is the problem that Sammy cannot solve—what does Sammy mean by freedom?

The Spire tells how Jocelin, Dean of Barchester Cathedral, determines to build a spire on the cathedral. The incidents take place in the fourteenth century, but as in *The Inheritors* there is no attempt to build up an accurate and detailed picture of the period. In the course of the building tragedies occur and Jocelin's ambition causes the death of innocent people. Golding is not condemning Jocelin, for in the end, after Jocelin's own death, the spire is completed to the glory of God. Before he dies, Jocelin reflects: 'There is no innocent work', and this is the truth of the book.

In *Lord of the Flies* Golding started from the same situation as R. M. Ballantyne's adventure story for boys, *Coral Island*, but showed that the probable course of events would not have been an idyllic life with difficulties painlessly smoothed over, but a reversion to primitive brutality. Jocelin's motives in *The Spire* are those of the Abbot in *Past and Present*, based by Carlyle on a manuscript by Jocelin of Brakelond, but he does not inspire everyone with his own idealism and energy as Abbot Samson did.

Golding's work will always be interesting, for he has great powers of invention, a supple prose style and an adventurous, speculative mind. He can penetrate the minds of the main characters in his books. He has moved steadily away from plot and diversity of character in his later books, but in his last two books it has been harder to see what he is moving towards. It is certainly not a formula.

Lawrence Durrell

LAWRENCE DURRELL (born 1912) belongs to the same generation as Golding, but he has been a professional writer for much longer. An amusing, but one-sided account of part of his early life is provided in *My Family and Other Animals* written by his brother, Gerald Durrell. Although his poetry and a short book about his experiences in Cyprus, *Bitter Lemons*, won praise, Durrell made only a limited impact until the publication of *The Alexandria Quartet*. This consists of *Justine* (1957), *Balthazar* (1958), *Mountolive* (1958), and *Clea* (1960). In the preface he explains that he adopted the relativity proposition in working out the form of the Quartet. The first three books are accounts of the same set of events, but each is told with a different character, indicated by the title of the book, as the pivot of the action. Although the events of the three books overlap, each contains many incidents not found in the others; the interpretation of events and characters differs from book to book, and sometimes the incidents themselves seem inconsistent with the other books. Durrell is showing that in human affairs there is no absolute truth, that to the participants what happens does not merely seem different, it is different. The author implies too that this process of looking at the events from various standpoints might be extended indefinitely, that the Alexandria Quartet does not exhaust the possibilities, for 'if . . . the axis of the work has been properly laid down it should be possible to radiate from it in any direction without losing the strictness and congruity of its relation to 'a continuum'.'

The first three books correspond to the three dimensions of length, breadth and depth, these giving solidity to the action. The fourth book, *Clea*, introduces the dimension of time, for it takes place at a later period, in which the events already described take on a new pattern. These four dimensions constitute 'the relativity proposition' Durrell refers to in the preface.

It is tempting to compare the four books to the movements of a string quartet, and the four characters who give their names to the books, two men and two women, to the instruments. It is also easy to identify the narrator, Darley, an artist, with Durrell who shares the same initials, L. D. After his passions for Melissa and Justine, he finds contentment with a fellow artist, Clea. In the Quartet Durrell shows how Darley grows to emotional maturity and in the process finds himself as an artist.

Durrell depicts Alexandria as a corrupt city in which the foreign residents exploit and debauch the local population. The basis of this exploitation is sexual, and adultery, incest, homosexuality, lesbianism, and perversions all flourish. The reader with a taste for pornography will, however, find the Quartet disappointing, for Durrell does not gratify him by embellishing these episodes. Sexual gratification is a motive for many of the characters and is used as the power-source for the development of the plot. The tendency of the Quartet might be regarded as conventionally moral, almost Wordsworthian in contrasting the moral squalor of the city with the more wholesome life of Leila's country home and the purity of Darley's Greek island at the beginning of *Clea*. The last book seems also to add a moral dimension to the Quartet: Darley's relationship with Clea is all the finer by comparison with the feverish lust of his earlier life. Like the hero of an eighteenth-century picaresque novel he emerges from his experiences purged of his grossness. This is a one-sided view, but no more so than the opposite view that the actions of the characters make the Quartet an immoral work. In fact Durrell is examining the complexity of human behaviour without pronouncing verdicts, and one of his principal themes seems to be the refinement of Darley's consciousness and the development of his personality. As he becomes less self-regarding he becomes more likeable.

The Quartet takes a broad-ranging view of human character, from the predatory Justine to the pathetic, waif-like Melissa; from the unawakened product of public school and university, Mountolive, before he met Leila, to the patient, loyal, hare-lipped young Egyptian, Narouz. There are also some glorious comic characters, notably Scobie with his Dolly Vardens, and Pombal, the womaniser. Pursewarden too is often absurd for his intellectual excesses, though his relationship with his blind sister is one of the most pathetic episodes in the Quartet. Anyone who enjoys Dickens and who is willing to suspend moral judgment until he has finished the work will find much to enjoy in the Alexandria Quartet. The narrative sweep, the range of character, the mingling of passion, pathos, and humour are all to be found in Durrell's work; he always bears in mind Stendhal's saying which he prefaces to *Mountolive*—'Il faut que le roman raconte.'

Durrell writes with the sensitivity of a poet, but this does not impede the narrative flow:

On the night in question he must have dozed off, for when he woke he found to his surprise that all was dark. A brilliant moonlight flooded the room and the balcony, but the lights had been extinguished by an unknown hand. He started up. Astonishingly, the balcony was empty. For a moment, Narouz thought he must be dreaming, for never before had his father gone to bed alone. Yet standing there in the moonlight, battling with this sense of incomprehension and doubt, he thought he heard the sound of the wheel-chair's rubber tyres rolling upon the wooden boards of the invalid's bedroom. This was an astonishing departure from accepted routine. He crossed the balcony and tiptoed down the corridor in amazement. The door of his father's room was open. He peered inside. The room was full of moonlight. He heard the bump of the wheels upon the chest of drawers and a scrabble of fingers groping for a knob. Then he heard a drawer pulled open, and a sense of dismay filled him for he remembered that in it was kept the old Colt revolver which belonged to his father. He suddenly found himself unable to move or speak as he heard the breach snapped open and the unmistakable sound of paper rustling—a sound immediately interpreted by his memory. Then the small precise click of the shells slipping into the chambers.

(From *Mountolive*)

Narouz sees his father looking into a long mirror pointing the pistol at the reflection of himself in the glass. This image of the human reflection in a mirror often occurs in the Quartet, for Durrell keeps reminding us that the view of events presented is not a direct one, but is distorted and partial. From putting all the views together we may arrive at something like the truth, but no more. Blind, one-eyed, squinting people are also introduced into the action and disfigurement is a recurring theme. Like many twentieth-century works the Alexandria Quartet can be read with interest for its story, but it also has overtones which the reader may recognise for himself.

Poetry since 1945

IN the 1920s any discussion of poetry took for its centrepoint *The Waste Land*; in the 1930s Auden was the acknowledged leader of the new generation of poets. During the twenty years that have elapsed since the end of the Second World War no young poet of this stature has appeared. There has been a trend to lucidity, away from obscurity and the private allusion. Some of the younger poets have detached themselves from politics and social problems in reaction against the poets of the 1930s who were often committed to one solution of such problems. These poets, who included Philip Larkin and Thom Gunn, contributed to an anthology called *New Lines* (1956) and formed a very loose group sometimes referred to as the 'Movement'. This 'Movement' has already disintegrated as its members have each developed their own work. Another anthology, *Mavericks*, embodied the view that poetry was legitimately concerned with a man's political faith and was a vehicle for protest against nuclear war and social injustice. On the whole the poets of the 'Movement' wrote in precise verse-forms, whilst the contributors to *Mavericks* wrote a much freer kind of verse. Other poets do not fall into either of these vaguely-defined groups; notable among them is Ted Hughes.

John Betjeman

POETS of an older generation, such as Robert Graves and W. H. Auden, have continued to write, and one of them, JOHN BETJEMAN (born 1906) has achieved a surprising and belated popularity. He has described his verse as follows in a letter to F. E. S. Finn:

My verse is made to be said out loud. I regard verse as the shortest and most memorable way of saying things—or rather that is what I think it ought to be. I also prefer to use rhythm and traditional forms as I think that until you know and can use rhyme and metre, you cannot know from what you are breaking free to write 'free verse', nor distinguish between poetry and prose. I think verse is natural to all of us and is only killed by 'Eng. Lit.'. Nursery rhymes are what we all first know, and later, all sorts of people who never read poetry nevertheless know hundreds of popular songs by heart.

Accordingly Betjeman writes verse with an immediate appeal—distinct rhythms, clearly-marked rhymes, simple language. His scenes and characters are often familiar—suburban London, the Cornish coast, typical rural scenes like Upper Lambourne, parish churches, healthy middle-class girls playing tennis, business girls, churchwardens. Nostalgia runs through his poems with references to tramcars and trolleybuses, decaying houses, shops that have disappeared, Tortoise stoves in churches. His autobiography in verse, *Summoned by Bells* is a sentimental ramble through a vanished or vanishing past, but it fixes in amber a period and a class which ought not to disappear without a record of its existence. It is easy to think of Betjeman as a jolly middle-class poet with an amiably eccentric taste for Victorian architecture, but he is not always as comfortable as that. In 'Christmas' for instance, he describes the scene, though it is a rather old-fashioned print of 'the festive season'—the Manor House, the villagers admiring the decorations in church, the decorations on the Town Hall. Betjeman then asks a question that reduces these celebrations to insignificance:

And is it true? And is it true,
  This most tremendous tale of all,
Seen in a stained-glass window's hue,
  A baby in an ox's stall?
The Maker of the stars and sea
Become a child on earth for me.

And is it true? For if it is,
  No loving fingers tying strings,
Around those tissued fripperies,
  The sweet and silly Christmas things,
Bath salts and inexpensive scent
And hideous tie so kindly meant,

No love that in a family dwells,
  No carolling in frosty air,
Nor all the steeple-shaking bells
  Can with this single Truth compare—
That God was Man in Palestine
And lives today in bread and wine.

This is not of course an original thought, for the contrast between the pleasures that Christmas brings and the origin of the festival is commonplace enough, but Betjeman puts the familiar idea neatly. This, perhaps, is what has made his verse popular—he can present to his readers and listeners in a palatable form their own thoughts and feelings. The mixture of humour, pathos and nostalgia has a wide appeal. In 'Youth and Age on Beaulieu River, Hants', he describes how, watched by Mrs Fairclough, an elderly lady sipping tea

. . . to her craft on Beaulieu water
Clemency the General's daughter
  Pulls across with even strokes

In the evening

Clemency, the General's daughter,
  Will return upon the flood.
But the older woman only
Knows the ebb-tide leaves her lonely
  With the shining fields of mud.

The qualities of Betjeman's verse are here displayed with a craftsman's skill in the handling of the verse and the mood. Both in its movement and in its theme—reversed though it is—this poem carries echoes of Tennyson's 'Lady of Shalott' that add a flavour to its enjoyment.

Philip Larkin

PHILIP LARKIN (born 1922) also reflects in his poetry the attitudes of the class to which he feels himself to belong: in his case, a middle-class intellectual who, as a professional man, has been left behind in the rat-race towards affluence. He is a University librarian. In 'Church Going' he tells how he enters yet another country church, uncertain what he is looking for:

> . . . hatless, I take off
> My cycle-clips in awkward reverence

It is a sensitive, low-keyed, rather depressed poetry that the cyclist who looks hesitantly at churches writes. In 'Next Please' he deprecates the false hopes with which man deludes himself:

> Always too eager for the future, we
> Pick up bad habits of expectancy.
> Something is always approaching; every day
> *Till then* we say.

But 'the sparkling armada of promises' never delivers its cargo to us.

> Right to the last
>
> We think each one will heave to, and unload
> All good into our lives, all we are owed
> For waiting so devoutly and so long
> But we are wrong:
>
> Only one ship is seeking us, a black-
> Sailed unfamiliar, towing at her back
> A huge and birdless silence. In her wake
> No waters breed or break.

The same quiet, speculative tone of 'Church Going' is found again in 'An Arundel Tomb', and 'Wants' expects as little from life as 'Next Please'. Despite all the distractions of life,

> Beyond all this, the wish to be alone.
> Beneath it all, desire of oblivion runs.

Thom Gunn

IF Philip Larkin sometimes seems to express middle-aged attitudes towards life, THOM GUNN (born 1929) retains some of the standards of adolescence. One of his poems is in fact called 'Adolescence', though in this is he not carried away by the idea of violence as he is in some of his other work. Here he reflects that after the end of wars people still suffer from their effects:

> After the history has been made,
> and when Wallace's shaggy head
>
> glares on London from a spike, when
> the exiled general is again
>
> gliding into Athens harbour
> now as embittered foreigner,
>
> when the lean creatures crawl out of
> camps and in silence try to live;
>
> I pass foundations of houses,
> walking through the wet spring, my knees
>
> drenched from high grass charged with water,
> and am part, still, of the done war.

Gunn is fond of this device of going back in history to a period of violence ('A Mirror for Poets' and 'The Wound') or to a strange country where treachery and assassination flourish ('The Court Revolt', 'The Right Possessor'). There is no pity for the victims of this cruelty.

Nor is there any gentleness in the poems about the relations of men and women—love-poems would not be the right name for them. These concern the casual conquests of young men doing their period of National Service in the Army. For them love is predatory:

> . . . Like the world, I've gone to bad.
> A deadly world: for, once I like, it kills.

The same with everything: the only posting
I ever liked was short. And so in me
I kill the easy things that others like
To teach them that no liking can be lasting:
All that you praise I take, what modesty
What gentleness, you ruin while you speak.

and from 'Captain in Time of Peace':

And if I cannot gratefully receive
When you are generous, know that the habit
Of soldiers is to loot. So please forgive
All my inadequacy: I was fit
For peaceful living once, and was not born
  A clumsy brute in uniform.

Another recurring theme in his poetry is uncertainty about identity. In 'The Corridor' a man kneels to pry through a keyhole to a hotel bedroom; he sees in a mirror his own reflection spying on others, but at the same moment loses his view of the couple in the bedroom. He asks:

For if the watcher of the watcher shown
There in the distant glass should be watched too,
Who can be master, free of others; who
Can look around and say he is alone?

Moreover, who can know that what he sees
Is not distorted, that he is not seen
Distorted by a pier-glass, curved and lean?

In 'The Monster' he goes at night to look up at the window of the woman who has rejected him and sees there another waiting figure whom he recognises as himself.

What if I were within the house,
Happier than the fact had been—
Would he, then, still be gazing there,
The man who never can get in?

Or would I, leaving at the dawn
A suppler love than he could guess,
Find him awake on my small bed,
Demanding still some bitterness?

'The Secret Sharer', a title taken from a short story by Conrad, also turns on the duality of the poet's individuality. There is a demoniac element in Gunn's poetry. A desire for possession persists, but with it doubts of possessing even himself. His finest poem, perhaps, 'Tamer and Hawk' again stresses this theme, for although the hawk seems to live only to carry out the tamer's commands:

> You but half-civilize,
> Taming me in this way.
> Through having only eyes
>   For you I fear to lose,
> I lose to keep, and choose
> Tamer as prey.

Ted Hughes

Ted Hughes (born 1930) also wrote a poem about this bird which he called 'Hawk Roosting'. As the hawk sits in the top of the wood, resting, it contemplates with pure satisfaction its power to kill:

> I kill where I please because it is all mine.
> There is no sophistry in my body:
> My manners are tearing off heads—

and it concludes:

> Nothing has changed since I began.
> My eye has permitted no change.
> I am going to keep things like this.

In an interview printed in *The Guardian* (23 March 1965) he said: 'You'll have noticed how all the animals get killed off at the end of most poems. Each one is living the redeemed life of joy. They're continually in a state of energy which men only have when they go mad . . . . My poems are not about violence but vitality. Animals are not violent, they're so much more completely controlled than men. So much more adapted to their environment.'

Hughes admires the animals for their animal nature; there is no attempt to sentimentalise about them or to make them resemble humans. In fact, what he seems to like most about them is that they are utterly different from men: the pike which spares nobody and eats other pike; Esther's tomcat for its sheer indestructibility; the pig for its voracity:

> Pigs must have hot blood, they feel like ovens.
> Their bite is worse than a horse's—
> They chop a half-moon clean out.
> They eat cinders, dead cats.

He does not see thrushes as pretty song-birds, but as wonderfully efficient destroyers:

> . . . with a start, a bounce, a stab
> Overtake the instant and drag out some writhing thing.
> No indolent procrastinations and no yawning stares,
> No sighs or head-scratchings. Nothing but bounce and stab
> And a ravening second.

He contrasts the single-mindedness of the thrush with the aimless activities of man, 'carving at a tiny ivory ornament for years.' As he said in the interview, 'The last stanza of "Thrushes" shows how the life of man at the desk has completely cut across any life of the senses, through which he might have reached fulfilment.'

Hughes has also written some war poems, strangely not about the Second World War but of the First, which ended years before his birth. The impersonal killing by bombing could not arouse his feelings as did the hand-to-hand fighting of the First War, described in poems like 'Bayonet Charge'. In another poem, 'Six Young Men', he holds in his hand a fading photograph of six young men taken against a rural scene the poet knows well:

> This one was shot in an attack and lay
> Calling in the wire, then this one, his best friend,
> Went out to bring him in and was shot too;
> And this one, the very moment he was warned
> From potting at tin-cans in no-man's land,
> Fell back dead with his rifle-sights shot away.
> The rest, nobody knows what they came to,
> But come to the worst they must have done, and held it
> Closer than their hope; all were killed.

Hughes's style is direct, the words short and forceful. His usual theme, the threat of quick death in combat, does not lend itself to elaboration. There are no moral overtones to mitigate the violence in either Thom Gunn, one of whose characters repeats 'I regret nothing', or in Ted Hughes, for whose creatures the hawk speaks when it says, 'No arguments assert my right'.

None of these seems to be a major poet, and perhaps it will be some other writer of the period who will be recognised as the outstanding figure. Danny Abse and Jon Silkin, leaders of the *Mavericks* group, are deeply concerned about the sufferings imposed by what they regard as an unjust society, and communicate their warmth of feeling. An older writer, R. S. Thomas (born 1913), is among the most distinctive modern poets, his subject the poverty of Welsh hill-farmers and the preservation of a Welsh culture and way of life against the incursions of soulless, characterless materialism from England. Peter Porter, another left-wing writer, has produced some rumbustious satires which may outlast more earnest comments on modern life.

Conclusion

THE great literary activity that has been characteristic of the twentieth century shows no signs of slackening, and if there are no giants to be seen, the countryside seems to be all the better populated for that.

Some books have surprisingly established their places in the canon of English literature in past centuries, among them a book on fishing, a country parson's observations of natural history in a Hampshire parish, an Oxford don's nonsense rhymes, a series of stories about the absurd escapades of a vulgar London grocer passionately devoted to hunting, and a badly written and shapeless biography of an overbearing essayist and critic. No doubt some of the books that survive from the twentieth century will not fall into any of the principal categories of novel, poetry, drama, essay; equally certainly some of the authors, of whose work we think as highly as his contemporaries did of Lord Bulwer-Lytton's historical novels, will be mere curiosities a hundred years from now.

Some books may be read partly because their authors' lives will continue to interest people, and among these T. E. Lawrence's *Seven Pillars of Wisdom* and Sir Winston Churchill's *My Early Life* will probably figure. Bertrand Russell, also prominent in public life though not a man of action, has a clear, vigorous style which may wear well, and his books are full of matter. We have not had a really popular historian since Macaulay, but Churchill, George Macaulay Trevelyan and Sir Arthur Bryant have all been widely read during the last quarter of a century, and one of them may prove durable. A few books on sport have been handed down from past generations, and perhaps a modern writer like Neville Cardus or the very different American, Ring Lardner, will join them. Amongst writers for children Edith Nesbit has already persisted for over half a century, and there are more accomplished writers of children's stories working today than have probably lived in all past ages put together. Fashions in humour change as a glance at old magazines shows, but it will be surprising if our age does not produce one humorist whose work will make subsequent generations smile or laugh. James Thurber seems perhaps the likeliest candidate, but P. G. Wodehouse has created both a gallery of characters and a distinctive prose style that has been admired by fellow-craftsmen like George Orwell. In a more dignified manner, Osbert Sitwell's family reminiscences recreate eccentric characters, notably his father, and a past age of country houses, elaborate gardens, and holidays at watering-places not threatened by the descent of hordes of day-trippers. In contrast, Ogden Nash has mastered the art of being facetious in verse. Most of these have only an outsider's chance of permanent fame, but history shows that someone equally unexpected will almost certainly emerge. Perhaps some branch of writing now regarded with a tolerant superiority—the Western novel or science fiction—will produce a master of the genre and become respectable. Journalism, film-scripts, broadcast talks, modern folk-songs are all popular forms of verbal expression which may be taken more seriously in the future. We live in an age when the spoken word is becoming more important in comparison with the written word than it has been for centuries as new means of communication are developed.

The rate of change is constantly accelerating. One result of this process is that it is impossible to sum up the twentieth century neatly. No one writes epic poetry or essays that are exercises in style any longer; the novel has ceased to be a solid construction of plot and character; comedy in the theatre is out of fashion, for modern taste seems to prefer something stronger and more acrid. It is in fact much easier to point out what kind of works are no longer being written than to find common elements in what is being written. A few general tendencies are plain enough: poets, novelists, dramatists often take up clearly defined positions about social and political, as well as moral, problems—the fashionable word is that they are 'committed'. Many plays and novels have been set in that uncertain territory between sanity and madness which nevertheless does not yet seem to have been thoroughly explored; the plays of Tennessee Williams and Arthur Miller, for instance, are concerned with abnormal mental conditions. The part played by the sexual instinct in men's and women's lives has been frankly recognised and even emphasised in countless poems, novels and plays. The difficulty, sometimes the impossibility, that people have in communicating with each other—understanding others and being understood—is another favourite theme. We have had the theatre of cruelty and the theatre of the absurd, but these aspects of human behaviour have also been stressed in novels. For many of these developments, the study and popularisation of psychology have been largely responsible. It is significant that American writers have taken the lead in these directions, and that in their country psycho-analysis has become an accepted part of everyday life much more quickly than in Britain.

It is doubtful whether the reader should exert himself to track down these common tendencies. By putting novels in categories, by tracing the influence of this writer on that, by comparing this writer's treatment of a theme with another's, attention may be concentrated on what the books have in common to the neglect of what makes this book or this writer's work distinctive or unique. When he wrote the book, the writer probably thought that he had something different to say from any other writer, or that he had found a more effective way of saying it. These are the qualities we should be looking for.

Reading List

THIS list contains only those works described in some detail in the text. The page numbers indicate where they may be found.

Acknowledgements

THE author wishes to thank the following for permission to reproduce copyright material:

George Allen & Unwin Ltd, for extracts from *Riders to the Sea* and *The Playboy of the Western World* by J. M. Synge; Edward Arnold Ltd, for extracts from *Howards End* and *A Passage to India* by E. M. Forster; Mrs George Bambridge and Methuen & Co Ltd, for extracts from the poems of Rudyard Kipling; Mrs George Bambridge and Macmillan & Co Ltd, for extracts from *Kim* and *The Second Jungle Book* by Rudyard Kipling; D. C. Benson & Campbell Thomson Ltd, for extracts from *What Every Woman Knows* by J. M. Barrie; The Bodley Head Ltd, for extracts from *The Great Gatsby* and *The Beautiful and Damned* by F. Scott Fitzgerald, from *Ulysses* by James Joyce and from *Clerihews Complete* by E. C. Bentley; Calder & Boyars Ltd, for an extract from *Quatre Poèmes* No. 3 and extracts from *Murphy* by Samuel Beckett; Jonathan Cape Ltd and the Executors of the Hemingway Estate, for extracts from *A Farewell to Arms* by Ernest Hemingway; Miss D. E. Collins and Cassell & Co Ltd, for an extract from 'The Queer Feet' from *The Innocence of Father Brown* by G. K. Chesterton; J. M. Dent & Sons Ltd, for extracts from 'The Force that through the green fuse', 'After the Funeral' and 'The Map of Love' by Dylan Thomas and from *Nostromo* by Joseph Conrad; Gerald Duckworth & Co Ltd, for an extract from 'Lord Finchley' by Hilaire Belloc; Faber & Faber Ltd, for extracts from *Collected Shorter Poems* and *Look Stranger* by W. H. Auden, from *Waiting for Godot* by Samuel Beckett, an extract from *Mountolive* by Lawrence Durrell, extracts from *The Rock*, *The Cocktail Party* and *Collected Poems 1909–1962* by T. S. Eliot, from *My Sad Captains*, *Fighting Terms* and *The Sense of Movement* by Thom Gunn, from *Lupercal* and *Hawk in the Rain* by Ted Hughes and from the poems of Louis MacNeice, Ezra Pound and Stephen Spender; the Literary Estate of the late William Faulkner and Chatto & Windus Ltd, for extracts from *Intruder in the Dust* and *The Hamlet*; the Great Ormond Street Hospital for Sick Children, for an extract from *Peter Pan* by J. M. Barrie; Mr Graham Greene and William Heinemann Ltd, for an extract from *The Power and the Glory*; the Trustees of the Hardy Estate, The Macmillan Co of Canada Ltd and Macmillan & Co Ltd, London, for extracts from *The Collected Poems of Thomas Hardy*; William Heinemann Ltd, for an extract from *A Man of Property* by John Galsworthy; Holt, Rinehart & Winston Inc and Jonathan Cape Ltd, for extracts from *The Complete Poems of Robert Frost*; International Authors N.V. and Mr Robert Graves, for extracts from *Collected Poems 1965*; the Executors of the James Joyce Estate and Jonathan Cape Ltd, for an extract from *Portrait of the Artist as a Young Man*; C. Day Lewis, The Hogarth Press and Jonathan Cape Ltd, for three poems from *Collected Poems 1954*; the Executors of the Sinclair Lewis Estate and Jonathan Cape Ltd, for extracts from *Babbitt*; Macmillan & Co Ltd, for 'A Visit from Abroad' by James Stephens; The Macmillan Co of Canada Ltd, and Macmillan & Co Ltd, London, for an extract from *Red Roses for Me* by Sean O'Casey; the Literary Trustees of Walter de la Mare and the Society of Authors as their representative, for an extract from 'Fare Well' and 'Echo'; The St Martin's

Press Inc, The Macmillan Co of Canada Ltd and Macmillan & Co Ltd, London for extracts from *The Plough and the Stars* and *Juno and the Paycock* by Sean O'Casey; The Marvell Press, Hessle, Yorkshire, for extracts from 'Church Going' and 'Next Please' from *The Less Deceived* by Philip Larkin; the Literary Executors of W. Somerset Maugham and William Heinemann Ltd, for extracts from *The Summing Up*; Methuen & Co Ltd, for extracts from *The Collected Poems of G. K. Chesterton* and for extracts from *The Caretaker* by Harold Pinter; Mr Arthur Miller, for extracts from *All My Sons* (published by Cresset Press Ltd) and *The Crucible* (published by Secker & Warburg); John Murray Ltd, for extracts from a letter, *Collected Poems* and *Summoned by Bells* by John Betjeman; the Executors of the Eugene O'Neill Estate and Jonathan Cape Ltd, for extracts from *Long Day's Journey into Night* and *Mourning becomes Electra*; Mr John Osborne and Faber & Faber Ltd, for extracts from *Luther*; Mr Harold Owen and Chatto & Windus Ltd, for extracts from *The Collected Poems of Wilfred Owen*; the Owner of the Copyright and Methuen & Co Ltd, for an extract from *Anna of the Five Towns* by Arnold Bennett; Oxford University Press Ltd, for extracts from *The Poems of Gerard Manley Hopkins*; A. D. Peters & Co, for extracts from 'Forefathers' and 'The Survival' by Edmund Blunden and from *Brideshead Revisited* and *Vile Bodies* by Evelyn Waugh; Laurence Pollinger Ltd and the Estate of the late Mrs Frieda Lawrence, for extracts from *The Rainbow*, *Lady Chatterley's Lover* and the *Complete Poems* of D. H. Lawrence; the Public Trustee and the Society of Authors, for extracts from *Major Barbara* and *Saint Joan* by George Bernard Shaw; Mr Siegfried Sassoon, for extracts from his poems; the Society of Authors, for extracts from the poems of John Masefield; the Society of Authors as the Literary Representative of the Estate of the late James Joyce for an extract from *Finnegan's Wake*; Mr James Strachey and Chatto & Windus Ltd, for extracts from *Eminent Victorians* by Lytton Strachey; the Executors of the Estate of the late H. G. Wells, for an extract from *The History of Mr Polly*; Mr Arnold Wesker and Jonathan Cape Ltd, for extracts from *The Wesker Trilogy*; Mrs Iris Wise and Macmillan & Co Ltd, for 'Check' from the *Collected Poems of James Stephens*; Mr Leonard Woolf and The Hogarth Press Ltd, for an extract from an essay on Modern Fiction and extracts from *The Waves* and *Mrs Dalloway* by Virginia Woolf; Mr M. B. Yeats and Macmillan & Co Ltd, for an extract from *Countess Cathleen* and extracts from *The Collected Poems of W. B. Yeats.*